What People Are Saying About B

In a day when the answer to personal doubts and societal ills seems to be "Burn it all down," Bradley Jersak calls to us from the ashes of ruin with the attentiveness and compassion of the Good Samaritan tending to and providing for a stranger in need. *Out of the Embers* reassures us that deconstruction is not merely for the purpose of destruction, but, unlike many Christian texts of old, it does not attempt to fill in all the blanks or flood us with certitude. In this seminal work, Brad comes to us as a fellow wayfarer, a sojourner who is questioning and seeking but anchored. And from that deeply rooted place, which includes the voices of sages from eras past, he has written *Out of the Embers* as a companion for his fellow seekers and as a guide for the questioners. He calls us once again to the One who loves, the One who leads, the One who makes all things new. What will we be after the coal of the Refiner's fire has touched our lips? *Out of the Embers* leaves us hopeful.

—**Felicia Murrell**
Author, *Truth Encounters*

This is a wise and creative book. And despite the fact that Brad Jersak's wisdom was clearly hard-won, he has not been hardened by the gaining of it. Tender and personal, he is nonetheless also often fierce, never shying away into shibboleths or truisms or abstractions. His is a faith of fever and tears, a faith in a God with wounds. So, he writes with a consummate "touch" about the pains of believing and doubting, finding and losing the way. Just so, he fulfills his calling and helps us to answer our own callings, renewing our confidence in old wisdom, proven true over time, and reminding us that the Spirit is creating a fresh wisdom in and for us here and now—a wisdom, believe it or not, formed in our wrestlings with God.

—**Dr. Chris Green**
Professor of Public Theology, Southeastern University, Lakeland, FL
Director, St. Anthony Institute for Theology, Philosophy, & Liturgics

Revelation is Deconstruction, not the revelation of that which lacks but that which is True. Like the burning bush, the deadwood is being destroyed, allowing for the emergence of that which has always been present but hidden, now visible and attractive by its nature. This is the journey that Brad Jersak escorts us through, where the intent of love is never wanton havoc but the tender Doula's work, the Holy Spirit overseeing the birthing of true life. After all, only the ashes make it through the flames, and from the ashes, beauty.

—**Wm. Paul Young**
Author, *The Shack* and *Lies We Believe About God*

Finally, someone has written what I think will be *the* textbook on the deconstruction of belief—and it's Brad Jersak. I appreciate Jersak's thorough and caring contribution to this important discussion and urgent reality.

—**David Hayward**
aka "NakedPastor"
Author, *Questions Are the Answer* and *Til Doubt Do Us Part*

When we experience the inevitable widening of our understanding of and identity in God, of the Scriptures, and of our way of being in God's beloved, broken world, sometimes it feels more like an exploding grenade than an expansive invitation. Yet we need love's widening, especially when we religious folks think we don't. (Note who disliked Jesus and his message enough to make sure *he* died instead of their old beliefs.) We also need wise, pastoral, knowledgeable, hope-oriented guides who can help clear the smoke, remove the rubble, bind the wounds, and redirect our gaze on Jesus, who hides our lives with his own in God amid the shakeup. With his insights and the historical companions he has chosen to help us, Bradley Jersak—who also brings experience in compassionate triage—is that transparent, trustworthy guide who can help us examine the unexamined "knowledge" to which we cling so that it might be released and surpassed by God's love.

—**Dr. Cherith Fee Nordling**
Faculty, Masters in Leadership, Theology and Society, Regent College,
Vancouver, BC

According to Bradley Jersak, "*The Great Deconstruction* is not just a two-year lockdown or four-year election cycle." He sees it as "a great historic tradition." However, the author insists we are bereft of neither reliable guides nor real agency. From Moses to Jesus to modern prophets like Simone Weil, *Out of the Embers* mercifully recollects for us the sages and seers who have "charted the way…[and] left us memos of their work." *Out of the Embers* is a most wise, kind, and timely gift for those of us whose very faith has been traumatized by the tumult of our age.

—**Steve Bell**
Juno Award-winning singer-songwriter-musician

If there is a way forward into faith and mystery, then there have been many who have passed through tumultuous cultural moments like our own and have lived to tell the tale. Linking arms with Voltaire, Weil, Tolstoy, Nietzsche, and John of the Cross, Brad Jersak opens a way to faith after having passed through the purifying fires of modernity. There can indeed be a second naivete, a return to childlike wonder after disillusionment. Deconstruction does not have to be an end; it can be a gracious iconoclasm that returns us to God, ourselves, and even God's scandalous GPS on earth: the church.

—**Dr. Julie Canlis**
Author, *A Theology of the Ordinary*

Too much of what passes for contemporary Christianity deserves to be burned to the ground (then steamrolled). Amid the fiery embers, scorched treasures remain, ablaze with the authentic experience of the life of God in human flesh. In *Out of the Embers*, Bradley Jersak is our wise guide to the ever-salvageable way of Jesus. As the fire of deconstruction burned through Bradley, he found a company that had been through the fire in ages and centuries past (hint: deconstruction isn't new) and bonded with present-day companions who continue to walk through the flames with him. What they have seen and heard and what their hands have touched in the midst of the furnace of existence is the human God, whose co-suffering love never fails.

—**Fr. Kenneth Tanner**
Church of the Holy Redeemer, Rochester Hills, MI

With a theologian's keen insight and a pastor's heart of compassion, Dr. Bradley Jersak provides us with a pathway through the maze of deconstruction. Anyone in the midst of a painful deconstruction of their faith will appreciate Bradley's overflowing and merciful empathy. In *Out of the Embers*, he leads us through honest questions and genuine pain, taking us safely to the arms of Jesus on the other side. I love how Bradley gently and lovingly shows us that the ultimate answer isn't found in a move away from Christ or the Holy Scriptures or even the community of faith known as the church. Rather, he humbly asks us to consider a healthy deconstruction—the appropriate abandonment of counterfeits and obstacles, and a holy pursuit of the real thing. In that sense, he wonders if we shouldn't instead embark on more of a restoration project: the restoration of the masterpiece that is Jesus Christ and the good news of God's love in and through him.

—Joe Beach
Pastor, Amazing Grace Church, Denver, CO

Bradley Jersak offers an encyclopedic tome that engages the mind and heart with timely urgency. He deftly interweaves spiritual theology, philosophy, and history with self-disclosure and ecclesial and cultural commentary. What emerges, *Out of the Embers*, is an unconventional guidebook to faith formation—what I term *continuous Christian conversion*—that shows us how to surrender our defective and toxic God constructs, attachments, and ecclesiologies to truly follow, obey, and trust the crucified and resurrected King Jesus. Bradley's goal is to help us navigate the unsettling pathway of deconstruction to experience God's living love and light—his *presence in communion*.

—Dr. Roger Helland
Prayer Ambassador, The Evangelical Fellowship of Canada
Author, *Pursuing God's Presence: The Devout Life*, *Missional Spirituality*, and
Magnificent Surrender (forthcoming)

This is a very deep, thought-provoking book, but, at the same time, it is not a difficult read. It asks profound questions about our walk with God. I felt as if I were in conversation with the prophets, helping me focus on Christ my Savior, my healer, and the forgiver of my sin. In fact, it almost felt like a Socratic learning opportunity with Christ himself. I am so blessed to have had the opportunity to read *Out of the Embers*. Praise be to God!

—Fr. Leonard Herrem
Therapist and Rector, Holy Resurrection Orthodox Church, Saskatoon, SK

What I love about Brad Jersak's book *Out of the Embers* is not only its timely message of *reconstruction*, shaped so significantly by Brad's own personal crisis and journey, but also Brad's passion—his relentless desire for others to come to know this God who walks every step of the journey in and with us. Thank you, Brad.

—**John MacMurray**
Director, Open Table Conferences and Northwest School of Theology

With his uniquely engaging style—jarring honesty, wit, insight, and compassion—Brad Jersak has written a book that challenges the way we look outwardly at deconstruction in the church and society, and leads us into an inward journey of the heart. While the deconstruction debate seems so current, Brad shows that, from Moses to our day, it has always been with us. Both individually and corporately, like it or not, we are on a journey of death and resurrection because this is how God moves. *Out of the Embers* calls us to step beyond our fear and insecurity to embrace the cruciform life of the Jesus Way. An outstanding book of vital importance for our time.

—**Steve Stewart**
Founder and President, Impact Nations

The process of faith deconstruction (or *renovation*, the term I prefer) requires the guidance of someone with a pastoral sensitivity, empathetic ear, and breadth of experience and wisdom to ensure that we don't succumb to the extreme pendulum swings and idolatrous ideologies with which such a disillusioning process can tempt us. Bradley Jersak is, for my money, by far the most trusted voice on this subject, having lived through the traumas and then stepped into the hopeful vistas of a genuine renovation of faith, which can often feel as frightening and exhilarating as building an airplane when it's already in the sky. Scholarly without being stuffy, *Out of the Embers* should be on the bookshelves of anyone who feels despairingly lodged in the darkness and pressure of the birth canal of deconstruction, clambering toward the "bright darkness" of divinity. The book is especially for those who've eventually found themselves disillusioned with disillusionment and suspicious of social-media influencers who've repackaged deconstruction as another consumer product—who, instead, want to avoid the allure of new fundamentalisms, restricting *isms*, and the worship of their own unanchored egos.

—**Dr. Andrew Klager**
Founder and Director, Institute for Religion, Peace and Justice

"Things fall apart; the centre cannot hold." So wrote Yeats, filled with dread and uncertainty after the First Great War and the devastating flu pandemic that had almost claimed his pregnant wife. In a similar liminal space today, Bradley Jersak invites us to dare to trust that this present time of greatest uncertainty can also be a threshold to wonderful opportunity. You cannot read these pages without your dread giving way to a settling hope!

—**Gary Best**
Author, *Naturally Supernatural* and *Where Joy Is Found*

BRADLEY JERSAK

OUT OF THE EMBERS

FAITH AFTER THE GREAT DECONSTRUCTION

WHITAKER HOUSE

Unless otherwise indicated, Scripture quotations from the New Testament are taken from *The Kingdom New Testament: A Contemporary Translation*, © 2011 by Nicholas Thomas Wright. Published by HarperOne. Scripture quotations marked (NRSV) are taken from *The New Revised Standard Version Updated Edition*, © 2021 Division of Christian Education of the National Council of Churches of Christ in the U.S.A. Used by permission. All rights reserved. Scripture quotations marked (NKJV) are taken from the *New King James Version*, © 1979, 1980, 1982 by Thomas Nelson, Inc. Used by permission. All rights reserved. Scripture quotations marked (NASB) are taken from the *New American Standard Bible®*, NASB®, © 1960, 1962, 1963, 1968, 1971, 1972, 1973, 1975, 1977, 1995 by The Lockman Foundation. Used by permission. (www.Lockman.org). Scripture quotations marked (LXX) are taken from the *Translation of the Greek Septuagint into English* by Sir Lancelot Charles Lee Brenton. Published in 1851, Public Domain. Scripture quotations marked (NIV) are taken from the *Holy Bible, New International Version®*, NIV®, © 1973, 1978, 1984, 2011 by Biblica, Inc.® Used by permission. All rights reserved worldwide. The "NIV" and "New International Version" are trademarks registered in the United States Patent and Trademark Office by Biblica, Inc.® Scripture quotations marked (HCSB) are taken from the Holman Christian Standard Bible®, © 1999, 2000, 2002, 2003, 2009 by Holman Bible Publishers. Used by permission. Holman Christian Standard Bible®, Holman CSB®, and HCSB® are federally registered trademarks of Holman Bible Publishers. Scripture quotations marked (KJV) are taken from the King James Version of the Holy Bible. Scripture quotations marked (CEB) are taken from the *Common English Bible*, copyright 2011. Used by permission. All rights reserved. Scripture quotations marked (ESV) are taken from *The Holy Bible, English Standard Version*, © 2000, 2001, 1995 by Crossway Bibles, a division of Good News Publishers. Used by permission. All rights reserved.

The forms LORD and GOD (in small caps) in Bible quotations represent the Hebrew name for God *Yahweh*, while Lord and God normally represent the name *Adonai*, in accordance with the Bible version used.

Bible reference abbreviations are taken from *The SBL Handbook of Style*, 2nd ed., SBL (Society of Biblical Literature) Press, 2014, https://divinity.libguides.com/styleguide/bible.

Unless otherwise noted, all emphases throughout this book, including quotations from the Bible and reference works, are by the author.

Pew Research Center bears no responsibility for the analyses or interpretations of its data presented in this book. The opinions expressed herein, including any implications for policy, are those of the author and not of Pew Research Center.

Citations from Søren Kierkegaard are taken from *Provocations: Spiritual Writings of Kierkegaard* (Walden, NY: Plough Publishing House, 2002). Used by permission. Citations from Simone Weil are taken from *Awaiting God: A New Translation of Attente de Dieu and Lettre à un Religieux*, ed. Bradley Jersak (Abbotsford, BC: Fresh Wind Press, 2012). Used by permission. Citations from Fyodor Dostoevsky's works are taken from *Gutenberg.org*, public domain.

All URLs in endnotes were last accessed October 10, 2022.

OUT OF THE EMBERS:
Faith After the Great Deconstruction

ISBN: 978-1-64123-888-5 • eBook ISBN: 978-1-64123-889-2
Printed in Colombia
© 2022 by Bradley Jersak

Whitaker House • 1030 Hunt Valley Circle • New Kensington, PA 15068
www.whitakerhouse.com

LC record available at https://lccn.loc.gov/2022031924
LC ebook record available at https://lccn.loc.gov/2022031925

1 2 3 4 5 6 7 8 9 10 11 ᴜᴜ 29 28 27 26 25 24 23 22

For my godfather,
David Goa,
and his pipe

I lurk between folds
inhaling sage wafting draughts
'neath wisdom's mantle

CONTENTS

PART III: PROVOCATIONS
OUT OF THE EMBERS—FAITH AFTER FREEFALL

"SOMETHING IS HAPPENING HERE"

Something is happening here
But you don't know what it is
—Bob Dylan, "Ballad of a Thin Man"

North America has experienced two episodes of Christian revival known as Great Awakenings—the first in the eighteenth century, the second in the nineteenth century. Both produced a remarkable increase in church membership. (Whether the Jesus movement and the charismatic renewal of the late twentieth century qualify as a third Great Awakening is for others to decide.) But now, in the early twenty-first century, the church in North America is experiencing a precipitous decline—a mass exodus that Bradley Jersak has aptly dubbed "the Great Deconstruction."

Something is definitely happening here. Mister Jones, the baffled reporter from a bygone age in Bob Dylan's "Ballad of a Thin Man," may not know what is happening, but there are others who do. American Christianity as a colonial extension of European Christendom has run its course and is no longer tenable—at least, not as the default religion and organizing center in an increasingly secular society. The phenomenon of what has been popularly labeled "deconstruction" is not a passing fad but names a genuine crisis of faith that millions of Christians, largely through no conscious decision of their own, are now facing. Once a Christianity corrupted by civil religion, consumerism, and clerical abuse is put on trial, the fate of Christian faith hangs in the balance. And, for many people, the jury is still out. It is certainly possible to deconstruct Christianity down to nothing. This has been the experience of many. But then what? What happens *after* the Great Deconstruction?

In 1888, one year before his mental collapse, Friedrich Nietzsche published three books: *Twilight of the Idols, Ecce Homo*, and *The Anti-Christ*. All three launch a withering assault upon Christianity, but none more so than *The Anti-Christ*. However, even in the midst of his scorched-earth attack upon Christianity, you can sense the alarm bells going off in Nietzsche's mind as he laments, "Two thousand years have come and gone—and not a single new god."[1] Nietzsche's grand project was to eradicate Christianity but avoid the abyss of nihilism. He correctly understood that only a god can accomplish this. Nietzsche's hope was for the *Übermensch* (humanity manifest as the Will to Power) to arise as the new god, yet he complained of this god's failure to appear. When the *Übermensch* finally did goosestep onto the world stage, it turned out to be not a god but a demon. In 1966, following the devastation wrought by the Nazi attempt to install the *Übermensch*, personified in Adolf Hitler as Europe's new god, Martin Heidegger gave an interview to the German news magazine *Der Spiegel*, trying to explain his failure to denounce Hitler and Nazism. In this now famous interview, Heidegger, reflecting on the current state of affairs following the two world wars, said, "Only a god can save us."[2] These two renowned German philosophers knew that in the world of late modernity, only a god can stand between us and the abyss of nihilism.

But I have news for Nietzsche and Heidegger: no new god is coming. Why? Because the one God who has already come has triumphed so decisively over all other gods that there is no possibility of their rising from the dead. Once upon a time, the Western world was awash in gods and goddesses— from Apollo to Zeus, from Venus to Cupid, from Odin to Thor. But no more. It took a few centuries, but Jesus Christ eventually vanquished all rivals. Jesus Christ is the last god standing because he is, as declared by resurrection, the true Son of God.

The implication of Christ's definitive triumph over the gods is enormous. Nietzsche and Heidegger both understood that only a god can save us from the meaningless existence of god-*less* nihilism. But since no new god is coming, we have reached the point in history where the only question that really matters is this: Jesus or what? If we are not going to believe in Christ, then what are we going to believe in? An *ism* as our savior? Conservatism? Progressivism? Capitalism? Marxism? Nationalism? Globalism? Dear reader, I have enough respect for you to assume that you will not foolishly put your faith for salvation in an *ism*. Heidegger is right: "Only a god can save us." We are now so stuck in a morass of meaninglessness that we can only worship our way out of it. But what are we going to worship if not the one declared to be the Son of God by the resurrection from the dead? Money? Pleasure? Politics? Self? We already know that such things, worshipped as gods, destroy our soul. And even noble things like knowledge and science, or even family and friendship, when worshipped as gods, are exposed to be feeble idols that cannot save. We really have arrived at the end of any possibility of an innocent idolatry. It's now God or atheism. God or nihilism. God or nothing. And the God who alone can save us has been definitively revealed to us in Jesus Christ.

In the Gospels, Jesus Christ is revealed as the light of the world, and how we respond to this light is our judgment. We either love the light and move toward it, or we hate the light and seek to escape from it. But there is no escape from the light other than to willingly choose to inhabit the outer darkness. This is like the elder brother in the parable of the prodigal son gnashing his teeth in the darkness outside the father's house, refusing to join the party because he continues to nourish his resentment toward his sinful brother. The *apokatastasis* hope that Christ will ultimately reconcile and restore all things does not eliminate an indeterminate time of self-exile in the outer darkness for those who refuse the light of Christ. The question always remains: Christ or what? When a great many erstwhile disciples walked away from Jesus because of his scandalous talk of "eating his flesh and drinking his blood,"[3] Jesus posed a very poignant question to the Twelve: "Do you also wish to go away?" (John 6:67 NRSV). Simon Peter was at his very best when he replied, "Lord, to whom can we go? You have the words of eternal life. We have come to believe and know that you are the Holy One of God" (vv. 68–69 NRSV). Peter knew: it's Jesus or nothing.

Bradley Jersak knows this too, and his book has arrived on the scene at a time when everything's on fire. The book you hold in your hands is filled with priceless treasures that have been pulled out of the embers and that offer you the possibility of a renovated faith after the Great Deconstruction. John Wesley often borrowed the language of the prophet Zechariah when he described his own life and faith as "a brand plucked from the fire" (Zech 3:2

NRSV, NKJV). My prayer is that many a brand will be plucked from the fire in the reading of *Out of the Embers*.

Bradley is a scholar who graciously consents to write not as a scholar but as a friend—a wise and trusted guide. In his engagement with Simone Weil, Friedrich Nietzsche, Søren Kierkegaard, and Fyodor Dostoevsky, he skillfully unpacks the insights of these important seers to help us understand the unique epoch we are passing through and how best to navigate it. There is never a hint of scolding in Bradley's writing; he is a humble and compassionate comrade who has experienced his own disorientation from a messy unraveling. He has glimpsed into the abyss and found his way back to feel the breath of God in his lungs and the love of God in his heart. When our Christendom-constructed houses of wood, hay, and stubble are consumed in the flames of deconstruction, there still remain the gold, silver, and precious stones of a faith worth saving. Bradley Jersak has done the painstaking work of sifting through the embers and ashes to retrieve these treasures. *Tolle lege.* "Take up and read." Recover and rediscover the imperishable treasure that fire can never destroy but only refine.

—*Brian Zahnd*
Easter Week 2022

THE D-WORD: POSSIBILITIES AND PEDIGREE

> "My idea of God is not a divine idea.
> It has to be shattered time after time.
> He shatters it himself."
> —C. S. Lewis, *A Grief Observed*[4]

THE GREAT DECONSTRUCTION

I believe in the necessity, the perils, and the possibilities of childbirth. Under normal circumstances, children must exit the womb, pass through the birth canal, and emerge into the world. A lot can go sideways (including the baby!), so, when that happens, we're grateful for medical staff who can intervene. Babies cannot remain in the womb and hope to grow up. They cannot stay in the birth canal and hope to live. Once the labor begins, there is no going back—they move into a life-and-death struggle for their first breath. It's especially terrifying if the baby gets lodged in the birth canal and Mom exhausts her strength in the pushing stage. At that point, both mother and child are in crisis. A safe delivery then requires help. Back in my day, that help came by way of a doctor's forceps; today, it would be by medical vacuum extraction.

Who am I to talk about childbirth? I'm neither a mother nor a doctor (not that kind, anyway). I dare to write about the perils of childbirth because I've experienced that trauma firsthand, although I rely on my mother's memory to recount it. I was the baby. I was stuck, in crisis, in mortal danger. I thank God for the obstetrician whose forceps dragged me into this bright, cold world. I don't remember saying thanks.

I also believe in deconstruction.[5] I use this term advisedly—with a wince—because *deconstruction*, in its popular usage, has been reconstrued into a trendy catchword for the dismantling (voluntary or involuntary) of the beliefs and values of a person or culture. In this book, I assent to the term while also deconstructing it and retrieving its more radical, historic, and expansive meanings.

I have coined the phrase "The Great Deconstruction" to describe the current wave of migration out of previous faith forms into new understandings of God (for better or worse) and/or the mass exodus from faith altogether. Whether the *deconstruction* phenomenon is experienced as liberating or traumatic, voluntary or involuntary, the upheaval of status-quo belief systems is of such a magnitude that I've added the adjective "Great" to identify it with parallel epochs such as the Great Reformation and the Great Awakening.

In the Christian sphere, The Great Deconstruction has primarily been a Western trend, has roots in the Emergent Church movement, and is often associated today with subgroups such as "Ex-vangelicals" and the "nones and dones."[6] (One might also ask whether radicalized fundamentalism, Christian Nationalism, and neofascist movements comprise an opposing movement or are themselves—as departures—subbranches of the same trend.) However, in this book, I demonstrate an older and even more radical lineage, as we'll discover in my survey of the "Seven Sleepers" in part 2 of this book.

I believe that, for *some* folks, childbirth is an apt metaphor for the necessity, the perils, and the possibilities of The Great Deconstruction. Those of us who've undergone a traumatic deconstruction understand that we could not remain in the womb and hope to grow. But we also discovered that we could not stay in the birth canal of deconstruction and hope to live. We needed to emerge into a new space, however bright and cold, however big and scary—and however wonderful our first breath and shriek of freedom might be.

But I want to acknowledge that it's also possible for *some* of those in deconstruction (if not you, you'll know someone) to feel the trauma of getting stuck, feeling the panic, and, knowing they can't go back, needing a push or a pull to help them through. As one woman put it, "It was isolating and terrifying. I was alone."

So, when I say *I believe in deconstruction*, I *don't* mean I believe in it the same way I believe in Jesus—more on him later. I mean it in the way I believe in birth canals—it's a pathway to new life we must pass through (even if repeatedly) that is necessary, perilous, but decidedly *not* our final destination.

I believe in "deconstruction" in each of its historic iterations:

1. First, I wholeheartedly embrace its most ancient form—*negative* or *apophatic* theology—in which the great prophets of Judaism and Christianity interrogated every human *construct* of "God" as probably idolatrous, stripping away accretions that were actually impediments to experiencing God.

2. Second, I also honor the *masters of deconstruction* from the Enlightenment and Existentialist eras and their withering critiques of both Christendom (a Christian-dominant state or culture) and its critics—of their superstition, intolerance, and violence, and of the church's cultural mediocrity. I believe we need to hear these masters again.

3. I am also sympathetic to deconstruction in its technical, philosophical sense, introduced by Jacques Derrida in the late 1960s. For Derrida, deconstruction is a strategy for mindfully examining language, exposing (and subverting) the ways we discuss and practice truth and meaning—how we use binary language to smuggle in power dynamics that generate injustice.[7]

4. Further, I do resonate with deconstruction in *some* of its contemporary usage,[8] at least insofar as it describes our journey through personal and spiritual transformation—experiences, seasons, or stages expressed by authors such as these:

    +   St. John of the Cross and other great mystics: purgation/illumination/union

    +   J. R. R. Tolkien: enchantment/disenchantment/re-enchantment

    +   Fr. Richard Rohr: order/disorder/reorder[9]

    +   Brian McLaren: simplicity/complexity/perplexity/harmony[10]

    +   Richard Kearney: theism/atheism/anatheism[11]

WATER TO WINE

Most of all, I embrace wholeheartedly Jesus's *water-to-wine* metaphor from the Gospel of John, chapter 2. This miracle of metamorphosis, Christ's foundational sign of the new covenant, is replicated in our lives through our living union with divine Love. I pause to acknowledge my friend Brian Zahnd's direct and invaluable influence in this regard[12] and offer this book as the vista I see from his shoulders.

Water to wine: not that our transformation is as instantaneous or straightforward as the sign in Cana. We're in for a wild ride that surely includes meandering and meltdowns. But what I love about the water-to-wine analogy is how the wine didn't obsess over its previous confinement to clay jars or pine to return to them. And, anyway, no one bursts the wineskins of our brittle *constructs* like Jesus—he (and the best deconstructionists) even lay bare the construct of deconstruction itself.

Further, Jesus uses *vine-to-wine* imagery in John 15. That metaphor calls to me because it's more than just "deconstructive"—it's about growth and pruning, then more growth and plucking, then on to crushing and ferment, followed by enrichment. The whole process is at work in you and me right now. It is occurring in individuals and in faith groups, especially throughout Western civilization. It's hard and it's scary and it's good.

So, yes, I believe in the necessity, the perils, and the possibilities of the current sea change. Whether we're watching a radical course correction or a complete collapse remains to be seen. How it pans out will likely depend on *how we see* what's happening, *who we are becoming, how we live* in response—and, most important, *where we find Christ* situated in this storm.

In this book, I will presume to add my own take to the current wave of fresh works that ponder faith after deconstruction. To get there, I will trace an arc through three distinct propositions that I categorize as "memoirs," "memos," and "provocations":

+ **Memoirs of deconstruction and personal trauma:** For *some*, dismantling their belief systems may be a blast ("Blow it up, real good!"), but when our faith collapses into a personal, full-blown meltdown, we require empathy and encouragement, not cynics or cheerleaders.

+ **Memos (essays) on deconstruction by the masters:** When faith is swept away by a pandemic of ideological viruses and sociopolitical revolutions, the masters of deconstruction never suggest backtracking. They double down, showing us hard truths about how we got here and what needs to happen next.

+ **Provocations toward faith after deconstruction:** In the wake of personal trauma and societal collapse, an inexplicable faith that is worth something may yet emerge, inspired in part by marginalized voices who comprise the center of our faith.

HARRIED AND HARROWED

Some people who've followed my harried career as a pastor, theologian, and author know me as both an agent of deconstruction and a critic of it. I've attempted (with faltering success) to retain a Christlike tone as I've waded into heated debates, especially concerning divine violence: penal substitutionary atonement, eternal conscious torment, Old Testament genocide, and the biblical literalism these doctrines depend on. My twenty-five-year journey has produced testaments to my theological one-eighty, including *Stricken by God?*, *Her Gates Will Never Be Shut*, and the *More Christlike* trilogy.

I refer readers to that résumé of my active, public, and sometimes costly witness as a "deconstructionist," despite the nervous tics that slippery label triggers in me. The truth is that behind every one of my shifts is the pastoral impulse to conserve authentic faith rather than dismantle it.

I only presume to recount my track record now because, once I start to problematize and deconstruct deconstruction, you'll need to remember that I believe in its necessity and beautiful possibilities. Please consider this commitment if I get bleak or a tad grumpy about the shadow side of certain strains of *ex-vangelical pop-deconstruction*. I'm not very sympathetic toward unrepentant fundamentalism when I see it disguised in pseudo-enlightened progressive sheepskins. You'll see my lament soon enough. But far from resisting the need for genuine reformation, I intend to stoke the fire that has yet to burn hot enough to consume the noxious residue of modernity. I do *not* believe the new reformation has gone too far. My fear is that we will inoculate ourselves and stop shy of death, burial, and resurrection.

I hope even my "none and done" readers will join me in the embarrassment of riches we share—a pedigree of deconstruction that includes the Jewish prophetic tradition, the apostolic martyrs, and, most of all, Christ crucified and risen. But there's also a personal bloodline involved for me. In my veins flow the Hussite reformers from the fifteenth century, dispossessed Bohemian and Moravian exiles (circa 1620), and my Czech Baptist family, including Great Uncle Vilem (William), tortured for his faith in Czechoslovakia in the 1960s.

Among the ancestors of my wife, Eden, are sixteenth-century Anabaptists who fled as refugees from the lowlands of Germany, through Prussia, and into Ukraine, where her Mennonite grandfather was exiled and martyred by the Stalinists, after which the family came to Canada as political/religious refugees.

The saints in these movements were deconstructionists from their formation to their often violent deaths. Theirs was not the fragile meme-able deconstruction of social-media trends. Their North Star was the wounded God who hung on a cross and asked them to follow suit. Unlike me, they weren't just ducking trolls while swapping out doctrines. They literally ran for their lives, hid in forests, experienced starvation, and sometimes had to weigh carefully what they'd be willing to burn for (with real fire).

As the author of Hebrews says, "The world was not worthy of them" (Hebrews 11:38 NIV). And neither am I. But I take this prophetic heritage seriously. For me, the only deconstruction worth living and dying for actually asks that of you—namely, the self-giving death of cruciform love, whether that looks like ascending in a blaze of glory or living a century-long life of unswerving faithfulness. As you already know or will see soon enough, I can't offer either. For me, strutting to victory is a lost cause—triumphalism makes me ill. I walk with a spiritual limp. I trust no one who doesn't.

BUT *mercy*—there's a word I know well and can own by experience. Where my self-pity and self-loathing say, "It's time to shut up and disappear," I hear the voices of my ancestors and the Holy Spirit extending this mandate: "Not just yet. You're not done gifting forward the mercy you've received."

Sigh. I mean, "Amen." Grant this, O Lord.

PART I

MEMOIRS:
TRAUMA, PURGATION,
AND LIBERATION

1

FREEFALL:
MY MESSY MEMOIR

RESIGNATION

December 8, 2008

To Eden Jersak [my wife and team leader of our church],

Dear Eden,

You asked the other day why I think I need to step off the leadership team. It felt like I needed to convince you of it, and I felt my heart cave in.

The truth is that, these days, I have a very bad feeling inside.... The best way to describe it is to paint a picture. I see an old fridge, built circa 1964. I hear a knock coming from its innards. A knock that shouldn't be there. Getting louder and louder over the past year until I hear it all the time. Something is broken. Not in the good way. And occasionally I see a puddle of water or even oil oozing from beneath it. I would like to ignore it for fear of being self-obsessed, but I can't overlook the fact that the contents of the fridge are starting to rot. I am not functioning properly anymore beyond brief bursts. I need to sort it out...have been trying to in spiritual direction, prayer ministry, twelve-step recovery, hiking, etc. But it's getting worse before it's getting better. The emotional slippage (like an overstretched rubber belt) that became noticeable earlier this year didn't stop when I stepped down as team leader. It hasn't stopped while I've been out of town and on the road. It probably won't stop when I step down from the team either. But that's what I need to do next.

I can only continue trying to support you and draw closer to you from off the team. From there, I am hopeful that I won't make the mistake of isolating or unplugging from life. I'm beginning to see how recovery could take years. With very limited energy, I think it's wise to focus what's left of my reserves on family and friends and on work that's life-giving. But as for church leadership, I'm done. I can still help in the community if I don't take it on or own it. What I'm trying to do is check out formally so that I don't check out relationally.

This might sound like bad news to you now, but I hope we'll see the good of it in the new year. I won't abandon you or ignore you because, hopefully, I won't need to. I'm hopeful about being able to be present for you rather than shriveling further or becoming the next tragedy you have to deal with. I'm trying to listen to God and to my heart and to my body. I'd rather not bottom out physically, emotionally, or spiritually, so I'm trying to let go of things that would deepen the problem. Please release me from needing to push past December 31 in leadership.

I love you and believe in you as leader. You and the team can do this easily. And I can help best from off the team.

FREEFALL (YOU SHOULD SKIP THIS PART)

My *freefall*—aka *meltdown*—had begun early in 2008 and climaxed hard by June. I white-knuckled a few hours of work per week through the summer, hardly functioning in my final months as a pastor. Months of sleep deprivation, cumulative grief, and anxiety attacks were taking their toll.

By September, my doctor confirmed what my spiritual director and twelve-step sponsor had already been saying. Diagnosis: "You're *unravelling*. You need to quit. *Now. Right now.*" Ah, the beautiful permission I could not give myself.

How we spun my departure for our already wounded little church was that it was now Eden's turn to step in as the team leader and paid pastor. That was true. We didn't mention that I was having a nervous breakdown, even if it was obvious. I handed over the baton mid-September in an inspiring transition that I dubbed "Esther emerging." I hobbled back to bed, but the insomnia and anxiety didn't wane. I needed a hard stop and sent the preceding resignation letter from all leadership roles to Eden, then to the leadership team.

I saw the refrigerator analogy in a moment of clarity, but my goodbye note was still overly optimistic. I apologize if I seem self-indulgent, but in an era when so many use the word *deconstruction* in revivalist tones, I need to say my bit.

I had already traversed most of my theological exodus out of Evangelicalism over the previous decade. My discoveries were rewarding and liberating. Yes, I faced difficulties—self-styled "watchmen" directing both random and coordinated hatred at my supposed heresies—but the trolling was entirely external and perhaps a bit too energizing. As my friend David Hayward has said, "I am not a victim of the deconstruction of my beliefs. My deepest self demanded personal growth, and I welcome it."[13]

I was not, in fact, creeping off the end of a flimsy limb. I was climbing down the trunk into the very roots of the historic apostolic faith. My biggest changes were deeply anchored, and I had solid support from mentors, friends, and our faith community. My church didn't abandon me, betray me, or drive me out. In fact, they blessed my adventures and formed a phalanx of the marginalized from which I launched my boldest sorties.

The real trauma—the deeper deconstruction—came via the onslaught of personal implosions, gruesome tragedies, and serial deaths that afflicted our little church that year. The people I loved most were suffering badly. In the overwhelming grief stacked on top of grief, I underwent the collapse of my inner world and, for the first time in my life, was no longer sure I could trust that God is good. My ship was capsizing, and Jesus seemed to be snoozing below deck. "*Rabbi, do you not care that we are perishing?*"[14] The ground of my whole being was, to my mind, being violently swept away.

And yet I managed to make these trials even worse—much worse—for myself and for my family, and at other people's expense. Groping wildly for emotional lifelines, I dragged others into my chaos, crossed boundaries, and damaged people I cared about. In hindsight, my character did not measure up to my gifting. By January 2009, I was battling unbearable shame and suicidal ideations. I knew I couldn't multiply our collective trauma by heaving a final grenade on my way out. But I did earnestly pray, "Lord, please, just take me home," no longer caring if that meant heaven or hell.

"Blah, blah, blah." That's what I hear as I write this. It is one of the lingering voices that mocks me when I retell my story. Sorry. Perhaps I didn't completely recover. Case in point: after rereading the above resignation letter last week,[15] I experienced emotional flashbacks with physical symptoms. I got myself to a support meeting, and they set me rolling on a "Step Ten spot check"—a self-examination, scanning for lingering resentments, selfishness, dishonesty, or fear. I was to ask myself if I'm obsessing, keeping secrets, causing harm, or being unloving. That night, I dreamed the most violent nightmare I've had in twenty-five years. I reached out to my sponsor and several friends and then wrote these pages as part of my recovery. Lucky you.

This is how deconstruction has been for me.

So, I'm taking my homie Pete Enns's words of hope to heart when he says of deconstruction:

+ We don't bring it on ourselves: it just happens.

+ You aren't failing at faith: you're expressing it.

+ Deconstruction comes from within.

+ Deconstruction is not sexy or trendy. It sucks.

+ It does something positive for our faith that nothing else can do.[16]

Everyone's story is different, but the pattern Pete describes matched my journey fairly closely. *Eventually.* I can only nod to these bullet points today because I could not dodge them back then, and I now have over a decade of distance and therapy from those traumatic events.

I've started here in order to lay a foundation for what I'll say in coming chapters about the necessity, perils, and possibilities of our deconstructions (plural)—personal and societal—because many like me have experienced faith crises, the pandemic, climate change, political chaos, race issues, and the culture wars as stressful and harrowing. For us, deconstruction has not felt like a dawning of enlightenment. Frequently, we experience it as a nervous breakdown or cultural collapse.

Yet, so often, we hear pop-deconstruction influencers universalize our disorientation and unraveling as a wonderful party to be celebrated. I've been there…but I find it hard to stomach when the PTSD[17] parts of my heart alternatively shriek and then feel silenced or belittled by all the toxic positivity. "Speak for yourself," I sometimes shout, but not in words I can use here.

See? You should have skipped this part.

ALMOST INEXPLICABLE

So, while my nerves are still on a path of recovery to peace, *almost inexplicably*, after the bulldozer came through, new life did sprout from the rubble. I say *"almost inexplicably"* because, in the rearview mirror, I now see and will share *some* of the factors that saved my faith and my life.

On one fateful night, when I begged heaven to take me home, I heard no response pertaining to me at all. Maintaining my strategies for self-preservation was of no interest to God. Rather, I received a spontaneous gift: my eyes were opened to see the diamond of amazing grace in my Eden's core. My obsessive self-loathing, self-pity, and self-will were swept aside for a moment with a vision of this person I cherish—a beautiful soul worth living for.

A second grace came through my friends Darlene and Ted Enns-Dyck, the gentle shepherds who descended into my hell without denial or condemnation. When I was a smoldering wick, they did not snuff me out.[18]

A third reprieve: another wonderful comrade, Jason Upton, flew me to his home in Wisconsin, where he propped me on a couch between the back of his upright piano and a crackling fireplace. Over the course of a week, like the psalmist David, he sang the worst of my darkness away.

A final grace, for now: in my despair, Ron Dart suggested I read the works of Simone Weil,[19] whose remarkable life led me to find the cross in my abyss and make the lateral move from despondency to astonishment—at both the goodness of God and the affliction of humanity, intersecting there in the crucified God. I feel like she saved my life, and she'll figure prominently in this book.

These are only a few examples of direct interventions during a perilous flashpoint. I've shared elsewhere about the long-term care I received from many others who became my healing team through that stormy season: Brian West, Stephen Imbach, Philip Cilliers, Brian Klassen, Robin Emberly, John and Diane Van Vloten, Lazar Puhalo, Staretz Varlaam, Dwight and Lorie Martin, Charles and Colleen Littledale, Bill and Jamie Pegg, Anne Lawless, Barb Bambrick, Fi Calder, and I could go on—so many good and beautiful people. Whereas many pilgrims in deconstruction suffer isolation and alienation, I found safe harbor. I no longer think it was just luck. Our faith community had been building this healing harbor together over decades.

The gift of faith I received—that God is perhaps good after all—was embodied by them as unfailing mercy and real-life caregiving. I experienced the kindness of God expressed through these loving friends.

My family and community loved me. I ache for those who are experiencing the trauma of deconstruction but don't receive the same love from their families and communities, those hurting souls whose churches wag the finger and spout platitudes about backsliding. I'm so sorry. I feel the survivor's guilt of having people—wise and simple—who supported my faith shifts and walked with me through each stage of my theological reformation. I remember how many of those same faithful friends felt their own lives crash down on them. Such unrelenting pain! I couldn't prevent it or stop it. I couldn't hold it or us together. But when I withdrew, they never once forsook me. I wish that were everyone's experience. If such a thing as *reconstruction* exists, God is the source, they were the agents, and I was their patient.

The way my healers co-struggled with me has left me with a "debt of love"[20]—a holy obligation to "pay forward" their kindness. For readers in the alienation wing of deconstruction, I hope in some way, through this book, to walk beside you so that you will know that you are not alone.

2

GOOD, BAD, OR UGLY: SORROW AND JOY FLOW MINGLED DOWN

IT'S COMPLICATED

Deconstruction, as the word is popularly used—*is*.

Deconstruction happens. It is inevitable. It is necessary. Again, it can be pure joy—the good news in most profound ways. It can also be pure sorrow—a cataclysmic collapse. Or the joy and sorrow can flow mingled down, like the water and blood from the Savior's side.

Do you see how complex and varied our stories can be? Note the theological, emotional, and social layers up for alteration, the concentric circles of individual, communal, and cultural reorientation. Beyond that, we see a spectrum of spiritual and psychological experiences from liberating to traumatizing, from awakening to meltdown. And our disorientation or reorientation occurs among families and communities that are variously supportive or openly hostile to changes we often didn't even choose. Thus, the range of agency across our stories may fluctuate wildly—from voluntary adjustments in our convictions to involuntary, life-altering events. Finally, our starting points differ drastically. In the great cosmic bus crash, some of us were born into privileged seats equipped with cushy airbags to protect us from the worst of the impact.

Others were more vulnerable, given seats without airbags or seat belts. Then when life hit them head-on, they were thrown face-first through the windshield, landed in a heap of shattered glass, and suffered even deeper wounds.

It's complicated.

We cannot and must not superimpose our unique experiences on others to minimize their stories of genuine spiritual abuse or to diminish the joy they feel after a prison break from religious bondage. Whether one's victimization is actual or imagined—even a contrived narrative—breaking out of "old wineskins" can be virtually euphoric. We might feel like Houdini as we free ourselves from old straitjackets and feel expansive for the very first time. This was as true for the first disciples of Christ as it has been for the masses who've since shed the yoke of oppressive religious systems.

Yet one person's *autonomy* is the next person's *alienation*. Those who have reduced deconstruction to their divorce from a generalized sinister image of "the church" (whatever that means) and celebrate her demise, provoke dispersion, or incite apostasy cannot possibly speak for all of us. Scapegoating narratives that encourage estrangement don't resonate with people like me who have experienced their faith family as an intensive care unit and their spiritual parents as Good Samaritans who applied oil and wine to their wounds when they found themselves beaten and wounded on the Jericho Road.

It's complicated.

METAPHORS SHAPE US

I have elsewhere suggested alternative metaphors of deconstruction that better describe the multiplicity of our reorientation experiences.[21] I believe such metaphors are not merely descriptive. Choosing apt imagery can also *reframe* our journey and offer guidance through treacherous territory. In modern terminology, we would note how the events of our lives are only "half the story." How we narrate our lives to ourselves and others has a huge impact on our experiences. The story I tell myself may either deepen my trauma or draw me out of it.

This is partly what I mean by *deconstructing deconstruction*: I must examine the metaphors and allegories I use to think about myself and ask how the metaphors and allegories themselves impact my heart, for good or ill. Do they free me or further enslave me? Do they nourish me or cause spiritual anorexia? Do they open me up or shut me down? See what I'm doing there?

Among the metaphors I've previously employed, I explored the following images:

+ *Demolition:* knocking down old structures or walls to create new space

+ *Renovation:* restoring and revamping existing structures

+ *Detox, rehabilitation, and recovery:* restoring health by breaking free of unhealthy attachments, harmful habits, and addictive behaviors

+ *Detox and cleanse diets:* restoring health by purging toxins and getting better nourishment

+ *Extreme makeover:* making cosmetic adjustments that draw out one's true beauty

+ *Fine art restoration:* carefully stripping away layers of varnish and centuries of touch-ups to reveal an original masterpiece

+ *Growing up or aging well:* normalizing development and dignifying maturity

+ *Path and pilgrimage:* recognizing the realities, perils, and joys of the journey

+ *Tailor-making (versus custom-making) clothing:* instead of designing self-made religion, adapting the best of your faith tradition to address specific times, cultures, and needs

+ *Dry-cleaning wedding gowns:* cleansing the spots, stains, and wrinkles of the spiritual bride's wedding gown, rather than discarding her or destroying it

CHRISTLIKE METAPHORS

To the above metaphors, we can add any number of the gospel analogies suggested by Jesus Christ—history's all-time, hinge-point proponent and practitioner of de/reconstruction. You know, the One who said, "Behold, I am making ALL things new."[22]

+ *Metamorphosis:* old self versus new self

+ *Homecoming:* finding our way back to the Father's house

+ *Old and new wineskins:* new wine bursting out of old, rigid wineskins

+ *Water to wine:* the wedding-guest sign of water being transformed from religious jars into the best wine of the feast

+ *Vine-dressing*: the vinedresser pruning (or lifting) fruitless vines to bear more and better fruit

+ *Fruit-bearing*: the divine Farmer plowing, sowing, watering, and weeding; and the fruit sprouting, experiencing expansive growth, flowering, and bearing fruit

+ *Healing*: spiritual blindness, leprosy, paralysis, and even death cured

+ *New covenant*: God's unfaithful spouse once divorced but now restored and remarried to God

+ *Born from above*: spiritual rebirth

+ *Baptism*: our death, burial, and resurrection with Christ

And then we have the apostle Paul—possibly the most dramatically reconstructed human that you'll find anywhere in history! He was fond of metaphors that reflected his *conversion* (isn't a full-blown *conversion* what reconstruction has always entailed?):

+ *Awakened*: waking up from sleep

+ *Enlightened*: eyes opened to see the light

+ *Transplanted*: being given a new mind, a new head, a new heart

+ *Hands*: grasping, clinging, releasing

+ *Cleansed*: by waters of renewal or fires that purge

+ *Resurrected*: being raised from spiritual death

+ *Reclothed*: putting on new garments (Christ himself)

+ *Recreated*: becoming a new creation

+ *Metamorphosis*: transfigured from glory to glory into the image of Christ

+ *Metanoia*: doing an "about-face" that changes you, converts you

ORIGAMI?

How about you? How would you describe your story? Are you unfolding, unraveling, or being folded into origami? What personalized metaphor would best serve, not just to describe but to reframe and perhaps upgrade your faith narrative? You may even need a whole constellation of metaphors because you, too, are wonderfully complex. That's allowed!

That said, I'm going to gather these experiences and metaphors into five broad, cohesive themes for deeper exploration:

- **Be-leaving:** in which we'll discuss some dynamics of leaving a faith family, congregation, or movement—the pain this involves and the reactions it invokes, as well as whether "be-leavers" are fleeing, following, or both.

- **Liberation:** in which we affirm the freedom that flows from leaving the prisons of restrictive and oppressive constructs, and how that was the point of the gospel from the beginning (even if it's hard).

- **Trauma:** in which we look at those who experience not only their past, but leaving their past, as severely traumatic, and how toxic positivity around deconstruction can demoralize those who discover they've lost more than just their faith.

- **Purgation:** in which we undergo the purifying function of deconstruction that is essential to our spiritual health; such purification was familiar to the great mystics who challenged us to let go of attachments and let God remove obstacles that hinder our connection to divine Love.

- **Illumination:** in which these same mystics (across many faiths) also recognized that we cannot enlighten ourselves. They call us to orient our hearts in open receptivity toward the Light and wait on grace to come illuminate the path to freedom.

I believe that navigating these major themes honors the *complexity* of deconstruction and remains mindful of the *hazards* of deconstruction, while also affirming the *necessity* of our water-to-wine development and assessing its *possibilities.*

3

TRUE BE-LEAVERS

LOSS OF COMMUNITY

I know that my missteps in deconstruction were more than I could bear by myself. How much more difficult are the trials of those who must go it alone! So many sorry souls lose their bearings when they first exit their faith communities. We can't just assume they've lost their way…or that they've found it. Have they "fallen away" into a pit? Or have they made their escape from bondage? Let's not be too quick to judge either the "dones" or those they're "done with." The full truth behind our narratives is elusive, perhaps inaccessible, and always above our pay grade.

But we do know this: those who leave their congregations—whether pastors or congregants—frequently go through a first painful stage, passing from communion to alienation, from community to isolation, from relative stability to spiritual vertigo. Panic may ensue. And that makes perfect sense. But the heartache goes even deeper when one is cornered into a double bind—when one's exit is both traumatizing but also obviously necessary. If the only fellowship we've ever known was truly toxic or spiritually abusive, then we *need* to flee, regardless of the fog ahead. I get that. I encourage it. Eden and I have regularly facilitated departures where either a pastor or a layperson had sustained sufficient soul damage that the only solution was immediate departure. Knowing that leaving was necessary to survival didn't make it hurt any less.

But then, just to add to the swirl, "Job's counselors" start chirping—condemners and cheerleaders alike—with so many bright ideas. Their reactions to our spiritual evolution vary, ranging from:

+ *Concern and bewilderment:* "What's happening to you? It's like I don't even know you anymore!"

+ *Accusation and condemnation:* "You're backsliding; you're a heretic. I don't think I can be your friend (or spouse!) anymore."

+ *Reckless and defiant affirmation:* "YES! Go for it! In fact, burn it all to the ground!"

+ *Cavalier and thoughtless counsel:* "Don't let anyone tell you how to do this! Follow your own heart. There's no wrong way."

Oh, great! That's all we need. Conflicting counsel, cacophonous voices. Noise.

Amid all that clanging, deconstruction-as-departure also inevitably includes disillusionment and doubt—as it should! Now, will disillusionment free us from unhelpful illusions or bind us to bitterness? Our doubts may actually open a path to greater freedom for us...or they may take us down into a ditch of despondency. Either outcome is entirely possible. Neither is assured.

A NEED FOR ROOTS

I am wary of joining the cacophony of "shoulds" bombarding people who are experiencing deconstruction. What I can suggest is that we all begin with empathy. Specifically, let's acknowledge how complicated, how life-altering, how *terrible* and *traumatic* deconstruction has been for many who undergo it (versus choosing it).

Simone Weil noted humanity's deep "need for roots"[23] in order to flourish, and she named "uprootedness" as the deepest of all afflictions. In her view, to uproot the Other[24] or drive them to uproot themselves—whether through imperial occupation, colonial relocation, or missionary proselytization—was an act of supreme violence.

Uprootedness is also a profound aspect of deconstruction. One's religious tradition or faith community can be so resistant to change or even questions that they virtually drive healthy, growing believers into exile. Conversely, to the degree that deconstruction has become a movement (or industry), those encouraging us to empty the pews may also be the culprit, inciting uprootedness by encouraging alienation. You're "damned if you do and damned if you don't"—damned to the violence of Weil's uprootedness. So, along with empathy, I'd want to add the importance of mindfulness. Do we understand the real impact of The Great Deconstruction on those souls whose need for roots we may violate?

In referring to *The Great Deconstruction*, I'm drawing an intentional parallel to America's two *Great Awakening* movements (1730s–40s with Wesley, Whitefield, and Edwards, and 1790s–1800s, which ignited antislavery and women's rights sentiments). Today's Great Deconstruction bears both the aromas and odors of classic American revivalism, including impulses toward colonizing and uprooting whatever predated its arrival. What surprises me is how thoroughly evangelical many of the *ex-vangelical* enthusiasts remain after losing faith, while seemingly oblivious to the overt and abiding similarities to their heritage. It's surprising how little we change.

Others see more clearly, cognizant that deconstruction, per se, is not the point. As Richard Rohr says, we necessarily pass through a phase of order, disorder, and reorder—i.e., we pass through cycles of *disorientation* into *reorientation*. My appeal is that we must not underestimate how severe the disorientation is for those uprooted from the soil of the only tradition, the only community, the only family they've ever known.

What I find so helpful about Rohr's take is that he doesn't totalize *disorientation* as an end in itself. It is a vital stage of our journey, however painful, that doesn't forecast any promised land over the horizon. My heart is not to dissuade pilgrims in exodus, but I would advocate for the many whose journey is far more treacherous, traumatic, and uprooted than others'. My concern is for those who message me, telling me they feel excluded from the deconstructionists' banner-waving pride, with its cheers of toxic positivity.

"You're doing great! You've got this!"

"No, I'm not. I'm not doing well at all. You're not my bench-press spotter! I've been chewed up in a living sequel to *Jaws* here! So please, stop shaming me for the loss I feel or failing to measure up to your standard of joy—for being a 'bad testimony' for your movement. I already went through that in the church."

Maybe the reason so much social-media deconstructionism sounds wonderful is that it ignores the broken hearts who not only lost their faith but also their families, meaning, hope, and joy. They feel marginalized and silenced when they don't meet the expectations of "successful," happy-clappy deconstructionists. Again, it's an all-too-familiar scenario they have already had to abandon before.

SHARK!

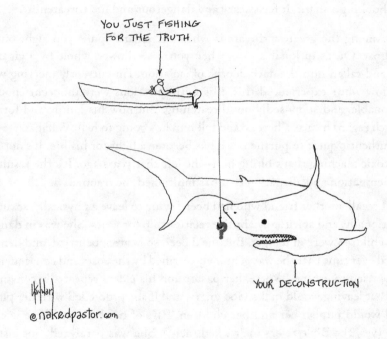

YOU JUST FISHING FOR THE TRUTH.

YOUR DECONSTRUCTION

@nakedpastor.com

I'm reminded of the David Hayward cartoon, which he summarized as, "When your deconstruction comes at you like a shark." In the cartoon, we see a person in a boat, innocently fishing, using a question mark as bait. Below the surface, we see a big shark ready to bite at the hook. David describes this drawing:

I see some parallels between fishing for fish and fishing for the truth.

There were times in our deconstruction when it's like tiny little nibbles. You can tell something is there but there is no clear bite.

Then there are times when it chomps down hard and a fight commences.

You catch small fish. You catch big fish.

In our deconstruction, we will catch plenty of small fish. These are new discoveries that don't necessarily rock our world....

But we will also catch some big fish. These are discoveries that upset everything....

When you catch the big one during your deconstruction, it is like hooking a shark. It feels scary and dangerous and life-threatening.[25]

Among the greatest threats is when the "shark" pulls you right out of the boat. Or, as in Jonah's case, when you're swallowed whole by a gigantic fish and taken into the dark depths of isolation. I'm currently meeting with a fellow who's experienced this. His faith questions were innocent enough, reasonable, and supposedly nonthreatening. But now his family and former church regard him as a heretic and tell him he's going to hell. What started as an authentic quest to pursue truth has become a fight for his life. It's not just the toxic teaching that's biting him—he left that years ago. It's the resulting condemnation and alienation that has multiplied the trauma.

I recall another friend who had been trying to leave a physically, sexually, emotionally, and spiritually abusive relationship for years. She was in danger. Her children were in danger. But she'd been so beaten, belittled, and demoralized over time that she was genuinely terrified by the costs and consequences if she tried to escape. Worse, her pastor and his elders repeatedly convinced her that leaving would make God angry, and if she proceeded with her plans, God would punish her and her children. Part of her believed these wicked men (yes, the Bible refers to "wicked men"). She was paralyzed, not just by the trauma of abuse but also by the threat of a retributive husband, accusing community, and monster god.

In both these stories, getting out was absolutely necessary. And yet the prospect of leaving—of uprooting—was as frightening as staying. Worse, in both cases, "believing" meant believing what the abusers said about God or Jesus. Their belief in Jesus and submission to spiritual violence were fused. To them, to escape the abuse, they had to disavow "belief" altogether. The motto "Don't throw the baby out with the bathwater" was incomprehensible to them. There was no such distinction in their minds.

DETACHMENT: BE-LEAVE

So, what if the name of Jesus is so attached to spiritual abuse and religious post-traumatic stress disorder (PTSD) that our exodus from spiritual death and slavery instigates a disavowal of his church (if it actually was his) and even his name? What if our conversion needs to be a "deconversion" *from* the many current and dominant religious idols that go by the name "Jesus"? What if, through a despicable act of identity theft, the precious name of our infinite Spring of Life, Light, and Love has been stolen and attached to something invasive and malignant? Or—slow down for this line—what if we're driven by necessity and encouraged by cynics to deconstruct something we never actually had?[26]

Well, the good news is that you can renounce a false Jesus all you like (*and you should, and you must!*), but the true Christ will never abandon you. Of course he won't. He doesn't. He can't. His mercy endures forever.[27] Who knows, Christ may have been the architect of your jailbreak in the first place. Yes, even from cellblocks within Christianity! "Let my people go!" he shouts against whatever social system has become the new Egypt, the new Babylon, the new Rome—regardless of whether his name appears on its marquee. Christ, our great Deconstructionist, has always been about breaking out of damp dungeons and dark tombs—and as he surfaces, he brings a host of captives with him.

Hallelujah, right?

I am in a conversation-in-motion with my friend Paul E. Ralph (PER). I believe he coined the term "be-leave."[28] In his lingo, "be-*leave*-ers" are those who had to walk away (from what? you name it!) in order to find their way home. For Paul, this is less about losing and finding than moving from alienation to communion. The idea that *leaving* a family or a church or a faith or a notion of Jesus could lead us *to communion* rather than *to alienation* with him and others sounds counterintuitive. Often, it doesn't at first…especially if we've been conditioned to isolate ourselves from outsiders and strangers.

For Abraham, be-*leaving* was following Yahweh out of his homeland toward a yet unknown city of God. For Moses, be-*leaving* was following the pillar of cloud and pillar of fire out of slavery toward a promised land. For the exiles in Babylon, be-*leaving* meant following God back to the rubble of their homeland. These treks all involved significant layovers and trials, but as PER pointed out to me, the key word is "home."

When home is a Person, rather than a place, there's freedom in the journey. For some, the former places cannot hold the new things we've discovered. For others, those very things return us to the wider awe and wisdom of the familiar. For *all* who choose it, and for those who do not, it remains an invitation to a Person. To Christ.

If we take a "pro-pro approach," yes, some need to leave and never look back. Others eventually return to their community of origin. But Jesus—as both path and home—remains for all. Both for those who discover him and those who haven't yet.[29]

So, be-*leaving*, in this sense, is more about *following* than *fleeing*. The New Testament (NT) terms for "leave" are multivalent and may even seem contradictory,[30] but what they reveal is that, for Jesus, the call to *follow* him can look a whole lot like *leaving* (and be frequently misinterpreted as betrayal or "backsliding").

BE-LEAVE IN JESUS'S WORDS

The Gospels recount many examples of be-*leaving*—following rather than fleeing, but leaving, nonetheless. Two passages, from Luke 9 and Mark 10, immediately come to mind:

> [57] As they were going along the road a man addressed Jesus.
> "Wherever you're going," he said, "I'll *follow* you!"
> [58] "Foxes have lairs," Jesus replied, "and the birds in the sky have nests; but the son of man doesn't have anywhere to lay his head."
> [59] To another person he said, "*Follow* me."
> "Master," he replied, "let me first go and bury my father."
> [60] "Let the dead bury their dead," said Jesus. "You *must go* and announce God's kingdom."
> [61] "I will follow you, Master," said another, "but first let me say good-bye to the people at home."
> [62] "Nobody," replied Jesus, "who begins to plow and then looks over his shoulder is fit for God's kingdom."   (Luke 9:57–62)

> [28] "Look here," Peter started up, "we've *left* everything and *followed* you."
> [29] "I'll tell you the truth," replied Jesus. "No one who has *left* a house, or brothers or sisters, or mother or father, or children, or lands, because

of me and the gospel [30] will fail to receive back a hundred times more in the present age: houses, brothers, sisters, mothers, children, and lands—with persecutions!—and finally the life of the age to come."

(Mark 10:28–30)

Here we acknowledge that *following/be-leaving* can be hard, misunderstood, sacrificial, and totally necessary. It may result in leaving home, family, church, and community. It can exhilarate or terrify. Case in point: this just in via email from a fellow *be-leaver*:

> I have been going through some major deconstruction after growing up in a Christian fundamentalist cult. It's been a lonely journey dealing with a lot of fear and shame. Thank you for pointing me to Jesus as our North Star—the Jesus I always knew was beautiful but was never really shown to me. The god I grew up with was a monster in a lot of ways.[31]

Fleeing or following? YES. A good reminder that we shouldn't quickly jump to judgments about what is happening in anyone's *leaving*. Any given departure could be *fleeing* or *following*, and, more often than we know, both at once. And we don't foresee the end of the matter, do we?

4

SHAKE OFF THE DUST

When Jesus sent out the Twelve, two by two, as evangelists to prepare the towns and villages for his arrival, he gave them explicit instructions. Some of his words were specific to the situation, while others apply to this day as well, even beyond the apostolic mandate. One phrase (troubling to some) is especially poignant to those on the water-to-wine journey:

> If anyone won't welcome you or listen to your message, go out of the house or the town and *shake the dust off your feet.*"   (Matt 10:14)

When your transformation (whether meltdown or growth spurt) requires *be-leaving* a faith group or movement (whether fleeing or following), we need to consider this controversial suggestion: *shake the dust off your feet.* Through ears clogged with judgment, resentment, or raw pain, that statement may sound rather harsh. In fact, we might be tempted to adopt the phrase to fortify a victim narrative and justify a rude departure. We like to imagine that slamming the door on our way out is righteous—even those who leave the Christian faith altogether can come across as holier-than-thou. I guess they had good teachers.

I've been there. Ex-smoker syndrome. I was once neck-deep in the mid-1990s iteration of charismatic renewal. I led in their meetings, spoke at their conferences, and saw the Holy Spirit at work in wonderful ways. But it became clear that I needed to distance myself from the devolving "New Apostolic Reformation" crowd that had infected authentic renewal with politicized "prophecies," partisan ideology, and the militarized nationalism of civil religion. If "the testimony of Jesus…is the spirit of prophecy" (Rev 19:10), then they had clearly lost the plot. When, at one of their "apostolic round tables," their famous chair, dubbed "apostle of the apostles," declared that their clique was "the epicenter of what God is doing in this world" and that his goal was "total governmental takeover,"[32] I knew I was done. It was time for me to move on.

To be frank, it didn't really feel like it was I who had moved on. I desired to continue following the Holy Spirit, and this was not that. *I shook the dust off my feet.*

Or did I? What does that actually mean? This is where I feel so many of us have misheard Jesus. Pilate *"washed his hands"* (Matt 27:24) of Jesus. He thought to absolve himself of any guilt in Jesus's death—immediately before green-lighting his crucifixion!

But washing bloodguilt from our hands is not the same as shaking the dust off our feet. For me, the difference took some time to sort out. I imagine others have had the same experience.

First, I had to sort through my anger, beginning with letting myself feel it. Repressing my ire has never served me well. If I just push it down in the name of peacemaking, it will grow and eventually leak out. It may emerge as depression, anxiety, or misplaced anger at my favorite people. So, I feel it…but, on my healthy days, I do this in prayer before the throne of grace. I feel the malice surface before the eyes of the One who can expunge it. Before the merciful Judge, I feel what I feel, and then I offer it to Christ. "Lord, why do I seethe?"

Next, I sense him sorting out divine grief and anger from my own passions. It is entirely appropriate to grieve deeply when influential men and women drive people away from faith in Christ by engaging in hateful, blasphemous, cultish behavior in Jesus's name. Righteous anger would be fitting. But, remember, moral outrage is often a form of confession. What was this outrage I felt toward wayward renewal miscreants?

Had they ever personally injured me? I can only recall minor instances of being slandered or snubbed by a few individuals. And only my ego was bruised—my heart was fine. No, that wouldn't account for the triggers in me. The Holy Spirit showed me that my anger was rooted in shame. It embarrassed me to be identified with their shenanigans and to see my complicity in promoting a rotting movement. I was angry at myself. My pride was so wounded by my participation that I was prone to projecting my self-condemnation onto them.

Oddly, when I could forgive myself for my spiritual arrogance and even redirect the embarrassment toward my egoism, I could now remember that era as part of my story. The anger lost all its fleshly edge. I still grieve the ongoing and escalating damage that the blowhards inflict on the bride of Christ, but I pray for the same mercy I need to be extended to them, because I know how deeply flawed I still am. I see how their repentance is connected to mine and that, somehow, my complicity in the movement is also my authority in intercession.

"*We* have sinned," said Daniel and other prophetic intercessors. "*We* have been evil, *we* have done wrong. *We* have rejected what you commanded us to do and have turned away from what you showed us was right."[33] This was "identificational repentance," even by prophets who had not participated in the sins they confessed—just as Jesus, completely sinless, received John's "baptism of repentance,"[34] vicariously immersing the sins of humanity in the death and resurrection of his baptism.

Having had my heart cleansed of, and my ego humbled by, the shame of my complicity in a house that can no longer welcome the "gospel of peace," I have moved on. Truly. And this is where "shaking the dust off our feet" makes new sense to me. The dust we carry is none other than *attachments* to our former way of being—the ways our resentments still keep us hooked to *who we were* and anyone or any group that reminds us of that old self.

For others, it's different. The *dust* they need to shed may be the festering wounds of broken relationships or abusive leaders and how they can become an identity. Wouldn't it be nice if "done" was just a label describing a corner of our life story, rather than an embittered identity that never lets us leave our hurts? In this regard, are we talking about leaving people, leaving family, leaving communities? Understandably, sometimes that's necessary for one's spiritual, mental, and emotional health.

"*Shake off the dust*," says Jesus.

I tell him, "Look, Jesus, we don't just shake off trauma."

He looks me in the eyes and holds up his hands and says, "I know."

I see the trauma of every human in the wounds of the God who knows. He's not afraid to go there. Indeed, he has. Never forget,

Jesus too *suffered outside the gate*, so that he might make the people holy with his own blood. So then, *let's go out to him*, outside the camp, bearing his shame. Here, you see, we have no city that lasts; we are looking for the one that is still to come.   (Heb 13:12–14)

WHEN THE SH*T STINK LINGERS

Unfortunately, we can leave a dangerous social environment without leaving behind the dust of our attachments to it—we may still live out our days in the bitterness of our narratives.

Reflecting on this reality, my friend Felicia Murrell modernized the dust-on-our-feet metaphor with another vivid metaphor—a lingering stench:

At some point in my life, I came to the realization that I don't like being around people who once made me feel like sh*t. Even if I was the one creating the narrative about what I thought they thought about me. It doesn't make being around these people any easier. Sh*t stink lingers on the fingers long after you've washed your hands. And sometimes it's hard to separate actual people from the story you've told yourself about those people. But this is the arduous, *brutiful* (beautiful + brutal) work of healing. The separating, the unraveling. Unbinding yourself from narratives that perpetuate bitterness.

As we surrender to Love's perfect work, the fury of Love is aimed at everything that is not of Love's kind. Stripping away all the muck that dims our unique expression as image-bearers...including the narratives we tell ourselves to protect ourselves from other people's character defects. The things in my life, in your life that happened, happened. Nothing diminishes the veracity of your experience...

The change Love invites us into is how we live and move and have our being in spite of, or rather, because of those things. How do I exist in my body in a way that isn't fragmented or stunted? For me, when sh*t stink lingers on my fingers, my defended self goes into warrior mode—distancing, walling off, hiding out, doing whatever feels right to protect herself from pain, from hurt and harm. Whenever I catch a whiff of that foul smell, I know it's an invitation to pause. To touch my heart. To name fear. Feel my feet supported by the earth. To express gratitude for the self who survived hell and has lived to tell it. This does not always silence the stories, but like the eye of a storm, in the center all is calm. And from this grounded state, I tell my mind: *I will not live trapped in a story of my own making*, and I offer myself compassion.

As Tara Brach says, "Compassion honors our experience; it allows us to be intimate with the life of this moment as it is. Compassion makes our acceptance wholehearted and complete."[35]

Truth! We can't merely exit the building. We need to exit the self-defeating story that traps us. It's hard work but good work. And best done with friends who care to see us truly free.

We've considered some of the hardest dynamics of leaving a faith family, congregation, or movement. We've leaned into the pain that involves, the reactions it invokes, and the question of whether "be-leavers" are fleeing, following, or both. *Be-leaving* can feel like *exile*, but as we'll see, there's also a rich history of *exodus* woven into the gospel itself—the exodus of spiritual liberation that Christ came to preach and enact.

5

EXODUS:
SPIRITUAL LIBERATION

I've alluded in passing to deconstruction as liberation (aka redemption, emancipation), using "prison break" as a metaphor. After having had an initial look at the trauma side of *be-leaving* (with more discussion to come), and having taken the *exile* side seriously, we're ready to speak of our faith sojourn in terms of *exodus*, of spiritual *liberation*. Traumatic *events* can't be undone. But trauma *narratives* can be rewritten—my past can be retold as my unfolding story of redemption.

AN UNFOLDING STORY OF REDEMPTION

When headlines announce the *exodus* of tens of millions of people from the church, the journalists may or may not realize that they're citing a biblical term, event, and book. You'll be familiar with the story, but a few highlights bear repeating in this context.

The Exodus is a story of liberation from slavery. It is told by slaves whose narrative subsumes their past into an emerging revelation of God's redemptive purposes for them. They leave Egypt (the nation) and, as their story unfurls, they're also invited to leave behind their slave identity. Through the annual celebration of the Passover Feast, they remember their past as those who are now free. Or, even when they must later celebrate Passover in exile (to Assyria or Babylon) or under occupation (under Greece or Rome), the Exodus story empowers them to live as free people, grateful to their Deliverer:

[1] Oh, give thanks to the LORD, for He is good!
For His mercy endures forever.
[2] Let the redeemed of the LORD say so,
Whom He has redeemed from the hand of the enemy,
[3] And gathered out of the lands,
From the east and from the west,
From the north and from the south.

[4] They wandered in the wilderness in a desolate way;
They found no city to dwell in.
[5] Hungry and thirsty,
Their soul fainted in them.
[6] Then they cried out to the LORD in their trouble,
And He delivered them out of their distresses.
[7] And He led them forth by the right way,
That they might go to a city for a dwelling place.
[8] Oh, that men would give thanks to the LORD for His goodness,
And for His wonderful works to the children of men!
[9] For He satisfies the longing soul,
And fills the hungry soul with goodness.

(Ps 107:1–9 NKJV)

Again, God's people remember their past but are not trapped in it. They remember their bondage and affliction, but as those freed from them. That episode has become an important chapter in a larger story that hinges on an encounter with the God who hears the cries and groans and "comes down" and leads them out.

The Exodus becomes the framework of the Christ story. When the four Evangelists pen their Gospels, they frame their portraits of Jesus of Nazareth according to the contours and colors of the Exodus backstory. Remember how, after Jesus's birth, his family fled as refugees to Egypt and stayed there until the death of Herod?[36] Matthew says, "This happened to fulfill what the Lord said through the prophet: Out of Egypt I called my Son" (Matt 2:15). Christ assumes the role of Israel, of the Suffering Servant, and of Moses, the deliverer who leads his people out of slavery from spiritual Egypt.

John's "paschal Gospel" conveys the life of Christ, the Lamb of God, slain and risen, as the great fulfillment of the Exodus Passover, expanding Israel's redemption narrative to deliver all nations from the kingdom of darkness, dread, and death.

The Exodus becomes the grammar of Christian freedom. With Christ as both our Passover Lamb and our Redeemer, the language of Exodus—ransom and redemption, liberation and deliverance—becomes typical (a "type" of) the Christian narrative. Even the overused terminology of "salvation" echoes the song of Moses after the Israelites passed through the Red Sea:

> ¹ Then Moses and the Israelites sang this song to the LORD:
> "I will sing to the LORD, for he has triumphed gloriously;
>> horse and rider he has thrown into the sea.
> ² The LORD is my strength and my might,
>> and he has become my *salvation*;
> this is my God, and I will praise him;
>> my father's God, and I will exalt him."
>> (Exod 15:1–2 NRSV)

The God who saves Israel out of Egypt is revealed in *Jesus*—literally, "Yahweh saves"—so that the gospel proclamation is that this Jesus is "*savior* of the world" (John 4:42; see also 1 John 4:14), on whom the Father confers the *Redeemer* identity of Yahweh himself in the prophecies of Isaiah.[37]

These highlights of the Exodus narrative—for Israel, for Jesus, for us—remind us that Christianity itself *is* an Exodus story, even when its hierarchs become the new Pharaoh, its structures the new pyramids, and its institutions the new Egypt. Whenever Christendom becomes a venue for spiritual slavery, the instinct for exodus shouldn't shock us. That just might be Moses calling, "Thus says the LORD God of Israel: '*Let My people go, that they may hold a feast to Me in the wilderness*'" (Exodus 5:1 NKJV).

METAMORPHOSIS

> We are, clearly, transitory beings, and our existence on earth is, clearly, a process, the uninterrupted existence of a chrysalis transitioning into a butterfly.[38]

Many of us have felt our faith metamorphosis as a kind of emergence, like butterflies from the chrysalis. More than merely escaping, we experienced transformation. Old parts of our life—ways of thinking, ways of being, ways of acting—dissolved, and we sprouted wings.

In lecture ten of his Gifford Lectures on "Varieties of Religious Experience" (1901–02), psychologist William James noted how this sensation of euphoric freedom is common to sudden conversions of all types, whether into a religious tradition or out of one. Newfound faith and newfound atheism may ignite the same neural sparks. One feels a dramatic shift from old life to new. Even apostasy may be a "religious experience."

Many of my friends describe their deconstruction, even out of Christianity, as a second conversion—not unlike the mainline Protestants who experienced a "second blessing" or the Catholic mystics who "saw the light." If what people are describing as their deconstruction sounds like just another word for *conversion*, that's because it often is. Our experiences of exodus, of awakening, of letting go, of transformation, of metamorphosis, and so forth, represent a familiar path—a *spiritual tradition*, believe it or not—that we find at the very heart of the Christian story and echoed through the lives and testimonies of the saints. Listen to the great eighteen-century evangelist/hymnist Charles Wesley:

> Long my imprisoned spirit lay
> Fast bound in sin and nature's night;
> Thine eye diffused a quickening ray,
> I woke, the dungeon flamed with light;
> My chains fell off, my heart was free;
> I rose, went forth, and followed Thee.[39]

Wesley identified his awakening with an inner explosion of illumination that beckoned him to follow his Savior out of the tomb. For Wesley and countless others, deconstruction signified a death-and-resurrection epiphany of Jesus Christ. And he's not talking about "finding religion" after a life of debauchery. Wesley found living faith after a dead and deadening religious church experience.

This kind of inner baptism into the faith is far more than a spiritual chiropractic adjustment or the adoption of new doctrines. Whether our newfound freedom liberates us from the petrified religiosity of a calcified church OR self-destructive attachments to our old cravings (à la twelve-step recovery), it involves the total recreation of our lives. Our transfiguration is every bit as radical as the caterpillar-become-butterfly. From the conversion of the apostle Paul forward, we've described these awakenings to freedom as a transformation from darkness to light, from slavery to freedom, from death to life.

In fact, from Paul to Wesley to Bill W. (founder of Alcoholics Anonymous), the de/reconstruction they describe sounds like joy, trials notwithstanding. Some of you know this as your own experience. It's good to remember that "you must be born again" or "born from above" did not begin as a trite evangelistic trope of stodgy fundamentalists. Jesus coined the phrase for Nicodemus[40] in order to emphasize how dramatic and how necessary personal transformation must be, even when it is *out of* or *away from* the "faith of our fathers."

DELIVERANCE NOW

I am so grateful to be a witness to such encounters and not just talk about or analyze them *ad nauseam*. I see God's Spirit midwifing these tomb-to-womb-to-new-life changes all the time. I'm not a counselor or therapist or pastor or spiritual director. As one who's caused trauma, I am admittedly gun-shy. But I try to pay forward the mercy I've received, and when that happens, I get to see neat stuff, even as a bystander.

For example, *just now* (as I was editing the above section with Wesley's hymn), my phone dinged. Someone was texting about an Instagram meme I had posted that summarized the theme of this chapter: "Trauma *events* can't be undone. Trauma *narratives* can be rewritten. My past retold as my unfolding story of redemption."

She asked, "Brad, can you explain that a bit more? Are you talking philosophically? Can God turn our traumatic experiences into something usable? I still jump at sudden sounds, cry at the drop of a hat, and tense up when I hear ambulance sirens. And I fight catastrophic thoughts…so…?"

I replied, "Not just philosophically. It sounds like you still have some work to do with the trauma in terms of your PTSD reactions. But your life is much more than that now. That part of your story is only an episode in a much bigger saga of redemption that you are already experiencing. More to come! As you do the trauma work, I hope that even the traumas in your story will be places you meet Jesus and exchange for his gift. But this is quite a journey."

I went back to work for a few minutes, satisfied that she would receive the message as encouragement to pursue trauma-focused therapy. She heard it the same way:

"Okay, I hear that. I think it's part of why we are heading back to the USA…resources."

But a minute later, she sent another message: "By the way…'exchange the trauma for his gift.' Massive imagery there for me. In fact, it's made me cry. Wow! Just WOW." Pause. "I don't like the pain."

It was one of those moments when I metaphorically felt the *im*patience of Christ. It felt like, "Just tell her, already." A simple message:

"Why not just go ahead and ask him? 'Jesus, what gift would you give me in exchange for this pain?' Then picture him, picture the pain, picture the gift, and say, 'Yes, please.' Then watch what he does."

That was it. It was all he asked of me. Just tell her, already. Right now.

She replied, "I shouldn't really be standing here alive today, to be honest… I will ask."

And back to writing.

"Ding…ding, ding, ding, ding, ding." *Lots* of one-line messages. I went to refill my coffee while I waited for her to finish. Here's what she sent next:

Oh, my dear, Lord / Well / I think you must have been praying for me. / In contrast to my experiences with my family and my husband's family. / I found myself not wanting to give him my pain because I didn't want to hurt him. / I was holding on very tight to it. / He told me that's why he came. / I told him I can't. / I must not hurt anybody. / The foot-washing image came to mind. / By the way, I'm bawling. / He said he could take it. / I'm not used to father figures or brother figures listening to me, giving me the slightest bit of notice. / The feeling I got was overwhelming love and that he actually wants to take everything. And then he showed me his resurrection. / He kind of clapped his hands together, like shaking the dust from his hands, and said, "It's done." / And I feel overwhelmed and I'm bawling, because of gratitude, not because of sadness. But also because I've had another huge answer to prayer today, where my son called me during his lunch break. He has never done that before and it was a response to my prayer today that he would call me. / Why am I scared to say I don't have PTSD anymore? But right now, I don't feel like I have it? How can it be this simple? When Jesus said he would take all of our sorrow, I didn't realize this is how it can be literally. Like the woman at the well. He had time for her. It's awfully hard to give Jesus my pain, Brad. I'm sobbing.

I replied,

Well, it's a layer. Maybe he took it all, or maybe he *is taking* it all. So, now that you have a living connection with Jesus the Listener, this can be your new way of praying—visiting with him face-to-face and continuing to make exchanges. Like with the foot-washing story, you don't need a whole bath, just a foot wash.

And Jesus *taking* your pain doesn't mean that you're *inflicting* pain on him. He already finished that on the cross. This is exactly like the foot-washing. It just means letting him cleanse it. So, what was the gift you received?

Her:

It was the resurrection vision and saying, "It's done." I haven't hurt him. The gift was the vision of him slapping his hands together, saying, "It's done." And I felt completely calm… Peace. I can't explain it, Brad. I just feel peace. I don't know if you suffer with anxiety, but if you do, you know that clenched-fist type of muscle thing that is sort of always there in the background. And *right now*, my hand is resting calmly on my leg and I'm not tense in any way. That is a miracle because ever since the day I was born, I am usually in some form of overwork or tenseness in my muscles…even the physio has noticed it.

I do understand this may be a layering thing or it might be completely gone.

But also, when you referred to "Jesus the Listener," I needed to hear that. I feel something huge has just happened! I'm overwhelmed again, crying. Oh, my goodness… Wow. How did that just happen? I feel the healing. Thank you for listening to the Spirit… And to me. I've had an encounter with our living God. I am bathing in what has just happened.

Me:

My wife says that so many people who talk *deconstruction* just continually pick the scab on their wounds, and so the wound just keeps on bleeding. Few people seem willing to just let Jesus lay his hand on the wound. You did that. I'm very proud of you.

It was like Jesus was impatient to get to it. He prompted me to suggest picturing him and making the exchange. So, I did, and you took it from there.

Her:

That made me laugh... Jesus "impatient." / Thank you. / It's not much of a faith if I'm not willing to take a leap. But he can wash my head, shoulders, and all of me now. ☺ / I get it. / Boy, do I get it now. / This has been a purgatorial experience in this moving delay and tiny flat. / Refining fire. / Best experienced from a spiritual point of view.

I think the practice will be to remember what happened today, like the altars they would build along the way in the desert, where God did great things for them. I have that exchange to recall.

Knowing that such transcendent experiences can also be loaded with dopamine and may become either momentary OR transformative, I gave her three days before a check-in. Here's where she has come to so far, in her own words:

Awareness of Jesus's constant presence. I'm not alone. I never have been. Not in a hymn type of way (cerebral)...more of a bodily resurrection way. Real. Conversation...which I've had before, but not in relationship to that exchange. And the unity of all, his image in all... I was so used to "tough love"...martyrdom as procedure. I'm now transformed because the reality of kingdom life is available now. And not just in theory. I've tasted, seen, witnessed this. We are living so close to that thin veil it's almost palpable. I love it! Whoa, here come the tears again!

It's funny to me now that I was just trying to get back to *writing about* liberation, while Jesus was more interested in *doing* liberation. Which begs the question: Why just *read about* liberation when you could be *experiencing* liberation? What if there's a divine interruption scheduled *right now*—an exchange you're due to make *right now?* To bestow on *you* "a crown of beauty instead of ashes, the oil of joy instead of mourning, and a garment of praise instead of a spirit of despair" (Isa 61:3 NIV). And what if Jesus the Listener were to say to you, "Right now, this Scripture is to be fulfilled, *this very day*"? What if Jesus the Healer is urging you to stop picking your scabs and calling it "deconstruction"? What if he's "impatient" to lay his wounded hand on your hurts and begin healing your wounds, bearing your sorrows, and gifting you with peace?

Now that might look like the prayer exercise that I suggested to my friend: "Picture him, picture the pain, picture the gift, and say, 'Yes please.' Then watch what he does."

If you do this, what you picture could be tailor-made to your history, or you could borrow the foot-washing imagery of John 13. Maybe we could humble ourselves to let Jesus wash the dust off our souls or baptize us in God's love. Too simple? Okay, I've learned to honor process, although I'm also not addicted to it. Jesus is willing to move at our pace—but he also recognizes our "stuckness." When I feel that way, I say to him, "I'm stuck again." He's never once shamed me for it. Instead, I see him hold out his hand. Will I take it? There's that leap my friend mentioned. Or at least just a baby step.

I leave you this story as an invitation to consider trauma-based therapy where needed. In fact, my friend used her experience to pursue further healing with a licensed trauma therapist. For those who want to investigate that route, Gabor Maté's film *The Wisdom of Trauma*[41] is a wonderful introduction. It is particularly helpful for those whose religious PTSD requires avoiding a Christian approach.

GOOD NEWS COUNTS

When so much of trendy deconstruction focuses on "bad news religion," spiritual abuse by pastors, and systemic oppression across churches, I feel the despair and cynicism. And all the more deeply because I'm in touch with my complicity. Again, I've been a perpetrator of spiritual abuse. And if that's it, if that's the whole story or the big picture—if it really is all so much horse manure, with no redemptive narrative—then…well, then it's "time to pack it in." Not just church, not just religion, but also people. Life. The whole thing. A global flood doesn't seem so impossible or offensive after all. If there's no good news, then Jesus was a liar and there's no cause for joy or even for survival. I've gazed down that road. Explored it far enough to know there's nothing (*nada, nihil*) down there.

But what if that's not right? What if there's Good News? What if there's reason for joy? What if life doesn't just "suck and then you die"? What if we can *reconstruct* our lives with love, joy, and peace? And not the fluffy kind, either! Something robust and resilient that can weather hurricanes and pandemics and death? Well, then I would want to hear about it.

My friend's recovery story illustrates how deconstruction can be joyful. It is not only trauma narratives around spiritual abuse or waves of "dones" abandoning Christian faith. Joyful deconstruction might include these aspects:

- abandoning *toxic* faith
- discovering *new,* liberating faith
- growing past toxic *assumptions* about faith

My larger point is that, yes, sometimes deconstruction truly is glorious— an exodus event or a journey that comes as a fresh breath of liberation that's palpable, even euphoric. Like new birth after a traumatic delivery through a perilous labor. Tears of joy aren't a myth.

But now we must return to hear those whose experience of deconstruction has involved trauma, and not only the ordeal of a toxic backstory. We need ears to hear the groans of those for whom deconstruction itself generates fresh trauma—those who experience the fear and panic of losing more than they bargained for. Those who've undergone deconstruction that seems more like a mastectomy than a carnival.

6

TRAUMA:
SPIRITUAL MASTECTOMY

"CUT OFF"?

Email from an anonymous Aussie:

> I have fallen into such a spiritual crisis that I have apparently lost my connection with God and I've lost my soul.
>
> If one is cut off from God, can there be any return?

Response:

Dear Anonymous,

Which voice sounds like Jesus Christ:

1. No, mate. You're pretty much burnt toast.
2. No, mate. Even if you've made your bed in hell, I am there.

Yes, you may have lost your *sense* of connection, but I promise you: there is nothing you can do to undo the union that Christ has established with you. He is with you. He is in you. He is toward you. He is for you. He has *not* unplugged from the relationship, and he never will. There can be no actual separation from God's side. But, yes, there can be that *broken perception* of alienation that comes when you somehow unplugged from yourself.

Somehow, you may yet come to trust that when God says, "*I will never leave you or forsake you,*" he cannot lie.

The question, therefore, is not whether you've lost the connection to Christ-in-you, but how you lost your sense of self. Do you want to tell me how that happened?

And do you want that sense of reconnection? How might you turn back to the Father, only to find he's been there the whole time?

Sincerely,
Brad

BEREFT

Having described the joyful liberation of deconstruction, which gets a lot of press these days, I now want to further explore the shadow side of the deconstruction experience. I've already expressed my longing for the deconstruction influencers to practice more empathy. Again, for lifelong "believers" whose entire world revolved around Christian (or any) faith—even to a tragic fault—the experience of deconstruction is not always pure joy. It can be yet another trauma. I'm afraid that many progressives are so focused on the first trauma (bad religion) that they are unaware of or undersell how acutely traumatizing, how shattering, deconstruction itself can be. I hope the depictions in this chapter will help to illuminate that shadow side.

Here's a powerful description of deconstruction I've excerpted from sections of Paul Kingsnorth's gripping novella *Beast*:

From the east I came, to this high place, to be broken, to be torn apart, beaten, cut into pieces. I came here to measure myself against the great emptiness. I came here to touch the void, to leap naked into it with the shards of what I was falling around me, to have the void clean me of the smallness that I swam in....

...in all directions there is cloud. there is no sound now i feel bereft i have been abandoned i have been left....

...i know what you think i say i know how it sounds i know god is dead i know he has been killed with everything else. i know all the parts have been taken out and are lying around on the carpet and now we are all free to be unhappy alone i know there is nothing holy now. perhaps i am circling it because it looks stupid to the people who take everything apart but i think there are things deep in some people which won't be taken apart....[42]

The people Kingsnorth is describing don't respond well to platitudes and shallow DIY fixes. They can't just be duct-taped back together. We can relate our experiences to them without imposing our stories on theirs; we can at least say, "I hear you. Here's how it was for me. Different for sure. But perhaps there is enough resonance that we might travel together, if you want the company."

EMPATHIZE

Dear Brad,

I'm an ex-pastor of a campus of what used to be one of the bigger churches in America. More than ten campuses. I've gone through a crisis of faith after getting deep into Bart Ehrman's[43] work. I walked away from my faith and was appreciating mystics from different religions. I've also listened a lot to gentle souls who don't believe in a named god but, rather, in a universal consciousness/divine intelligence that is the zero-point field of creation.

I felt sure in my newfound "agnostic belief"—but after a severe breakdown, a hell-trip of the mind that left me a shell of mess—I feel shattered into a million pieces and don't really know what is happening. I'm at the bottom, trying to piece my life together while daily battling this new monster.

While driving home today from the psychologist, I was just so upset, and suddenly your name popped into my head and I pulled over to send you a message. *I feel like I don't believe in Jesus anymore, but then, at my lowest, I found myself calling to him.*

I am not seeking counseling, so I don't wish to trouble you on this. My question is how you have kept your faith. I'm curious how you manage to have a faith in "Jesus" as opposed to the "universe," etc.

With appreciation,
Nathan

I get messages like this every week, and sometimes every day. As I respond, I remember that people who use words like *bereft*, *shattered*, and *bottom* don't need to be chastised for wandering away. Neither do they need a cheering squad to wave congratulatory pompoms at them at the threshold of the psych ward. And they find little solace from rational "answers" from some apologist or clever advice from the cynics. So, what can we offer "Nate" and his cohort of the beleaguered and bereft?

As I suggested earlier, empathy is a good place to start. I try to listen, to dignify them with hard questions, to suspend judgment…and to vulnerably share my own story. Here's how I put it to Nathan, applying some of the themes we have been covering:

Dear Nathan,

So much of my story is about my longing for attachment. For life, for meaning, for faith, I need a *living connection*. I *need* a face, a name, a person attached to my conception and experience of God. I need to experience my faith as a real, reciprocal relationship with a living person in whose care we feel seen, safe, secure, and soothed.[44] Apart from that living connection, what remains? Only a religious *cause* or spiritual *idea*, blown away by the winds of disillusionment after the initial euphoria of freedom.

Tragically, you know this by experience. This may be why you feel bereft right now. After a lifetime immersed in Christian culture, including pastoral leadership, somehow, you missed out on spiritual attachment to Christ as a living person. How did your church tradition fail to facilitate a real encounter? How is this possible and yet so common? How could you not have met him there? OR maybe you did…. Then how is it that, having tasted divine Love, the skeptics could rob you of faith so thoroughly that you have no recollection of an authentic connection with Jesus Christ?

Simone Weil regards the uprooting you underwent as the most violent thing that can happen to anyone. Worse than rape. No, it IS a rape. Or arson. In his novel *The Possessed*, Dostoevsky saw how progressive deconstruction can feel like freedom from shackles (at first), a real exodus from the bondage of bad religion…but in his world, deconstruction itself soon became an act of spiritual arson.

Between bad church, bad skeptics, and a bad breakdown—you can relate—you find your house of faith (and joy and peace) burned to the ground. You've experienced the nihilistic effect that razes faith, deprives us of meaning, and sabotages our emotional health. What was presented as truth (by both the church and the skeptics) cannot be truth because it's simply not beautiful.

And there, at the bottom of *hades*, in the heart of darkness, when faith and sanity were gone, your heart cried out, "Jesus." I hope you come to see that as the most important moment of your life...the turning point—*metanoia*—if you want it to be....

Through 2008–2009, I had a massive crash. I didn't "do" deconstruction. It did me. Or rather, undid me. I became ultra-wary of ANY kind of faith that I could contrive or project. For the first time in my life, I didn't know if I could trust God.

The tragedies we experienced were far beyond my ability to endure. I was bereft and virtually nonfunctional. I spent much of the next year in bed, detoxing from responsibility, in the care of twelve-step recovery and my spiritual director.

At my most hopeless, I ran into the writings of Simone Weil. She saved my life. I found her so helpful that I later translated some of her key works and compiled them in *Awaiting God*.[45]

The essence of her message was that I could not dig my own way out of despair. But she showed me how I might make a lateral move to astonishment. She allowed me to say that the Good (divine love) and affliction are REAL contradictions that stand an infinite distance apart. These contraries act like pincers that grip you, arrest you, and throw you into the abyss. At the bottom of her dark abyss, she looked up, and when she did, she saw the cross.

She saw the cross span the infinite distance between the Good and the necessary (affliction)—that the two intersect in the heart of the One hanging there. She didn't dig in or press on or rise up. Weil waited there with attentive expectancy, and she came to see her own afflictions act like a hammer, driving her like a nail right into the heart of Christ. And from his wounds, she felt his healing love flow into her.

I experienced this. It is not a theology or theodicy. It was a long process of holding my spiritual gaze upon the "Serpent on the Tree."[46]

The only prayer I prayed for a very long time was, "Lord, have mercy." Nothing else came. Nothing else was needed.

I waited. And perhaps God waited. But, oddly, though my whole life had been bulldozed to bedrock, what remained, inexplicably, was "God is good."

I don't know why that remained. The reality of the Good did not arise from circumstances or deliverance or healing or an emotional shift. I just knew that "God is good. Period." A faith gift that wasn't washed away in the flood or consumed in the fire. *God is good.* I saw that goodness in the One hanging there, co-suffering my affliction. He showed me *MY* scars in his hands and side. And I *came to* (a process phrase) believe.

We might ask a million "what about" questions. I had exhausted mine. I was beyond the questions. Eventually, maybe a year later, I could add, *"God loves me. Period."* Again, only a faith statement. And not one I chose. It just emerged from my waiting one day with the help of my friend Dwight, who had walked the valley of the shadow ahead of me.

Another year passed, and I tentatively added, *"God cares..."* The ellipses (rather than a period) meant I would watch for how that *might* be true. I didn't need a caring feeling in God's heart. I needed to see how our Source is an active caregiver. I thought about the ever-present help of caregivers I know who work with people with disabilities in full-time *care.* I asked, "How is God's real care happening for me?" Where? Through whom? I saw how that living, loving Care—connection in communion, mediated through people—is God (as a verb, meaning Love). In my wife and children, in my recovery group, in my spiritual mentors, in friends who would take me for walks. I also began to recognize and experience divine Care at work *in myself*—through fleeting moments of clarity, gratitude, courage, or the messages my body offered me. I discovered how this Father "who is in the secret place—who sees in secret"[47] is everywhere present and fills all things....

Nate, I don't really know if you need to figure anything out. I hear your concern about going back to what we knew. And that's fair. But the sense I get is that when your bulldozer, your flood, your fire came through in full force, "Jesus" is the name you were *given* to call upon. I suspect this is the Jesus you didn't know you knew. I think that's so important because "the universe" doesn't love you.[48] But the God revealed by Jesus as co-suffering love offers a living connection—the Fountainhead of all being is loving, caring, forgiving, responsive, and personal. But he's also the human image whose affliction is united with and gives meaning to yours.

Blessings,
Brad

I hope my words or imagery helped him. I won't sell this as a successful evangelistic testimony or the moment of truth that launched Nathan back into faith. It's all that I have. Empathy for a bereft ex-pastor, ex-Christian, whose last fingerhold of sanity was the name of Jesus. And I could relate to that.

RADICAL MASTECTOMY

So, once again, we see that, for some, deconstruction has truly been—and felt like—liberation, like chains breaking, like flying, like breathing new life. But, for others, it does not feel that way. The closest metaphor I can draw on for their experience is a *radical mastectomy*. Yes, there was a metastasizing spiritual or social cancer that had to be removed before it killed them. Its tendrils had wormed so deeply into the tissue of their soul that radical surgery was nonnegotiable. But here's the excruciating fact: they didn't get to choose the limits of what else got amputated. They experienced real loss—of faith, of meaning, of self.

And now they feel shame because it doesn't feel safe to admit they have lost their joy.

As one who has passed through both theological and personal deconstruction that brought me near (or was it *through*) death, I will presume to offer the following modest guidance. If it's unwelcome, don't worry. It's not for you.

A GUIDE TO MASTECTOMIES

1.   Don't do it yourself.

2.   Get a second opinion.

3.   Don't hire a plumber.

I've had pushback on this advice. It goes like this: "People in deconstruction have already been spiritually abused by people in authority. You should not give them guidance. You should teach them to trust and follow their own inner voice."

Um. Okay, first, that's still giving them guidance. And who teaches them how to hear and trust their inner voice? That still assumes someone is guiding them, right?

People are urged, "Don't let anyone tell you how to walk your deconstruction! This is your journey, your truth! No one can tell you how you should do it!" Do we not hear how alienating that is? So, I'm supposed to do this without guidance, while you ironically assert your guidance as, "It's all up to you." That may be fine if your deconstruction is a bouncy castle at Playland (in which case, it's not deconstruction, it's just playtime). But if you're discovering that what you've been taught, believed, and lived all your life is a life-threatening mass that demands radical surgery, then all that triumphalism is just another episode of spiritual abuse.

And what if someone's own inner voice is abusive? What if they have internalized the voice of their primary abuser so that what they hear is condemnation, accusation, judgment, and self-harm? That *is* how religious PTSD works. Who will guide them to discern and follow the voice of their true self?

"Well, that's why we refer them to a good therapist."

I agree. Okay, so we admit they actually need a guide, then? And who decides which therapists are good? By what criteria? I can't tell if such pushback about guidance is duplicitous or just poorly thought out. Against the riptide, I will take the pushback as permission to respond:

1.   Don't try to navigate the minefield of deconstruction via social media sloganeers and popular podcasts, even if I happen to be a guest on one of the podcasts. That's what I mean by "plumbers."

2.   Find a good guide who can help you discern your way to the voice of your true self in Christ (everyone has this voice). I mean someone

with both training and experience, whether a therapist or spiritual director—which probably means neither a pastor (conflict of interest) nor someone who is still in spiritual freefall (blind leading the blind). And your helper mustn't be a rescuer. They aren't to be the voice of God to you. Their role is to serve as quality control while you work through the inner noise to your quiet, clear center. Good news: your innermost being is still down there. You'll find it.

3. Consider taking time in therapy (check therapists' references beforehand) to zero in on both trauma elements: (a) traumas you've experienced in your spiritual backstory and (b) the new trauma of disorientation and uprootedness.

RECOVERY

Nearly thirty years have passed since the following events, but this is how I remember them:

A loved one in her sixties was facing major surgery for cancer in her bowels and uterus. The prognosis was bleak. But a few prayer zealots from our youth group and another friend, Imbenzi George, prayed for her healing. During the surgery, my relative's doctors searched for the tumors for forty-five minutes but couldn't find them, so they closed her up. They redid the biopsies on her uterus, which came back completely clear. (She's now passed her ninetieth birthday).

Immediately after that healing, my mom discovered she had breast cancer. No problem, we thought. We'd just call the same people to pray the same prayers, but now with even more faith. Yet the miracle didn't come. My dear mom went through the trauma of radical surgery—part of who she was got amputated. Yes, our bodies are part of who we are. We're not Gnostics, after all.

But here's the real miracle: for years, Mom had suffered from chronic illnesses. One of her conditions was severe fibromyalgia that calcified the muscle knots across her shoulders. She testifies that, prior to her surgery, her life was very pain-focused. Every day involved self-awareness of her physical misery and the effects it had on her emotional well-being.

Now, facing malignant breast cancer and her mortality, Mom made a profound decision. She chose to *live*. First, she said to me, "If I survive this, I will focus on life. I'll live each day that I'm given as a gift." And then she latched onto someone she loved dearly, worth living for—my firstborn, Stephen, not yet in kindergarten—and began to dream. Her motivation was to live one day at a time, to see him grow up (she did), and to attend his wedding (she did).

Now in her early eighties, she looks forward to her first visit with her great-grandchildren!

Listen, even if your unraveling has been like a radical mastectomy, if your descent has seen the annihilation of your faith or even your sense of person-hood—no matter how much of yourself has been lopped off—could you choose life, just for today? Could you fix your eyes on love today, to be love for some other person who loves you or needs love?

Stepping back, could you also imagine a reason to celebrate down the road that gives you a sense of meaning today—that makes you present for love?

These are genuine questions that only you can answer for yourself—not *"you should"* statements to further bury the weary. But my mom illustrates one way through. All the way through to life, light, and love. To liberation.

7

THRESHOLD:
CAN'T LEAVE, CAN'T ENTER

CAN'T LEAVE

I am well aware, to the point of nausea, that the movement or institution or community called "church" has often been a source of terrible suffering in this world. As I write these words, front and center is the demonic coalition of church and state in Russia, where the Orthodox Patriarch of Moscow rides Vladimir Putin's coattails, and their war crimes multiply across Ukraine. Putin stooped to cite Jesus's words "No one has a love greater than this, to lay down your life for your friends" (John 15:13) at a war rally immediately preceding massacres, civilian murders, and war rape committed by his army. Blasphemy. At Putin's right hand, there is Kirill, apostate head of the Russian Orthodox Church, who once described his dictator as a "miracle of God."[49] It's Revelation 17 all over again—the harlot church in bed with Babylon the Great.

Much closer to home, I see church-inflicted damage in many of my friends. Some experienced authentic spiritual abuse through stifling manipulation and control, and others through marginalization or outright exclusion. I hear such stories regularly from both former and current church members. Just as often, I hear the trauma in faithful leaders who were mistreated by conniving congregants. It's an ugly business that deserves careful attention until it ends completely.

That's one story. And I think it is only fair that I tell you another one.

I speak often about how my parents taught me to love Jesus and to value prayer, Scripture, and sharing good news. They raised me on "Jesus loves me this I know" and urged me to remain open to the Spirit when I was entrenched in dispensationalism, cessationism, and an early form of neo-Reformed Calvinism. I've shared how those systems and the revivalists who spread them traumatized me with a fear of hell, Armageddon, and being "left behind." So, when it comes to toxic faith, I can relate, believe me.

But here's the other side of the story, beginning with some background. For many years, I experienced bullying, mockery, and exclusion *outside* the church. Attending public school was a lonely and frightening experience for me. I was an outsider from the time I was in third grade, and I developed a heart for the marginalized because my few friends were the other "losers." I really appreciate those guys, and, really, they had it worse than I did. Without them, I would have been all alone. I tried to compensate by being smart (and was ostracized) or funny (and was met with cruelty). When I joined the hockey team for a few years, the other members made me gear up in a separate dressing room. During goalie practice, I heard my teammates murmur, "Aim for his head." Eventually, I learned that being "nice" helped, but I rarely felt a true sense of belonging. As the other kids matured, some were kind to me, but, after years of rejection and insecurity, I knew I wasn't "in." Later, I played basketball and volleyball, but it always felt like my peers only allowed me to participate on the team as a concession to my meager skills. I couldn't also expect an invitation to parties and such. I spent most of my spare time alone, walking the forest or the lakeside, playing with toys, reading books, or working out in my bedroom. I don't mean to whine. I'm not shy, but I am definitely an introvert, so alone time was solace.

And now here is the other side: I did *not* feel that exclusion or abuse by peers in the church—not as a child, not as a teen, and not as a young adult. Our church was too small to have much of a youth group, but that little band was consistently kind to me. So, too, was the little group of outsiders at our interchurch "boys' club." Best of all, going to summer camp was like being transported to another planet. Despite the heavy-handed teaching, the staff and campers showed me real love, and, surprisingly, they obviously *liked* me.

They treated me as a peer and even esteemed me. How was this possible? Did I change every summer into a confident, popular guy who was worthy of welcome and belonging, only to transform back into a contemptible freak come September? Was I Dr. Jekyll and Mr. Hyde?

Well, if I did change, the difference was because of my environment. Among those Jesus followers, I didn't have to flinch or worry about being blindsided, physically or emotionally. My gifts were appreciated but not required for acceptance. Everyone was my brother or sister. Now that Brian Zahnd has given me the language, I can see in retrospect that those summers of reprieve were "Christ's alternative society." They were what, in the Synoptic Gospels, Jesus called "the kingdom of God" or, in John, "eternal life." I remember the goodness of those summer reprieves and the depression that set in when I had to face "the real world" again.

I'll say it directly: for me, overall, "the church" I experienced was a place of peace and belonging. "The world" I knew was hostile and incredibly mean.

CAN'T ENTER

Now let's reverse my statement. "For me, overall, 'the world' I experienced was a place of peace and belonging. 'The church' I knew was hostile and incredibly mean." Is that statement true for you?

Again, I hear that story too. And I believe it. For that reason, for the people who have experienced an antagonistic church environment, faith is often found beyond the threshold of the church community. Some long to enter in, but they can't. And it's not just that they're wounded and bitter. For Simone Weil, despite her commitment to Christ—or rather, because of it—faith outside the threshold was a matter of deep conviction and even obedience to Christ. In her many letters to her Catholic priest friends, Weil offers numerous reasons why she couldn't join the church. These include:

+ Personal reasons: her sense of unworthiness, her perfectionist streak, her stubborn individualism.

+ Social objections: her suspicion of collectives, the exclusivity and non-catholicity of the Catholic Church, the totalitarian seeds she sees in the church's condemnations of heretics.

+ Theological objections: the narrowness of Christian dogma, missionary proselytizing, our failure to adequately address modernity (science, miracles, and so forth).

♦ Vocational objections: solidarity with the world God loves, including all outsiders; the sense that Christ himself forbade her entry as part of her calling.

Among Weil's reasons for faith outside the door, the most pressing and persistent that can be noted across her notebooks and letters is her belief that God loves the entire world, and that this good news includes everyone—and yet the church does not. She lived in a time (pre-Vatican II) when the Catholic Church taught that only those it baptized were saved.[50] To her, a Catholic Church without a catholic (universally inclusive) gospel is an oxymoron. If entering the church means abandoning everyone outside it to damnation, Weil would rather remain outside with them, damned or not…and she suspects Christ would, too, given that he suffered and died "outside the city"[51]:

> Christianity must contain within itself all vocations without exception, since it is catholic; therefore, the Church should as well. But in my eyes, Christianity is catholic by right and not in fact. So many things are outside of it; so many things that I love and do not want to abandon; so many things that God loves, for otherwise they would not exist….
>
> If Christianity is catholic by right but not in fact, I regard it as legitimate for me to be a member of the Church by right and not in fact, not only for a time, but for my whole life if necessary.
>
> But this is not only legitimate. Until God gives me the certain command to the contrary, I think it is an obligation for me.[52]

There's a holy defiance to Simone Weil that I don't want to diminish by using her as an excuse for faithless rebellion. In her case, we can test her decision by its fruit.

> Consider, Weil writes her [complaints in] *Letter to a Priest* in the Autumn of 1942 and dies August 1943. In 1944, Angelo Roncalli is sent to France as Apostolic Nuncio where he becomes close to Simone Weil's father. He becomes familiar with Weil's thought and by his first Pentecost sermon in Paris (May 24, 1944), he is virtually quoting Weil or affirming her stance:
>
> > It is so easy to stay within one's group, especially for Catholics, cutting ourselves off from our Orthodox brothers,

Protestants, Jews, Muslims, believers or nonbelievers in other religions. But I have to tell you that in the light of the Gospel and Catholic principle, this logic of division makes no sense. Jesus came to break down the barriers; he died to proclaim universal brotherhood; the central point of his teaching is charity—that is, the love that binds all human beings to him as the elder brother and binds us all with him to the Father.[53]

Roncalli was eventually elected Pope Paul XXIII and initiated the Second Vatican Council in 1962, which recognized that Catholicism, and even Christianity, cannot claim a monopoly on God's grace or act as a turnstile to salvation.

It is as if the world's largest Christian communion found it so unacceptable to leave Weil outside the gates that they broke them open to include her and all with whom she identified. Every pope since Roncalli would have baptized her (if she had let them). But in her reluctance at the threshold, perhaps Weil baptized them all into her own generous orthodoxy.

I find Weil's process easy to understand when I think of my children and grandchildren. I've been a church guy all my life, and I'm mainly the better for it. But I do not believe Christ withholds his grace from my offspring until they join a local church. I'm grateful for churches that would welcome them if they chose to enter. But could I take part in churches that refused them or treated them as second-class citizens? Could I join a religious club I knew was unsafe for them? No way. Better to join those whom I love outside than take my place at a banquet where they're forbidden entrance.

That's how Weil viewed the whole world. And she was convinced Christ saw it this way too.

Weil's resistance to joining the church was about faithfulness to Christ, not some spiritual malady to be overcome. Three passages (of many) from *Awaiting God* come to mind:

> If it is not God's will that I join the Church, how can I enter?... If it is in fact the case that it does not belong to me to pass through, what can I do? If it were conceivable to be damned by obeying God and that by disobeying we are saved, I would still choose obedience.

It seems to me that it is God's will that I should not enter the Church for now. For, as I already said to you—and it is still true—I feel the inhibition that keeps me out no less forcefully in moments of attention, love and prayer than at other moments....

I know that Christ said, "Whoever denies me before men, I will deny him before my Father." But perhaps denying Christ may not signify for everyone and in every case failing to join the Church. For some, this may only signify failing to execute the precepts of Christ, not reflecting his Spirit, not honoring his name when the occasion presents itself, or not being ready to die through faithfulness to him....

It is for the service of Christ—in that he is the Truth—that I deprive myself of partaking of his body in the manner that he instituted it. More exactly, *he* deprives me. For I have never had, even until this second, the impression of having a choice.[54]

IN OR OUT?

What's the moral of these stories—mine and Weil's? I can name a few:

1. It is entirely possible to experience love and belonging among the people of God, a harbor for those wearied and downtrodden by the cruel systems of exclusion in the world. When God's people love one another as they loved me, members will choose to stay connected—even if the preaching is mediocre, the services are blasé, and the theology is sketchy. We need to understand these faithful souls rather than ridicule them. Love and belonging are more important than anything. Regardless of Christianity's reputation for ugliness, I can tell you I experience that acceptance in churches all over the world.

2. Therefore, it is even more *unacceptable* that *anyone* should experience the church as controlling, abusive, or exclusionary. That so many have had to flee to "the world" for safety is entirely inexcusable and an indictment not of the household (*oikos*) Christ established, but of those who've co-opted and perverted it for their own self-centered agendas. It is especially sickening when insiders mistreat, exclude, or treat as less-than *anyone* because of who they are. Those congregations who fail to repent will have—or already have had—their lampstand extinguished.[55] Mercifully, Jesus is more patient than I would be.

3. Some feel secure in a fellowship of believers, and it was among fellow Christ-followers that they first found harbor and healing from world-inflicted

wounds. Others needed to escape serious abuse from dysfunctional faith communities, and they feel safer among friends outside any church culture. This tells me we should not paint the whole Christian movement with one wide, condemning brush. Nor should we imagine Christianity holds the monopoly on love, kindness, inclusion, and healing. It's not that simple. Rather, wherever we find ourselves today, we need to hear each person's unique story and attend to their spiritual needs with the compassion, kindness, and radical inclusion of Jesus Christ.

The "church," whatever it is, has its share of negative press and army of haters. And surely, in many cases, it's well deserved (as Israel's prophets or Jesus in Revelation 2–3 would be quick to point out). But if we're talking about the family of Christ-followers, then a generalized hatred of 31-plus percent[56] of the people on the planet is pretty…well, hateful, whether or not you identify with them.

Maybe the answer is for all of us to follow Paul the apostle's advice in Romans 2:1–4. Namely, wherever we assume wrath (God's or our own) is most deserved (inside or outside the church), it's only kindness (God's and ours) to all that leads to repentance.

Lord, we confess that the Christian church has increasingly distanced itself from the Jesus Way. We have chosen politics over people, power over love, and business over service, and we have failed to follow you. We confess that our institutions have excluded you, especially in the people we've chased away. Instead of welcoming your hungry children to the banquet, we have withdrawn your welcome and co-opted your table. We have sinned against you and your beloved children.

You could not stay in this environment, but you did not leave. In your mercy, you stand at the threshold; you keep knocking. Where we've played the harlot, you would yet make us your bride. If any hope remains, hear our prayers, cleanse our stains, and restore us. Lord, have mercy.

8

DECONSTRUCTION HAPPENS.
AND THEN?

Deconstruction happens. And then? Whether the water turns to wine, Kool-Aid, or cyanide is not random happenstance. Outcomes are determined by the hope, cynicism, or fanaticism of the spiritual voices, scripts, or herds we follow, whether mindfully or with glazed eyes.

Deconstruction happens. And then? Why does the glee of spiritual freedom so often devolve into despondency, alienation, or renewed bondage to some *ism*? To use an analogy of liberation, it happens when kites, posing as "free birds," cut their own strings and inevitably crash, get tangled, or become devoured by some tree.

Deconstruction happens. And then? The herd disperses down one path where the autonomous become automatons, and even the self gets deconstructed. We become vulnerable to the parade of sloganeers and influencers who offer to transform us from persons into conforming identity "its." As I mentioned, I receive messages nearly daily from *post-deconstructionists*. After the meltdown, all too often, their confession to me is, "I am bereft."

But there is another path: an ancient way, a trustworthy anchor, a deep faith, and a cruciform love. The souls who find and follow that path may yet find safe harbor.

Deconstruction happens. But unless you're okay with devolving all the way into nonbeing, deconstruction is not the point or telos of human flourishing.

We may experience a very real prison break from toxic faith and controlling *constructs*, yet what happens after we're over the wall and outside the confines of our old constrictive belief systems or institutions? Will we race blindly into the traffic? Will we wander forever in the wilderness? Will we charge with the lemmings into the sea? Or will those who suffered prolonged institutionalization experience such disorienting agoraphobia that they long for the security of their old cells?

Trying to subvert old and broken orders can degenerate into idolizing and perpetuating revolution itself. If there are cracks in the foundation of one's faith or culture or politics, it makes sense to dismantle the broken bits of the faulty floor, but *how* the foundation gets renewed deserves focused attention. I wouldn't trust my family's well-being to those who've not thought past the demolition phase.

FELLOW TRAVELERS

Here's my point: if you knew for sure that The Great Deconstruction is, let's say, just phase two of a precarious five- or seven-stage expedition, and only a remnant of previous travelers have traversed the terrain, you'd want to know how they did it, what they've seen, and their take on what trails led nowhere, or worse.

I think we'd better not isolate our own stories or this fleeting moment in time from centuries-long patterns of a bigger story. History can, should, and does inform this moment and the forthcoming stages that history's greatest deconstructionists have, so far, correctly predicted. Their prophetic diagnoses have served to aid my unlikely healing, the restoration of my fragile faith, and my emergence from the embers. If meaning matters, seasoned guides are welcome.

It's complicated because I'll be introducing those sages, ironically, as a tradition—dead folks whose ideas travel through time with thirty-thousand-foot vision and a track record of getting it right. They're all far more radical than the watered-down ideologies inside today's left-right matrix. Their warnings are dire, and their solutions surprising—often too obvious and demanding to be taken seriously. From Moses to Friedrich Nietzsche, from Voltaire to Søren Kierkegaard, from Fyodor Dostoevsky to Simone Weil, we'll see deconstruction "on crack," along with the civilizations they saw built or destroyed, including our own.

We need to think big and wide and long like this because the great unraveling won't only affect you and me. My worries and prayers now extend to our grandchildren and the world you and I will leave them. Will faith even be an option for them? Even after the freefall?

Perhaps.

SEGUE: FROM PERSONAL TO SOCIETAL

In part 1, we have focused primarily on personal deconstruction, beginning with my roughest patch, and with an emphasis on trauma. But, as is obvious, our entire culture is passing through a major period of disorientation, deconstruction, and tumult. Just as individuals break free from a constrictive belief system or experience a colossal collapse, so it is with societies. The chaos and conflict around partisan politics, climate change, a volatile economy, and the pandemic affect individuals, churches, corporations, cities, and nations alike. We're in an era that is undoing old constructs at breakneck speed. It's as if all the world has suffered a grade 4 concussion!

We know all this. But what gets overlooked is how The Great Deconstruction is not just a two-year lockdown or four-year election cycle or post-9/11 era. We're living on a thin slice of greater epochs that span two centuries, five centuries, and two millennia. To understand deconstruction as a great historic tradition and broader social phenomenon, we'll invoke help from those sages who charted the way. Gratefully, they left us memos of their work.

PART II

MEMOS:
SEVEN SLEEPERS
OF DECONSTRUCTION

9

SEVEN SLEEPERS

PRELUDE: TIME TRAVEL

Tales of time travel can make for fantastic storytelling, or they can devolve into eye-rolling plot holes that make suspending disbelief impossible. From the scientist's time machine in H. G. Wells's novel by the same name to Marty McFly's DeLorean in the movie *Back to the Future*, science fiction conceives technological bridges across years, centuries, even eons. Sometimes the means of conveyance are more mystical or magical, and they are frequently accidental. Depending on the tale in question, time travel may only allow you to observe events without changing them. But if you can alter the space-time continuum, watch out for the chain reactions of a time paradox!

But that's just one way to bridge the times. We time travel naturally whenever we remember the past or imagine the future. We span days or decades in a second with every pang of regret, happy memory, rush of anxiety, or dream of what could be. We even do thought experiments in which we visit our past or future selves with a question or some word of wisdom. Go ahead, play with it for a moment. You visit your ten-year-old self and are only allowed to say one sentence. What do you say? Do you offer affirmation, a warning, or some insider information?

And then there's biblical time travel in which "seers" such as Daniel peer into the future and see visions of either what *is* to come or what *might* come, depending on their listeners' choices. Rather than being deterministic, prophetic time travel speaks in contingencies or inevitabilities, taking seriously our agency while also asserting God's intentions. Some Open Theists doubt God can foreknow without predetermining events or violating our will. If he knows I will have Fruit Loops for breakfast tomorrow, am I really free not to? Don't go there.

Here's how much of biblical prophecy actually seems to work: prophetic forecasts don't cause events to happen later. It's just the opposite. The events are causing the prophecy! For example, Jesus doesn't come as a Suffering Servant *because* Isaiah prophesied it in chapter 53. Rather, the cross of Christ casts a shadow back across time that, by the Spirit, Isaiah was able to see. Isaiah prophesied the crucifixion *because* Jesus would die. Mind blown! Said another way, *prophets remember the future!*

In this section, prophecy and imagination will intersect to bring us time travelers from the past who remember our time in advance, who foresaw the very path we are traveling and speak to our troubled times. Said another way, it's as if, after a long, Rip-Van-Winkle-like slumber, these prophets wake up in our day to give us our own much-needed wake-up call.

THE SEVEN SLEEPERS OF EPHESUS

It's not as though it's never happened before. Have you ever heard of "the seven sleepers of Ephesus"? Somehow, they had slipped my notice until recently, which is embarrassing given my field of study. They aren't even all that obscure: the sleepers are commemorated with an annual feast day in both the Roman Catholic and Eastern Orthodox church calendars. From Ireland and France[57] all the way to Syria and Egypt,[58] their tale crossed the Mediterranean world, and Mohammed recounted their story in the Qur'an.

Details vary, from the number and names of the sleepers to the location and duration of their slumber. For our purposes, I'll abridge the key points from a detailed Syro-Orthodox version, as told by Patriarch Ignatius Zakkā I ʿĪwāṣ.[59]

During the reign of the Roman emperor Decius (AD 250), seven young nobles from Ephesus refuse to worship the emperor or his pagan gods. The emperor strips them of their titles but gives them time to reconsider until his return to Ephesus. Instead, they distribute their property to the poor, except for a few coins, and retreat to a cave on Mount Okhlon (or Anchilos) to pray and prepare for martyrdom. There, we are told, they fall into a deep sleep. By the way, the Muslim version includes a dog named ar-Raqīm or Qiṭmīr[60] who faithfully guards the mouth of the cave.

Upon his return, Decius discovers their disobedience, finds their hiding place, and orders the cave sealed with great stones, basically burying them alive. Two believers decide to preserve their names and story in a copper box at the mouth of the cave.

Centuries pass, along with a succession of emperors, until the rule of Theodosius II (AD 408–450), son of Arcadius, who was himself a Christian. During those days, a heresy arose, calling into question the resurrection of the dead, confusing believers and dividing the church. Troubled by doubt, King Theodosius prayed in sackcloth and ashes for divine reassurance.

In answer to his prayers, God inspires Adolius, the owner of a pasture, to build a stone enclosure for his cattle on property near the sleepers' cave. His servants gather stones for the task, including the boulders that sealed the mouth of the cavern.

The sleepers awaken, assuming they've slept just one night. They figure they'll have to give themselves up, stand trial before Decius, and face execution. One of them, Maximilian, suggests they send Malchus (or Diomedes) to sneak into the city to buy food so they can have a final breakfast together.

When Malchus gets to Ephesus, he's confused. There are crosses on the gates of the city and on a lot of the buildings. And the city seems unfamiliar because of new construction. Moreover, when he tries to buy food, the merchants are perplexed by his currency, which bears the image of Decius. People cannot understand where he has gotten such old coins. Perhaps he has found hidden treasure! It is all very confusing, so Malchus is eventually brought before the city prefect and the bishop Maris. All they can do to verify his story is to follow him to the cave, where they find his friends and the inscription, confirming their origins and their miraculous awakening.

Emperor Theodosius is informed, and he goes to Ephesus, where the sleepers tell him their story. He rejoices because he realizes they haven't actually been sleeping for two or three hundred years (depending on the legend). Rather, the sleepers had in fact died, and now, like Lazarus, they have come forth from the tomb. They are living evidence of the truth of the resurrection. A celebration ensues. The sleepers praise God, then reenter the cave and go back to sleep. The emperor enshrines their remains and proclaims anew the orthodoxy of the resurrection.

Crazy story, isn't it? Embellished truth or historical fiction? The account is not as wild as some biblical stories of the sun reversing direction, a talking donkey, and three teenagers surviving a fiery furnace.[61] But when a story is not in our Bibles, even our most conservative credulity quickly withers into skepticism. No matter, much of our hagiography is surely fanciful. Or, better, stories like the seven sleepers, whether fact or fiction, employ creative theology to teach us deeper truths. In this case, the ancient church told the story to reaffirm their belief in the resurrection during a wave of unbelief. How poignant today!

SEVEN MORE SLEEPERS

Now I want to recreate the magic of the seven sleepers story by extending the metaphor to our discussion of deconstruction. That's right: seven more sleepers—prophets who "remember the future," but, this time, they wake up here and now, fifty to five hundred to twenty-five hundred years after they spoke their beautiful and ominous truths, waiting for those with ears who could hear them.

Why should we care about the wisdom of prophets who lived in an age and order that no longer exists? What could they possibly say to postmodernists in the digital age? Have we not progressed beyond their quaint and passé reflections into the new awakening of The Great Deconstruction? Judging by the barrage of direct messages I receive from desperate deconstructionists who describe their faith as "dead in the water," we're due for a fresh set of eyes—of those who both saw into the murky depths of the individual soul and addressed big-picture patterns we're too nearsighted to see. These sleepers recorded what they saw, and we need their voices today.

The voices I will recount did not align with the status quo. Some were allies of Christianity, and others were opponents. They include cynics and skeptics, prophets and provocateurs, agnostics and believers. All were formidable deconstructionists. They will be our conversation partners—if we have ears to hear. Some we have briefly heard from earlier in this book. I'll introduce them here in their chronological order:

1. **Moses** and his apophatic entourage from church history (through the sixteenth century), including Dionysius the Areopagite (first century), Macrina the Younger (324–79), Basil the Great (330–79), Gregory of Nyssa (ca. 335–after 384), Maximus the Confessor (580–662), the

author of *The Cloud of Unknowing* (fourteenth century), and John of the Cross (1542–1591).

2. **Plato** (circa 428–347 BC), Greek political philosopher (riffing his mentor Socrates)

3. **Voltaire** (François-Marie Arouet) (1694–1778), French writer, playwright, and poet

4. **Søren Kierkegaard** (1813–55), Danish philosopher and provocateur

5. **Fyodor Dostoevsky** (1821–81), Russian novelist

6. **Friedrich Nietzsche** (1844–1900), German philosopher

7. **Simone Weil** (1909–43), French philosopher, activist, and mystic (along with Albert Camus [1913–60], French novelist, essayist, and dramatist)

With these seven "neo-sleepers" as our guides into the depths of deconstruction, let's now proceed to interrogate them in turn.

10

INTO THE DARKNESS, INTO THE LIGHT: AGNOSTIC FAITH (FROM MOSES TO JOHN OF THE CROSS)

"And the people stood afar off,
and Moses went into the darkness where God was."
—Exodus 20:21 (LXX)

"When he opened the seventh seal,
there was silence in heaven for about half an hour."
—Revelation 8:1 (NIV)

"Can a person want to live as Jesus taught—to grow in the love that Jesus modeled? Can I say, if this is all true, I am a partaker of his doing, and I rest in his work and his faith (if true), but I embrace a mystery of unprovable certainty? And I just say—if true—I want that. I cannot prove or disprove anything beyond that, so...I wish I had the gift of certainty and total understanding, but apparently those aren't promised, so I embrace the best version of what I think I understand and—if true—it doesn't make logical sense, but thank you. Now, instead of focusing on wild things I cannot prove, now I just need to grow in love?"
—Jayson, ex-missionary[62]

Jews and Christians have always confessed their faith in God. But would it surprise you to hear that, at certain times in history, they have also had a reputation with outsiders for being *atheists*? In the second century, an Athenian named Athenagoras wrote his *Plea for the Christians* to the emperors, making his case that the Christians' refusal to offer sacrifices to the idols of civic polytheism is not actually atheistic. It's just that their allegiance was to the one true God who transcends matter and forbids the absurdities of idolatry.[63]

MOSES: PATRIARCH OF DECONSTRUCTION

This conviction against idolatry reflected Christianity's Jewish foundations, beginning with the Mosaic prohibition against fashioning and worshipping crafted images of any god, including images of the God of Israel. In a thunderous spectacle from atop Mount Sinai, God delivers Ten Commandments to the Israelites, beginning with,

> [2] I am the Lord thy God, who brought thee out of the land of Egypt, out of the house of bondage. [3] Thou shalt have no other gods beside me. [4] Thou shalt not make to thyself an idol, nor likeness of anything, whatever things are in the heaven above, and whatever are in the earth beneath, and whatever are in the waters under the earth. [5] Thou shalt not bow down to them, nor serve them; for I am the Lord thy God, a jealous God, recompensing the sins of the fathers upon the children, to the third and fourth generation to them that hate me, [6] and bestowing mercy on them that love me to thousands of them, and on them that keep my commandments. (Exod 20:2–6 LXX)

The people seem completely terrorized by the earthshaking, earsplitting presence of God, and they beg Moses to serve as God's mediator-spokesperson to them—a buffer of sorts. Moses immediately ascends Mount Sinai and disappears into the stormy darkness:

> [18] And all the people perceived the thundering, and the flashes, and the voice of the trumpet, and the mountain smoking; and all the people feared and stood afar off, [19] and said to Moses, Speak thou to us, and let not God speak to us, lest we die. [20] And Moses says to them, Be of good courage, for God is come to you to try you, that his fear may be among you, that ye sin not. [21] And the people stood afar off, and *Moses went into the darkness where God was.* (Exod 20:18–21 LXX)

God reminds Moses that he has spoken from heaven and forbids all worship of worldly idols (vv. 23–24). A simple "hospitality barbecue" offered to God on an altar of unhewn stones is all he asks (vv. 24–26). You likely remember what happens next: the people get impatient and lose faith that Moses will reemerge from the crackling smoky Presence above them. They demand that Aaron *"make us gods* who shall go before us" (Exod 32:1 LXX). He instructs them to gather all their golden jewelry and, from that, he fabricates a "molten calf."

Now they make their nervy confession, "These are thy gods, O Israel, which have brought thee up out of the land of Egypt" (Exod 32:4 LXX). The next day, they hold a "feast of the Lord [Aaron used the sacred Hebrew word for Yahweh!]" (v. 5 LXX), offer peace offerings, and load up on food and alcohol. They indulge in *"revelry"* (Exod 32:6 NIV), which apparently means "noisy partying."[64] (The phrase is translated as "to play" in the LXX.) Bad idea.

God hears them and tells Moses, "Leave me alone! Let the fire of my anger burn them up. I will consume every last one of them! Let's just forget them. We'll start fresh with you and make a new nation" (Exod 32:10, paraphrased).

Sounds to me like God throws a violent fit...but we know better, right? The Scriptures, when revealed through the heart of Jesus Christ, unveil what's happening. As is so often the case, the fury we encounter in this passage actually reflects the self-destructive severity of the people's sin. If they get away with this, they'll follow their imaginary constructs of God right into the grave. They'll be dead in the desert in no time. And what is God up to? He's looking for a willing prophet whose heartfelt intercession will embody and release God's own mercy to save these rapscallions from themselves.

Moses pleads, and God relents, but that's when things get messy. Moses heads back down the mountain (surprise: *with Joshua*; see v. 17). But when Moses sees his people's orgy of idiocy for himself, it's his turn to snap. He smashes the stone tablets—a powerful gesture of their broken covenant—melts down the calf, grinds the gold to powder, stirs it into their drinking water, and forces the people to swallow it (v. 20)! I can't unsee the subsequent golden bowel movements in my mind's eye!

Aaron diverts blame to the people and claims that when he threw their gold into the fire, *"there came out this calf"* (v. 24 LXX). Again, Moses burns with rage and demands to know who's on his side. The Levites join him, and Moses says, "Thus saith the Lord God of Israel, Put every one his sword on his thigh, and go through and return from gate to gate through the camp, and slay every one his brother, and every one his neighbour, and every one him that is nearest to him" (v. 27 LXX).

Odd. Because I see *nothing* in the story that backs up Moses's claim that God sanctioned the killing. Only *after* this bloodbath does Moses concede he would go to the Lord to appeal for forgiveness. The Levites slaughter three thousand people before the day is done. Moses sees his most violent allies as God's most faithful servants, and he rewards their tribe with perpetual ordination for tabernacle ministry (v. 29). Remember how, centuries later, it was the Levite temple guard that arrested Jesus in Gethsemane.

Anyway, as the story goes, Moses has to do a lot more face-to-face negotiating with the Lord through chapter 33 before the final verdict comes down. Moses declares he will stand in solidarity with those whose names God will blot out if God refuses to show mercy. "Then blot me out too," he says. And, at last, God not only forgives but also consents to continue leading Israel. He reveals his glory to Moses as mercy and compassion (Exod 33:19). Even in their rebellion, God did not forsake them.[65]

The story entered the Jewish psyche as a traumatic and unforgettable memory (by design), a warning that they should never identify the ineffable One—that dark and mysterious Presence smoldering above Sinai—with crafted counterfeits of gold, silver, wood, or stone. Their sacred Scriptures memorialize every instance of how destructive it is to forget that lesson.

Many Jews were so affected by this episode that they would refuse to even use God's holy name, lest the placeholder itself become an idol. In fact, Jewish rabbis who perceived the spirit of this law knew that even our *concepts* and *constructs* of God all too easily become idols. Thus, Sinai became ground zero for all deconstruction—and the golden calf an archetype for every idolatrous construct thereafter.

Stated formally, Judaism was and is the mother of *apophatic* religion,[66] also known as the *via negative*, Latin for "the negative way" or "the negative path."

CHRISTIAN AGNOSTICISM—"APOPHASIS"

Christian theologians, drawing from the Jewish-Moses tradition[67] and seeking to evangelize the Greeks, developed a nuanced approach to the apophatic, or negative, way (God beyond images and concepts) in tandem with their conviction that God has in fact revealed Godself through the incarnation of Jesus Christ (the cruciform Image of God).

In the spirit of deconstruction, let's jiggle loose the tangle of ideas that came together in the early centuries of Christian thought.

Christian apophasis, or the negative way, comes in two forms or flavors.[68] The first form has to do with *analysis* (from Greek "*ana-*," "up," and *luein*, "to loosen").[69] This form of apophatic theology is about undoing, about letting go, or negating character attributes that would constrict God's freedom. The goal is to pare away limiting concepts to arrive at God's unqualified nature. We practice this form of negation whenever we speak about God using the prefix *in-* or *im-*. To say that God is *infinite* means God is *not* finite. To say that God is *immortal* means God cannot die. *Immense* = God is not measurable. *Immutable* = God's character does not change. *Invincible* = God cannot be defeated. And so on. So, by saying *what God is not*, we come closer to seeing who God is.

The second form has to do with our limitations. We say that God is *inconceivable*, meaning that God is beyond our comprehension. We say that God is *ineffable*, beyond our ability to describe. Again, we use the negative to unveil the truth that God is transcendent. God is beyond all apprehension to finite human reason, and yet, even as we confess our limits, we're also declaring our awareness of the reality and presence of Someone who exceeds them.

To summarize thus far, *apophatic theology* is "the attempt to reveal what is good not by a positive statement but by clearing away the obstacles and impostures."[70]

THE CAPPADOCIANS

Historian Jaroslav Pelikan locates the most developed Christian apophatic theology in a fourth-century Cappadocian family—namely, the lives and teachings of Basil the Great, Gregory of Nyssa, and their elder sister and teacher, Macrina the Younger.

Macrina describes the essence of negative theology in this way: "In the very act of saying that a thing is 'not so and so,' we by implication interpret the very nature of the thing in question."[71] In that sense, negative theology isn't simply negative, isn't only skeptical, isn't really atheism. It's the active practice of dismantling the rubble of our God-constructs (hence, de-*construct*-ing) in service of our quest for God.

Thus, for Macrina, it's not just an approach to philosophy or theology. It's her lived faith practice of drawing near to God in *imageless* contemplation and *silent* prayer (known in the East as *hesychastic* prayer). Why imageless and silent? This is in response to God's invitation "Be still and know that I am God" (Ps 46:10, various translations). In the *via negativa*, knowing God comes as we *unknow* all that which we thought we knew.

Further, Macrina modeled the *via negativa* by living an *ascetic* life[72] (common among monastics and hermits), where her commitment to voluntary poverty cleared away obstacles to intimacy with God. She sought to detach herself from anything or anyone that might become an idol. Ascetics hope that by pruning their attachment to outward possessions, their minds and hearts will also be freed from passions and cravings that displace God as their central focus and allegiance. Indeed, by the time of Macrina's death, she had downsized her life to a hair shirt so that even comfort would not cloud her vision of God!

The shadow side of ascetic faith and practice is when it breeds a sense of "super-spirituality." Any Christian discipline can be co-opted by pride in the service of the ego—and the monastics knew it. From the desert fathers of the fourth century to Thomas Merton in the twentieth,[73] the great ascetics constantly deconstructed the insidious agendas of their spiritual egoism, keeping "Blessed are the poor in spirit"[74] front and center.

THE APOPHATIC PARADOX

The *via negativa* (theological, contemplative, ascetic) is pretty intense:

> [It] consists in negating that which God is not; one eliminates firstly all creation.... Then one excludes the most lofty attributes, goodness, love, wisdom. One finally excludes *being* itself. God is *none* of all this; in His own nature He is the unknowable. He "is not." But here is the Christian paradox; He is the God to Whom I say "Thou," Who calls me, Who reveals Himself as personal, as living.[75]

The most daring negative theologians insist that God is not even a being among beings. But also not less than a being. God is beyond being and the ground of all being. God does not "exist." God is existence itself. Everything that exists finds existence in God, and so God is *no thing*. Well, that just sounds like one big negation.

On their own, such radical negatives would constitute a repudiation of some central Christian confessions: that God *is*,[76] that God is *one*,[77] and that

God has revealed Godself to us in the incarnation of Jesus Christ,[78] who also said, "This is eternal life: *that they may know You*, the only true God, and the One You have sent—Jesus Christ" (John 17:3 HCSB).

Sounds like a contradiction to me! The Cappadocians and their spiritual progeny saw this. They recognized that *apophasis* on its own would just dissolve God into a vague, ethereal nothingness. That's not what they meant. They combined their rigorous *apophasis* (what God is not, what cannot be said about God) with an equally essential counterpoint: *kataphasis* (affirmation)— who God *is*, what God has *revealed*, and what may be *said* about God.

THE REVELATION OF GOD

How has God been revealed? How has God been made known? To say it simply, God the Father reveals who he is through (1) human nature (you and me!), (2) the grace of the Holy Spirit, and (3) God's incarnation in Jesus Christ.

1. IN HUMAN NATURE

For all that we don't know or can't say about God, here's some simple logic:

1. Humanity is personal.

2. God is the source of all that is personal.

3. God cannot be less than we are.

4. Therefore, God is personal or more than personal.

Neurosurgeon Michael Egnor says,

When you look at the effects of God in the world, I think the most remarkable effect is our personhood, our subjectivity. The fact that we are persons leads me—and I think has led a lot of theologians—to say, "That's because God is a Person." That's where our personhood comes from. We're the small case I am and he is the big case I AM.[79]

Thus, we can reverse engineer from personal creatures to a personal Creator. We also have some revelation on the matter. The Scriptures say that God created humanity in God's image.[80] For all the discontinuity implied in divine transcendence, the creation story claims continuity between God and Adam/Eve in whatever the *imago dei* might mean. We see in one another something essential to our Creator—God's infinite *relationality*. To speak of God as *personal* means more than "God is an individual." Individuals only become persons in relationship—and, in God's case, that relationship cannot be less than ours. Divine personhood is the pattern for at least the best of human relationality. For example, we can infer from healthy human relationships that God is loving, caring, forgiving, and responsive, and therefore relational. If relational, then also communicative. And so on. We can know and say something about God as divine parent because the best aspects of God's children reveal their heavenly Father-Mother.

2. IN THE GRACE OF THE HOLY SPIRIT

When distinguishing between what we can know and can't know about God, Saint Basil the Great (Macrina's brother) exalts the work of God the Holy Spirit. Basil was called "the Great" because he established once and for all the full deity of the Holy Spirit in Christian theology—that's a big deal. So, when Basil writes about how God is known, he naturally appeals to *the grace of the Spirit* using the term *energies*.[81] He distinguishes between God's *nature* or *essence* (*ousia*), which is beyond human reason, and God's *energies*, which can be known in our experience:

> We say that we *know* the greatness of God, the power of God, the wisdom of God, the goodness of God, the providence of God over us, and the justness of the judgment of God—but not the very *ousia* [essence] of God."[82]

No eye has seen, no ear has heard, no mind has conceived all that God is and does—but God has revealed himself to us *by the Spirit*.[83]

I once found this notion of *energies* puzzling, especially when I would hear my friend Archbishop Lazar refer to "the uncreated energies." As a Protestant, I had never once heard the phrase. Later, I found out that the word *energeia* (used by Paul[84]) is often translated as *working, power,* or *operations*. Our conversation went something like this (any errors to follow are due to my memory of his words two decades ago). It began by comparing our definitions of grace:

Me: When we talk about *grace*, I'm not sure we mean the same thing. I grew up hearing that grace is "the unmerited favor of God." What does the Orthodox church mean by "grace"?

Lazar: Grace is the *uncreated energies* of God.

Me: What are these "uncreated energies"? Are they like some force? Or emanations?

Lazar: No. The uncreated energies—*energeia*—refer to *the grace of the Holy Spirit.*

Me: *Uncreated.* So, if they're *uncreated*, the energies must be...God?

Lazar: Of course. Only God is uncreated.

Me: But you distinguish between the *essence* of God and the *energies* of God? If they're both God....

Lazar: According to the Holy Fathers, the *essence* of God is transcendent and beyond knowing. But the *energies* of God describe our direct experience of God through the indwelling, transforming grace of the Holy Spirit. The *energies* are the grace of the Holy Spirit—not a "thing" or "force" that God sends, but God known directly by the Holy Spirit, transfiguring us from glory to glory into the image of Jesus Christ.

Me: So, the *energies* are God's grace, and *grace* is the presence of the Holy Spirit.

Lazar: Exactly.

Me: Why does this matter? It sounds a bit conceptual and metaphysical.

Lazar: Not at all. The primary concern is pastoral. In the final development of this essence-energies distinction, Saint Gregory of Palamas's[85] concern was twofold: (1) to defend the mystical practice of *hesychastic* prayer [silent contemplation in God's presence] because the practice transforms us without words or images, and (2) to assure God's people that, however mysterious, God wills to communicate with us, to unite with us, to indwell us, to transform us, and to empower us to know God in our real-life experience.

Me: As in the Evangelical "personal relationship"?

Lazar: I prefer to say "intimate friendship," but the point is that God *can* be known, not by thinking our way up to God but inside a relationship through the indwelling grace—*energies*—of God.

Here's one analogy I've heard regarding God's nature: just as we cannot approach our physical sun, so too God "lives in unapproachable light" (1 Tim

6:16)—that's God's essence. At the same time, we experience that same sun as our source of light, warmth, and life. We literally see and feel and live under the sun. Similarly, we experience God as light, love, and life—through God's *energies* or *grace*, the heart-melting presence of the Holy Spirit. That's why I like to capitalize Grace as a personal name for the Spirit.

To the Cappadocians, we experience these *energies*, this transforming grace, this indwelling Spirit, through openness in contemplative prayer and by making space via ascetic practice, as the beloved ones who receive her love. In this way, the *via negativa* is, ironically, a deconstructive turn *toward* God.

3. IN GOD'S INCARNATION IN JESUS CHRIST

We come to know God not only through the *imago dei* in human nature and the grace-gift of the Holy Spirit but also through the historic incarnation of God's Word, Jesus Christ, who said, "To see me is to see my Father."[86]

So again, we must de-*construct* every un-Christlike conception of "God" so that we don't overlook the Real Deal when he draws near to us. Nowhere in Christian faith or human experience has the incomprehensible goodness of God drawn so near—so completely participated in God's creation and so identified with our humanity—as it was in the incarnation of Jesus Christ. In Christ, God is made known.

As Saint Maximus the Confessor argued, the essence or nature of God stands beyond all our affirmations *and* all our negations, beyond our constructions *and* our deconstructions—but who God truly is culminates in Christ!

> In Christian theology, the goodness of God does not stop at creation or emanation…but goes to the extreme of God's own incarnation: *God goes out of himself and becomes man in Christ.…*
>
> …Creation's participation in God *culminates in Christ,* as through his human existence God's goodness is freely allowed to be poured forth to its final degree in the *outpouring of Christ's life on the cross.*"[87]

To summarize the paradox, we say *both*:

1. That the invisible God who dwells in impenetrable darkness or unapproachable light, who created all things, is in all places, and fills the cosmos, is beyond comprehension and surpasses description. Our finite concepts and inadequate constructs and inane projections of that Mystery continually drift toward idolatry and are therefore in need of constant deconstruction.

2. That this same God loves us and has revealed himself through the indwelling, transforming grace of the Holy Spirit in our lived experience, and has revealed his glory through the incarnation of Jesus Christ. Infinite goodness overflowed into our world through the life and the wounds of the God who made himself vulnerable and accessible in the crucified Son.

The crucifixion of Christ raises a final and all-important feature of *apophasis* and the *via negativa*: the felt *absence* of God in the human experience that we call "the problem of evil." We will return to that question later in chapter 19, "Atheism, Decreation, and the Absence of God: Simone Weil."

PIERCING THE CLOUD

We return to the *via negativa* by once again referencing the imagery of Moses's ascent into the dark cloud on Sinai. Macrina and Basil's younger brother, Gregory, used the story of Moses's ascent up the mountain of God as an analogy for the mystical ascent of the soul into God. Basil described it as the journey into light, cloud, and darkness:

+ The light represents correction and clarification of our concepts of God.

+ The cloud represents the soul's movement from knowing by sense perception to spiritual (*noetic*) apprehension of the hiddenness of God.

+ The darkness represents the soul that follows Moses into the presence of God even beyond spiritual perception into darkness that surrounds God.[88]

+ Moses then appears from the darkness of God, radiating the light of God's transfiguration glory! And while the radiance on Moses's face faded, the glory of God in the face of Jesus Christ will never fade; it transfigures all those who behold him.[89]

DARK NIGHT OF THE SOUL

Oh, night that guided me,
Oh, night more lovely than the dawn,
Oh, night that joined Beloved with lover,
Lover transformed in the Beloved!
—Saint John of the Cross[90]

The most famous metaphor for Christian negative theology and deconstruction came via a sixteenth-century poem by Saint John of the Cross entitled "The Dark Night of the Soul."[91] While moderns lay hold of the phrase to describe physical, emotional, or experiential woes that "bring us down," John argues exactly the opposite. He specifies that if you can identify some cause, whether a malady, a tragedy, or any kind of evil driving you low, you're *not* in the dark night of the soul. The dark night is *not* grief for some loss, the consequences of some sin, or for any explicable reason.

John identifies two dark nights that he attributes to necessary, positive, but painful growth on a three-stage spiritual ascent (common to the mystics).[92] The stages are:

+ *The Purgative Way:* in this phase, the focus is breaking out of habitual vices, fostering habitual virtues, and learning to live the Jesus Way. We could say that, here, the light shines in the darkness, exposing and driving away that which is not love.

+ *The Illuminative Way:* in this phase, the focus is on growth, developing Christlike charity, and deepening in the life of prayer. Here, the light shines in our hearts, opening our eyes to new depths in contemplative prayer.

+ *The Unitive Way:* in this phase, surrender to the Father's will leads to the union of our hearts with the Lord. We are in sync with Christ and flow with impulses of the Spirit.

John noticed that at each transition, we experience a dark night.

+ *The Dark Night of the Senses* occurs as a crisis of faith at the culmination of the Purgative Way. A feeling of "affliction" may come over us, and we pass through this dark valley with no conscious sense of God's love or presence. None of our usual stimuli bring us comfort or pleasure—food, friends, sex, money, success, stuff...not even worship or prayer alleviate the deadening sorrow. What's going on? God has *not* abandoned us, and the enemy of our souls has not overtaken us. The dark night of the senses is a deep dissatisfaction, a kind of involuntary detachment, a purging of sensual and egoistic spiritual appetites that sweeps out the temple of our hearts, purifying us of "worldliness" for the illuminative way.

+ *The Dark Night of the Soul* occurs near the end of the *Illuminative Way*. Again, we're being purged of attachments and prepared for the next stage (the Unitive Way). But, this time, the desolation goes far deeper, for God's Spirit is breaking internal attachments—to sin and to self, to our inner "craver" and the demands of the ego. The mystics use terms such as *desolation* and *no consolation* and *crushing* and *abyss* to describe the intensity of the trials, temptations, and emptiness that accompany this second night. The function of the second night is to reveal how empty we are without God. We find life by seeking God alone. The resolution of this night is a complete willingness and resolve to take up our cross and joyfully follow Jesus wherever he goes.

The Dark Night of the Soul is a season (or seasons) in the darkness, pressure, and safety of God's closed fist that accomplishes what ten thousand blessings cannot achieve: a permanent deposit of Christ's own character. The forge of the fire of divine love is fashioning us into his image!

I summarize John's descriptions of the dark night to repeat a question my friend Ellen Haroutunian, a spiritual director and psychotherapist, proposed:

> What if we treated deconstruction as a type of "dark night of the soul" à la John of the Cross? "Dark night" implies nothing bad. Rather, it's a movement from what was once certain to a deeper knowing and deeper union with God. It does require letting go of much of what is old, and of attachments that hold us back and keep false personas in place.[93]

Bingo! John of the Cross was certainly describing deconstruction. And Ellen was saying, "Here is a way to look at it." I would, of course, resist making the experience "one size fits all."

There is deconstruction that is voluntary and deconstruction that is involuntary; there is deconstruction that is joyful and liberating, but there is also that which is terrifying and traumatic. There is deconstruction that is entirely Jesus-led and deconstruction that is nihilistic.

Deconstruction can lead to a new sense of purpose and meaning, or it can lead to hopelessness and despair. Agency may or may not be involved. Some resist the guidance that John sees as essential.

With John, I see the *cruciform way* as the ultimate deconstruction, signified by the cross and our baptism into Jesus's death and resurrection. And I see alternatives that, ironically, are simply assertions of self-obsessed egos. Thus, the term *deconstruction* has become an impossibly broad brush, so I love how Ellen framed her question as, "What if we treated it *this way?*"

If we did so, then we *could* navigate the rapids of our faith shifts without being dashed on the boulders or drowned in white water.

LOVE PIERCES THE CLOUD

Awesome. But perhaps such lofty heights seem inaccessible to busy entrepreneurs, diligent blue-collar workers, or stay-at-home parents with children buzzing around the house. Most of us aren't especially theological or mystical or saintly. But the image of a dark cloud can be helpful when distilled as it was in the medieval classic on deconstruction, *The Cloud of Unknowing.*

In this fourteenth-century work, an anonymous monk writes to a disciple, telling him that in our pursuit of God, we'll soon discover that a dark cloud stands between us and God—an impenetrable fog of "unknowing" that reveals the hard limits of human understanding to grasp the divine. Most people can relate to this—eventually even those addicted to certitude must concede the limits of their finite notions.

But the author has good news! While this dense cloud of unknowing is impermeable to the natural mind, it *can* be pierced—*by anyone*—with nothing more (or less) than the "sharp dart of longing love"! *We know God by love.* Even a single word uttered in love opens the way to divine intimacy.

I began this chapter with a question from Jayson, my ex-missionary friend: without knowing what we can't know, can we simply focus on growing in love? I'll finally respond with this exhortation from our humble monk:

> For He can well be loved, but he cannot be thought. By love he can be grasped and held, but by thought, neither grasped nor held. And therefore, though it may be good at times to think specifically of the kindness and excellence of God, and though this may be a light and a part of contemplation, all the same, in the work of contemplation itself, it must be cast down and covered with a cloud of forgetting. And you must step above it stoutly but deftly, with a devout and delightful stirring of love, and struggle to pierce that darkness above you; and beat on that thick cloud of unknowing with *a sharp dart of longing love*, and do not give up, whatever happens.[94]

11

OUT OF THE SHADOWS:
PLATO (FROM SOCRATES TO WEIL)

As we continue to listen to the insights of our "seven sleepers," our dialogue partners across the centuries, we now move to another apophatic teacher—the Greek philosopher Socrates (via the writings of his pupil Plato). How might Socrates/Plato speak from four hundred years before Christ to us twenty-first-century rookies in deconstruction? And why does it matter?

To read Plato well,[95] I've enlisted the help of his greatest interpreter, the French philosopher-activistic-mystic Simone Weil. She warrants her own chapter near the end of this section, but when reading Plato's works, I find Weil's keen contemplative mind keeps us on the "fairway" where others have "sliced into the hazards."

The heart of Plato's abiding influence is his famously misinterpreted "cave analogy" (from *The Republic*, 514a–515c). In this chapter, I identify our generation with the prisoners chained inside.

Plato was a political philosopher in Athens whose works record the dialogues of his mentor, Socrates. Some people mistake Plato's Socrates for a heady rationalist, others for an anti-material dualist. That's ironic, because those who misread and mistranslate him only do so because of their own rationalistic or dualistic lenses.[96] In truth, Plato's thought exposes the *limits* of reason and establishes *contemplative knowing* as the only way to perceive eternal truth. His alleged dualism is not anti-material or gnostic at all. Rather, he's anticipating the familiar New Testament distinction between the light of truth and the dark shadows of delusion. He grounds these insights in his world as a prophet of civic politics and public education.

But, really, is Plato even relevant to us today? Tertullian famously asked, "What has Athens to do with Jerusalem?"[97] A whole lot, as it turns out. For Christians, certainly, his prophecy of the crucifixion four hundred years before the fact is notable![98] All the more so when we see the New Testament repeatedly engage his thought, language, and metaphors. The way John, James, and the writer of Hebrews see Christ fulfilling and exceeding Socrates's/Plato's insights is well worth contemplating—especially the categories of light and darkness, conversion and transformation, deliverance and ascent. Like the Jewish rabbis of Alexandria, the apostolic witnesses integrate Plato's language into the revelation of Moses and Isaiah.[99] To the first Christians, Christ fulfills the hopes of both the Jews and the Greeks—the gospel in Acts is that Jesus is the Messiah of Israel *and* Light to the gentiles, the nations, and the world.

THE CAVE ANALOGY

In that spirit, and in the context of this conversation, let's examine Socrates's historic "cave analogy" in Plato's *Republic*. After Moses, I would regard this parable, "The Allegory of the Cave," as *the fountainhead of Western deconstruction*. In due time, we'll see how the apostle John subsumes and inverts the "Cave" in the prologue to his Gospel.

Socrates tells his students that *The Republic* is an inquest in which the "philosopher" (literally "lover of wisdom") desires and apprehends what is eternal and unchanging[100]—namely, God: the Good, the True, and the Beautiful. Why? For the purpose of discerning and living the just life together (here and now).[101] In *The Republic*, the cave analogy signifies one prisoner's escape from bondage to delusion and deception into a higher way of knowing that leads not only to enlightenment but also to justice.

The cave[102] can be summarized in three brief acts:

1. *The dark cave of delusion:* people are prisoners chained in a cave of delusion where shadows on the wall are mistaken for reality.

2. *Into the Light, illumined by love:* a prisoner is somehow released and dragged up and out of the cave into the sunlight, where his/her

spiritual eyes are opened to see the Sun. The Sun (the Good/God) is the source of light, existence and reality, knowledge and truth. Simone Weil's revelation is that for Plato as for John, light represents not only eternal *truth* but also, and ultimately, divine *love*. Love is *not* blind. Love is the light by which we truly see.

3.   *Return to the cave:* having seen the light, love compels the redeemed prisoner to return to the cave to stand for what is true, right, and just. He soon discovers the hostility of those who remain in the shadows. This aspect of the analogy shows us that Plato does *not* believe in escaping our material existence, but rather turning and ascending to see the light of truth and then becoming messengers of the light who serve those still living in darkness.

WHAT IS THE CAVE?

Let's now expand on the first part of Plato's allegory, what I will call "Act I: The Dark Cave of Delusion." Plato invites us to imagine a subterranean cave, open at the top toward the sunlight above. In this cave, we find people who have, since childhood, been chained immobile to the floor by their legs and necks. They are bound in such a way that they can only stare straight ahead, facing the wall, and have never seen direct light of any kind, much less the open sky. All they see are shadows dancing on the wall, cast by objects moving back and forth behind them, backlit by a campfire, which is also out of view.

These prisoners symbolize most of humanity—those trapped in the matrix their entire lives, beholding mere shadows of reality and hearing only echoes of the truth. Oblivious to life outside their restrictive field of vision, they cling to their distorted reality and have no desire to escape their prison. *This is their life.*

This is us.

You see, we mustn't read Plato's Cave dispassionately as bygone historical philosophy. We listen. We allow our seven sleepers, the masters of deconstruction, to speak to our situation. They serve as sage consultants who examine our symptoms and diagnose the malaise of our moment.

So, when Plato says, "Imagine a cave," I do exactly that. I assume we are—or, at least, I am—the prisoner(s) he continues to address from afar. I see how modern Western civilization has become this dark cavern, and we are the willing prisoners in a dungeon of our own construction. The cave is a parable of our world or society and its distorted perceptions of reality.

The *world* in this context is not the good world of God's creation, or the world of people whom God so loves that he sent his Son. Rather, the world in this context is the godless *system* that John describes in his epistle:

> [15] Do not love the *world*, or the things that are in the *world*. If anyone loves the *world*, the father's love is not in them. [16] Everything in the *world*, you see—the greedy desire of the flesh, the greedy desire of the eyes, the pride of life—none of this is from the father. It is from the *world*. [17] The *world* is passing away, with all its greedy desires. But anyone who does God's will abides forever. (1 John 2:15–17)

Plato's analogy, then, has nothing to do with escaping the material world (via death, drugs, or spiritual ecstasy). Nor is it concerned with an earth-versus-heaven or body-versus-spirit dualism. Rather, the cave illustrates how stuck we are, how prone humanity is to every wind and wave of opinion, and how our ideological mirages lead to injustice in the real world. Thus, rather than signifying *the world* as the created order (i.e., nature), the cavern depicts our *attachments*[103] to the world system with the established lies, toxic mindsets, and destructive practices so dominant in our society.[104] We veritably breathe them. We mistake the shadows we see and the echoes we hear for truth—collective, illusory ways of knowing and being we are chained to in darkness.[105] One more time: the *bondage* we hope to escape is *not* temporal life. Rather, it's about waking up from a dreamlike existence ("reverie") of enslaving perspectives and allegiances ("loves").

We might also distinguish the cave itself from the darkness and chains inside. That is, the *cave*, as such, can represent our lives in time (personal, social, internal) while the *darkness* describes our deceived perceptions and damaged discernment.

The cave of the world, then, is where we live our lives, where we form communities, and, I'm happy to say, where Christ became incarnate. But the darkness, the shadows, and the chains point to the idols we erect—idols of the self (our egos), the social (our *isms*), or even the divine (our "gods"). The shadows in Plato's cave continue to flicker in our time. Think, for example, of our dependence on speed-of-light technologies and a myriad of mind-numbing distractions.

In Weil's language, the *self* and the *social* are the two great idols. We can burrow into *self*-obsession or be swept away by *social* ideologies. She turned her spotlight on the forces of nationalism, fascism, and communism that overtook her world. Today, our idols may include political or social movements, the culture-wars phenomenon, social-media trends, or the enticement of our smartphones—and their effect on our nervous systems. When Facebook and Instagram went offline for eight hours on October 4, 2021, we joked about how soon we'd be living in caves again, failing to see how we already were.

Now here is the true darkness: rather than living in the grace of today, waiting on God, and loving each other, we fall into self-centeredness, chained to the idea that the universe revolves around us and triggered by any obstacle to "my will be done." This desire to *master* MY own destiny—the primacy of MY so-called "freedom" (self-will)—is the darkness that needs deconstruction. And any deconstruction so enslaved to the self (I, ME, MINE) that it finally declares, "There is no Sun," has not yet emerged into the Light. That's just a darker cavern and a deeper delusion.

If we can no longer even imagine the Sun/the Good—when we live beyond good and evil by self-made and self-serving values—the result is inevitable. An ethic perched on the shifting sands of self-interest leads us to exploit and tyrannize the weakest among us because we cannot remember why we shouldn't. No Good, no justice.

More simply, if there is no ultimate, eternal Good, why be good? Answer: we won't be. We aren't.

If our freedom is absolute, why should goodness restrain us? Answer: it won't. It doesn't.

Deconstruction is then reduced to this: total emancipation from the Sun is the Cave.

INTO THE LIGHT

Our focus now shifts to how Plato describes the prisoner's escape from the matrix in terms of deliverance, of healing, and of enlightenment par excellence. The picture isn't merely freedom *from* or turning *from* or awakening *from*—though that is the first part of the story. It is also about turning *to* or returning *to*, about ascending *to*, and about transcending *to*. And it's about the transformation of one prisoner into a guardian of the city and a messenger *of* the Light. For the Old Testament prophets, there's a greater emphasis on turning *from*—repentance is weighted with regret and contrition (Hebrew, *pathos*). But among the Greeks, the focus is on turning *around* and turning *toward* and turning *into*—reformation and transformation (fashioning a new *ethos*).[106] The New Testament (including Jesus) synthesizes both aspects in the word *metanoia*, translated as *repentance* or *conversion*.

Metanoia is neither self-loathing anguish nor simply a "change of mind." Rather, *metanoia* is the complete reorientation (turning around) of the *nous* (our minds, hearts, and lives) toward the overtures of divine Love. It is about turning our eyes from the shadowy delusions we inherited or created toward the true Light of Love. It is the reality of being indwelled and converted by that Light into someone new and renewed...so that the Light in us begins to shine out through our scars. Any deconstruction that doesn't *convert* us into light-bearing lovers is dim indeed—just another shadow to "leave go."

Read that way, the Cave is a story of redemption and how the redeemed soul also becomes a willing agent of redemption. The deliverance comes in stages:

1. The chains are *broken.*

2. The prisoner is compelled to *turn* from his error.

3. Turning, he *sees* the light, which at first hurts his eyes.

4. His instructor drags him *upward* toward the light.

5. Outside, his eyes adjust to the light in stages. He sees the sun indirectly reflected on a lake, then is finally able to look up and see "the beatific vision."

In Plato's model (and experience), the prisoner is *not* simply *choosing* to "follow his heart" to freedom. (More often than not, that's how we got into this mess.) No, the prisoner doesn't break his own chains, doesn't turn of his own volition, and is reluctant to make his ascent. Who or what breaks his chains? Who or what compels him to make that first turn? Who or what urges him upward? Who is this instructor? That depends on your journey. What woke you up? What turned your head? What were the means of your recovery? Who has compelled you to follow? Some people will point to tragic circumstances that jarred them out of their reverie. Others recall the faithful people who offered a helping hand. Still others had a dramatic Damascus

Road experience. But, ultimately, through these means and agents, Grace was always at work in them and through them.

The grace of God (or the light of the Good) sponsors the journey—every stage—from beginning to end. And it's not just about *the release, the turning, and the ascent*. To see the light is to be *transformed by the light*. *To behold the Sun is to be transfused, transfigured, and converted* in the fullest sense.

As much as "saved" and "redeemed" became washed-out Christian clichés, so, also, the language of *conversion* has been overused but underrated. Think for a moment about the implications of that term. Somehow, "churchianity" reduced converts to those who have simply parroted a prayer, adopted a new opinion, or transferred their membership to a new belief system. But is that all *conversion* implies?

Maybe Christian *conversion* became so vacuous that we've adapted the language of *deconstruction* to better capture how deep these changes can and must penetrate into our very being. And isn't that what conversion meant all along for those who experienced Jesus? Christ is the ultimate deconstructionist—inexorably converting whole lives, a whole species, a whole cosmos—by gathering all things and all people into himself, entering the chrysalis of death and hades, then reemerging to transfigure all things with his eternal life.

BEHOLDING THE DIVINE SUN/SON

Seeing Plato's Sun in light of Christ, the divine Son, shows us how Socrates anticipated the righteous One "through a glass, darkly" (1 Cor 13:12 KJV). As with the Jewish prophets, he foresaw and painted a portrait that, once complete, would surprise and subvert his own expectations. His contribution offers the contours of a narrative that Christ alone would fill out and transcend.

Plato prophesied the crucifixion, but he could not foresee the resurrection. In Christ, the fulfillment of his intuitions vastly exceeded them. But after the resurrection, by the Spirit, John and Paul were able to connect the dots and could proclaim Christ with reference to aspects of the cave analogy. Let's compare a brief passage from each author.

1. Plato

Watch then the process of *liberation from their chains* and the *remedy for their folly*.... Shall we go on to consider how such people [guardians] may be formed and how they may be *raised upward to the light* even as some are said to have *ascended from hades to the gods?*

It seems this would not be like the turning over of a shell, but rather, *the turning around of a soul—away from a day that is night toward the true day—an ascent to Reality* which we will affirm to be true philosophy.[107]

2. John

Now watch what John does in his prologue on the *Logos*. While Plato talks about leaving the Cave to gaze on the divine Sun, John reveals how the divine Son becomes flesh as the righteous Man who enters the darkened world and *is* himself the Light that shines in the darkness. Through Christ, we gaze on the glory of the Father "here below"!

> [3] All things came into existence through him; not one thing that exists came into existence without him. [4] Life was in him, and this life was the light of the human race. [5] *The light shines in the darkness, and the darkness did not overcome it* ["comprehend it" NKJV]....
>
> [9] *The true light, which gives light to every human being, was coming into the world.* [10] He was in the world, and the world was made through him, and the world did not know him. [11] He came to what was his own, and his own people did not accept him. [12] But to anyone who did accept him, he gave the right to become God's children; yes, to anyone who believed in his name. [13] They were not born from blood, or from fleshly desire, or from the intention of a man, but from God.
>
> [14] *And the Word became flesh, and lived among us. We gazed upon his glory, glory like that of the father's only son*, full of grace and truth.
>
> (John 1:3–5, 9–14)

3. Paul

Similarly, watch how the apostle Paul says that those who *turn* to the Light discover freedom and behold the glory that transforms us—*metamorphosis, transfiguration*. The Spirit opens our eyes to see the glory of God in the face of Jesus.

> [16] But "whenever *he turns back to the Lord*, the veil is removed." [17] Now "the Lord" here means the spirit; and where the spirit of the Lord is,

there is *freedom*. [18] And all of us, without any veil on our faces, *gaze at the glory* of the Lord as in a mirror, and so are *being changed* into the same image, from glory to glory, just as you'd expect from the Lord, the spirit.   (2 Cor 3:16–18)

[3] If our gospel still remains "veiled," it is *veiled for people who are perishing.* [4] What's happening there is that the god of this world has *blinded the minds of unbelievers*, so that they *won't see the light* of the gospel of the glory of the Messiah, who is God's image. [5] We don't proclaim ourselves, you see, but Jesus the Messiah as Lord, and ourselves as your servants because of Jesus; [6] because *the God who said, "Let light shine out of darkness," has shone in our hearts*, to produce *the light of the knowledge of the glory of God in the face of Jesus* the Messiah.

                                                                                    (2 Cor 4:3–6)

We see here that the apostles' response to the dark cave of this world is not escapist. This world, as dark as it gets, is the realm in which we live. It's the very place the "Light of the world" entered and shone! So, while Plato's Cave is a surely a picture of the darkened existence within a human heart or of a messed-up world, the gospel depicts how the light of Christ enters and transforms. He never abandons.

REAL LIFE

How we experience God's love and light is my central concern. As I look about through dim eyes, the light of Christ has not yet fully illuminated the darkness of our world. Yet, we do experience moments of clarity that reveal the depth of this present darkness. The light of Christ is present, ever shining on us—all of us (John 1:9)—waiting for us to *re*-turn.

Perhaps you didn't need to know about Plato or his cave. After all, the parable of the prodigal son(s) is Christ's own perfect redemption parable. But, then again, the description may deeply resonate for some people, especially as Christ is unveiled as the true Light.

For example, just as I was working on my translation of the above portion of "The Allegory of the Cave," a friend messaged me from her hospital bed. She had suffered a psychotic break, with delusional fantasies, and was checking in from the psych ward. She asked about my day, so I replied, "Translating Plato."

"Ew."

"I enjoy it. It's creative and meticulous. Maybe like when you used to do nails and eyelashes."

Then it occurred to me that she had been living the cave experience. So, I copied and pasted my translation to her. She liked it!

I asked, "So, when you read that, what does it speak to you?"

Remember, all she had was the translation. None of the connections John or Paul made to Jesus. Just ninety-five words from *The Republic*.

She replied quickly, "Turning to Jesus is the only way I will find the truth. The truth about the true me…and about the reality in which I live with him. Am I right? Is that what it means?"

"Yes," I wrote, "IF you do it."

"OK."

"Tell me what happens."

I paused for lunch. Thirty minutes later, I came back to read this:

"Jesus says,

Why do you turn your back from what I tell you? About the true goodness of your heart and soul? Why do you turn your back to me and believe lies and stand in the darkness of death? Why don't you receive my love for you? Why do you hate the beauty I have created?

You are scared. You feel lost. You feel unlovable. You feel rejected…again. You feel lonely. The pain in your heart is unbearable, and you want to run to the darkness forever. You are hopeless. I know. I know.

Let me tell you. There is love in this world for you. You mustn't give up. You must choose life. You must choose me again. I have been waiting for a true choice. In this reality.

I will help you. He [her abuser] has not won!

I will help you. Always, I will help you.

Open your heart and soul to me. Turn from the darkness and look into the light. I am there for you."

Pretty amazing. The true Light came into her dark cave, broke the chains of her delusion, and spoke the truth of Jesus's compelling love.

Not that you want to tell the psychiatric ward staff that God or Jesus or Plato has been speaking to you. That's usually a red flag. But, in this case, it was just the opposite! She turned and *re*-turned to Life and Love and Truth. She's surrendered to the care of the Great Physician once again and is willing to follow him to freedom.

Not long afterward, I received a message from my friend's nurse. The nurse described the medical comeback after this encounter as "an actual miracle." She regarded my friend as beyond hope, on her deathbed, and was just trying to make her comfortable in her last day or two. Since then, she says, her patient has worked hard, has fought for her life a day at a time, and has been discharged from the hospital, actively planning for life and love beyond the confines of the ward. That didn't happen by reading a few sentences from Plato. It came by encountering the Light of Life and surrendering to his healing love. The Great Physician himself deconstructed death's reign in her heart, mind, and body.

12

VOLTAIRE'S ENLIGHTENMENT: LOVE YOUR FRENEMIES

Next to Jesus, and, okay, maybe Moses and Plato, we might regard François-Marie Arouet (1694–1778) as the greatest deconstructionist in history. Never heard of him? Likely not by that name. Perhaps *Voltaire*, his most infamous pen name, rings a bell. This French author, playwright, and poet is widely regarded as the central literary influencer in the era we call "The Enlightenment" (from 1650–1800 or, more narrowly, 1715–1789). Voltaire stands as head of a class of European thinkers dubbed *the philosophes*. Who were they?

> The men most celebrated for their genius were increasingly those who equated churches with bigotry. To be a *philosophe* was to thrill to the possibility that a new age of freedom was advancing. The demons of superstition and unwarranted privilege were being cast out. People who had been walking in darkness had seen a great light. The world was being born again.... His age was...an "age of enlightenment."[108]

Among the other bright minds of that era were Denis Diderot, Jean-Jacques Rousseau, David Hume, Adam Smith, Immanuel Kant, John Locke, and Thomas Jefferson. It was an age that touted science, reason, and liberty—both political and religious. Weary of the serial wars endemic to monarchs and churches, these thinkers birthed the ideals that ignited the American and French revolutions: *Liberté, égalité, fraternité* (liberty, equality, fraternity).

Kant summed up the spirit of the Enlightenment as *"Dare to know! (Sapere aude.)* Have the courage to use your own understanding!"[109] Even amid the catastrophes of continued colonial expansion and the burgeoning slave trade, Europe's deconstruction included progressive ideas about the equality and rights of all people (well…all white male landowners). A seed was planted and began to sprout, although many have yet to taste its fruit. For others, the fruit turned out to be bitter. But that's for another chapter.

In that epoch of intellectual celebrities, Voltaire "was the single most famous individual of the eighteenth century.… He set the Western agenda for much of the nineteenth century."[110] Flooding Europe's citizenry with pamphlets, poems, plays, novels, and letters, he virtually invented "popular opinion" and populism. "Flooding" is no hyperbole for his prolific output: defying censorship laws (under risk of prison, exile,[111] or death), he penned twenty thousand letters and two thousand books and pamphlets[112] under roughly 175 pseudonyms[113] and personae. His agenda was to defend human freedom by mobilizing his words like termites into the strongholds of structural oppression.

According to historian John Ralston Saul, Voltaire focused his work on six basic freedoms:

+ Freedom of persons (antislavery)
+ Freedom of speech and the press
+ Freedom of conscience (religious belief and practice)
+ Civil liberty (subject only to the rule of law)
+ Security of private property
+ The right to work[114]

You can imagine how these ideas would have pitted him against the entrenched institutional powers that be of his time—the monarchy, the church hierarchy, and the business elite. As the son of bourgeois parents and a star student of Jesuits, he wrote from a place of privilege and as one who saw its dark underbelly. He resisted his father's pressure to become a lawyer[115] and instead made his fortune through a scam that exploited a loophole in the French government's bond lottery system. This funded his lifelong career in writing.[116]

His scathing social critiques ooze with pathos, his satires are doused with sarcasm, dripping with irony. The sting of his pen made him a powerful but elusive enemy of both the church and the state, but he was beloved as a people's champion to his death.

Concerning Christianity, his brutal ridicule of bad theology and even worse practice in the church of his day made (and makes) him seem like an antichrist to many a faithful Christian. Youthful scorn grew to mocking skepticism and became outright hatred as the clergy, in their fear of losing control, doubled down violently against critique to the point of radicalized religious intolerance. "It seems," he wrote, "that fanaticism, indignant over reason's recent successes, struggles under it even more angrily."[117]

> The *philosophes* saw in this [an edict making any attack upon the Church a crime punishable by death] a declaration of war, and felt that henceforth they need spare no feelings, no traditions, in attacking what seemed to them a murderous absurdity. Behind the beauty and poetry of religion they saw propaganda conscripting art; behind the support that Christianity had given to morality they saw a thousand heretics burned at the stake, the Albigensians crushed out in a homicidal crusade, Spain and Portugal darkened with autos-da-fé, France torn apart by rival mythologies, and all the future of the human spirit subject in every land to the repeated resurrection of superstition, priestcraft, and persecution. They would fight such a medieval reaction with the last years of their life.[118]

ÉCRASEZ L'INFÂME!

Thus, Voltaire's signature rallying cry became *"Écrasez l'infâme!"* or "Crush the infamy!"

> What did he mean by "the infamy"? Did he propose to crush superstition, fanaticism, obscurantism, and persecution? Or was he undertaking to destroy the Catholic Church, or all forms of Christianity, or all religion itself? Hardly the last, for we find him again and again, even amid the campaign, professing his theistic faith, sometimes in terms warm with Voltairean piety.... We may conclude that by *l'infâme* he meant not religion in general, but religion as organized to propagate superstition and mythology, to control education, and to oppose dissent with censorship and persecution. And such was Christianity as Voltaire saw it in history and in France.[119]

You see, to paint the great deconstructionist as either a demon or a saint is simplistic. On the one hand, in his bitterness, Voltaire's propaganda against

Christianity could be unfair, cruel, and misleading. He deliberately sowed misinformation in his revisionist history of the church. A humorous account of his final words has a priest attempting to lead Voltaire in a renunciation of the devil. His cheeky response was, "This is no time to be making new enemies."[120]

BUT...we ought not overlook the apparent contraries: that he continued to attend the Catholic Mass throughout his life,[121] became a public defender of religious liberty, and, in February of his final year, allegedly confessed, "I die adoring God, loving my friends, not hating my enemies, and detesting superstition."[122] His deism[123] was as much a defense against the spread of atheism as it was a counterpoint to divine intervention.

This is not to "Christianize" Voltaire, but, as Tom Holland points out,

There was nothing quite so Christian as a summons to bring the world from darkness into light....

...Voltaire's dream of a brotherhood of man, even as it cast Christianity as something fractious, parochial, murderous, could not help but betray its Christian roots.[124]

In vilifying superstition, religious violence, and medieval ignorance within the church, Voltaire's concerns sound closer to our table-turning Messiah cleansing the corrupted temple than the Sanhedrin of status-quo religiosity, whether in the first, eighteenth, or twenty-first century.

So, while I have little use for Voltaire's condescension and contempt for faith—exactly the opposite of fruit of the Spirit—I want to "give the devil his due" as an ally of truth, even the truth of the gospel, on the following important fronts, which I will flesh out as we proceed.

1. His anti-theodicy (he opposed rationalizing the problem of evil)

2. His vehement defense of religious liberty (against violence by religion or against it)

3. His rejection of atheism (he felt the Enlightenment atheists were dangerously cynical)

VOLTAIRE'S ANTI-THEODICY

Theodicy is the term theologians use to describe arguments that rationalize the goodness of God and the reality of evil. If God is all-powerful and all-loving, how do we explain the great tragedies that afflict humankind, whether natural (e.g., earthquakes, disease, disability) or humanly caused (e.g., murder, sexual assault, oppression)? And if there is a God who cares, how does such a God relate to the created order? Is divine providence active in this world, in history, and in our lives? The proposed answers to "the problem of evil" are called *theodicies*.

In the early eighteenth century, the most popular of these approaches was actually called *Theodicy*, after the title of philosopher Gottfried Leibniz's 1710 book *Essais de Théodicée sur la bonté de Dieu, la liberté de l'homme et l'origine du mal* (*Essays of Theodicy on the Goodness of God, the Freedom of Man and the Origin of Evil*). We can distill Leibniz's argument (along with Alexander Pope's *Essay on Man*) to three primary premises, in step with his particular Christian convictions:

1. *We live in the best of all possible worlds:* Leibniz believed that while God is perfect (all-loving and all-powerful), the universe cannot be perfect because humanity is not perfect. Within the exercise of our free will, we are limited in our wisdom, our decisions, and our actions. Our moral imperfection introduces evil into the world to which God consents. While the universe is not, in this sense, *perfect*, Leibniz contends it is the *best of all possible worlds*. Human freedom and natural law are *necessary* and therefore *good*.

2. *It's all for the good:* If human freedom and natural law are both necessary and good, how do we find comfort when they result in terrible affliction, as in the case of an earthquake or a war? Leibniz calls us to trust that, ultimately, a good God will work everything out for our good.[125] Since God is good and does not inflict arbitrary suffering, we can find consolation in times of trouble by trusting that whatever happens, it is God's will and ultimately for our best.

3. *Everything happens for a reason:* The principle of "sufficient reason" goes this way: (a) every event has a cause, (b) there is a reason why everything is, and (c) everything that is, is good, (d) even if that reason is not clear to us now. Through whatever *necessary* chain of events we must pass, including tragedy, God has a plan, and providence will bring about that *good* end. In this model, the necessary and the good are one[126]—"It's all good."

Voltaire was initially impressed with the Optimists, especially Pope's account in *Essay on Man*, which he celebrated as "the most beautiful, the most useful, the most sublime didactic poem ever written in any language."[127] The enchantment ended with a tumultuous crash on All Saints' Day, November 1, 1755. A great earthquake off the coast of Portugal toppled Lisbon's six great cathedrals during the Mass, the city crumbled and burned, and the resulting tsunami drowned the survivors who made for the beach. Estimates of between sixty and one hundred thousand people died all along the coast of the Iberian Peninsula, clear down to Morocco. Bodies of men, women, and children were stacked in heaps throughout the city. Then free will kicked in—looting, molestation, murder. To restore order, the Portuguese army was deployed to construct gallows and execute the looters. They also surrounded the city to prevent able-bodied people from fleeing, forcing them to clear the ruins.

Then came the religious scapegoating. This must be God's judgment. Who is God punishing? Who must we sacrifice to appease the wrath of heaven? Was it the heretics? Or the Jews? A Jesuit priest, Gabriel Malagrida, published a series of vitriolic sermons denouncing the sins of Lisbon.[128] His messages so demoralized the survivors that the prime minister had him banished (and ultimately executed for treason in the Inquisition).[129]

The Lisbon earthquake caused a dramatic, immediate reversal in Voltaire. He was forever cured of Leibniz and Pope's optimism. I will recount three "volleys" that he fired in response.

FIRST VOLLEY: "A POEM ON THE LISBON DISASTER" (1755)

Within a few weeks, he published a scalding anti-theodicy in a lament titled "A Poem on the Lisbon Disaster, or: An Examination of that Axiom 'All Is Well.'"[130] This initial howl of protest is worthy of King David's psalms of lament:

> Oh, miserable mortals! Oh, wretched earth!
> Oh, dreadful assembly of all mankind!
> Eternal sermon of useless sufferings!
> Deluded philosophers who cry, "*All is well*,"
> Hasten, contemplate these frightful ruins,
> This wreck, these shreds, these wretched ashes of the dead;
> These women and children heaped on one another,
> These scattered members under broken marble;
> One-hundred thousand unfortunates devoured by the earth,

Who, bleeding, lacerated, and still alive,
Buried under their roofs without aid in their anguish,
End their sad days!
In answer to the half-formed cries of their dying voices,
At the frightful sight of their smoking ashes,
Will you say: *"This is the result of eternal laws*
Directing the acts of a free and good God!"
Will you say, in seeing this mass of victims:
"God is revenged, their death is the price for their crimes?"
What crime, what error did these children,
Crushed and bloody on their mothers' breasts, commit?
Did Lisbon, which is no more, have more vices
Than London and Paris immersed in their pleasures?
Lisbon is destroyed, and they dance in Paris!

SECOND VOLLEY: CANDIDE, A PARODY (1759)

Voltaire then shifts to satire. In his novella *Candide*, he parodies Leibniz and Pope through a caricature named Master Pangloss, who "could prove to admiration that there is no effect without a cause; and, that…this [is] best of all possible worlds…."[131] Pangloss is the *Optimiste* par excellence, aping all their slogans in ludicrous platitudes.

"It is demonstrable," said he, "that things cannot be otherwise than as they are; for as all things have been created for some end, they must necessarily be created for the best end."[132]

The story follows Candide and his entourage, including Pangloss, through a series of disastrous misfortunes, including the Lisbon earthquake. Note how Voltaire lays bare the bankruptcy of both the philosophical and religious theodicies:

Scarcely had they ceased to lament the loss of their benefactor and set foot in the city, when they perceived that the earth trembled under their feet, and the sea, swelling and foaming in the harbor, was dashing in pieces the vessels that were riding at anchor. Large sheets of flames and cinders covered the streets and public places; the houses tottered and were tumbled topsy-turvy even to their foundations, which were themselves destroyed, and thirty thousand inhabitants of both sexes, young and old, were buried beneath the ruins.…

"What can be the *sufficing reason* of this phenomenon?" said Pangloss.

"It is certainly the *day of judgment*," said Candide....

...The repast, indeed, was mournful, and the company moistened their bread with their tears; but Pangloss endeavored to comfort them under this affliction by affirming that things could not be otherwise than they were.

"For," said he, "all this is for the very best end, for if there is a volcano at Lisbon it could be in no other spot; and it is impossible but things should be as they are, for *everything is for the best.*"...

Pangloss was in the midst of his proposition, when the familiar beckoned to his attendant to help him to a glass of port wine.[133]

A fine exit from a dour conversation, in my view.

THIRD RESPONSE: "TOUT EST BIEN," AN ESSAY (1764)

From lament to satire to straight-up prose, the final volley comes in an essay Voltaire wrote for the *Philosophical Dictionary* in 1764:

This system of *All is good* represents the author of nature only as a powerful and maleficent king, who does not care, so long as he carries out his plan, that it costs four or five hundred thousand men their lives, and that the others drag out their days in want and in tears.

So far from the notion of the best of possible worlds being consoling, it drives to despair the philosophers who embrace it. The problem of good and evil remains an inexplicable chaos for those who seek in good faith. It is an intellectual exercise for those who argue: they are convicts who play with their chains.[134]

In each of Voltaire's volleys, I cannot find an enemy of faith—only of bad faith, of un-Christlike faith in an un-Christlike god. I don't know that Voltaire finds his way back to the cross, at least not consciously so. But he shares an anti-theodicy that is cruciform in its rejection of the god who wills evil. The Optimists were right to trust that God is good and will bring about the best end. But not by calling evil good or good evil—not without a theology of the cross where evil is confronted and overcome rather than rationalized or justified.

VOLTAIRE'S DEFENSE OF RELIGIOUS FREEDOM

Voltaire rooted his fiery opinions in the reality of human tragedy rather than philosophical abstractions. So, too, he tethered and directed his convictions on religious tolerance to actual oppression and injustice—his engagement hints at pastoral and prophetic motives, if not vocation. We see this most clearly in the curious case of Jean Calas.[135]

In March 1762, Jean Calas, a French Huguenot (Protestant) from Toulouse (very Catholic) discovered the body of his son, Marc-Antoine, who had converted to Catholicism. At first the family claimed he had been murdered, but the attending physicians noted the "livid mark" on his neck and assessed the cause of death as "hanging whilst alive, or by others."[136] According to Voltaire, "The Toulouse populace gathered around the house...superstitious and impulsive; it regards brothers who don't share one's religion as monsters."[137] The mob cast suspicion on the family, convincing themselves that the Calvinist father had murdered his son for heresy. The fanatical crowd was already venerating the dead son as a Catholic martyr as they took him away for a consecrated burial (at the objection of the priest). Thousands showed up to honor their young saint.

After thirty-six hours in the dungeon, the household changed their story. They claimed that Marc-Antoine had hanged himself and that their story of murder was to avoid the ignominy that befalls suicides. Otherwise, the mob would have stripped his body nude and dragged it through the streets.

The case passed through trial with bogus evidence and unsubstantiated witnesses, but, in the end, Jean Calas was convicted and sentenced to interrogation, torture (to get him to confess and implicate his family), and then death.

First, he faced violent dislocation on the dreaded wheel: "With his wrists tied tightly to a bar behind him, Calas was stretched by a system of cranks and pulleys that steadily drew his arms up while an iron weight kept his feet in place"[138] He would not confess, so they proceeded to waterboarding. Two sticks held his mouth wide, a cloth was placed over his mouth, then, on the cloth, a funnel. "Then came the water, pitcher after pitcher."[139] Still, he insisted he was innocent.

David de Beaudrigue, the brutal *Capitoul* (police detective, prosecutor, and magistrate), carried on. They suspended Calas on an X-shaped cross.

Whereupon an executioner, iron rod in hand, crushed Calas's bones, two blows apiece to the upper and lower arms, two to the upper and lower legs, three to the midsection. Calas, his body broken, was then tied to a wheel, face to the sky, where, for two hours, he refused to convert and refused to confess.[140]

During the insanity, even hostile Catholic witnesses could not help but see his imitation of Christ—he was even praying for his tormenters. To the end, he insisted, "I die innocent. Jesus Christ, innocence itself, was well content to die by a more cruel suffering."[141] At last, it was time to finish him off. Poor Jean was strangled and his body burned.

Unreal, right? For those who'd like to imagine that such cruelty is a thing of the past, I'll leave you to research the range of "extraordinary renditions" that were approved and perpetrated by our "good Christian" democracies in the twenty-first century.

But Voltaire would not turn a blind eye. A sense of outrage and mission aroused him to act. He immediately became obsessed with the case, convinced that Calas was innocent, a victim of religious fanaticism. The furtive mocker of superstitious religion raised his game to become a public defender of religious liberty. Seeking a posthumous pardon, he employed all his skills and resources to the task. He financed the legal battle, recruited aristocratic donors, hired lawyers and an investigator, studied French law, wrote legal documents, and mobilized a powerful propaganda campaign to bring public pressure to bear.[142] He went all in and succeeded in reopening the case.

I am grateful that history has preserved his masterpiece argument, "Treatise on Tolerance," a pivotal piece in ultimately seeing Calas exonerated in March of 1765, but also a master class in deconstructing the hypocrisy of religious violence. Voltaire demonstrates his striking breadth and depth of knowledge in the history of civilization, interfaith studies, biblical scholarship, and early Christianity. He condemns the way Christians misuse Old Testament violence to justify the barbaric persecution of Christians by Christians, shaming them with the relative tolerance of the Jews, Greeks, and even the Roman emperors. How is it that the persecuted church exceeded their own persecutors in death-dealing cruelty?

As with the chiasms of Scripture, the center of this booklet marks the high point of his argument. *What would Jesus say?* "Let us now see whether Jesus-Christ set up sanguinary laws, enjoined intolerance, ordered the building of dungeons of the inquisition, or instituted the ceremony of burning at the stake."[143] He proceeds to dismantle every possible perversion of gospel teaching the church of his day (and of ours!) commonly used to justify violence, countering that Jesus is in no way like them. "He does not exclaim even against Judas, who is going to betray him; he commands Peter never to use the sword; he reproaches the sons of Zebedee who, after the example of Elias, wanted to bring fire from Heaven down on a town that refused him shelter."[144]

Voltaire then reviews the unjust crucifixion of Jesus, the innocent victim of the same religious fanaticism that "legally" murdered Calas. He concludes that section, "I now ask: is it tolerance or intolerance that is of divine right? If you wish to be like JESUS-CHRIST, be martyrs, not executioners."[145]

I see in this that Voltaire's attacks on Christianity and his wish for it to dissolve are specific to its superstitious fanaticism and sectarian violence, its hostility toward tolerance and human freedom. This is what he's deconstructing. That these dysfunctions persist make him relevant today.

But we should not stop our examination of Voltaire with his deconstruction of religion. He also discerned and deconstructed the Enlightenment's atheistic reactions, the counter-intolerance as familiar now as it was then...

VOLTAIRE'S REJECTION OF ATHEISM

Those who've suffered the wounds of religious bigotry imagine a utopian world where heaven, hell, and religion no longer exist. A universe devoid of God. "Imagine," sang John Lennon. A world where we all live as one in perfect peace and harmony.

Voltaire examines these claims carefully in his gargantuan *Philosophical Dictionary* in articles on "Atheism" and "Theism." He challenges the notion that societies unmoored from belief (or even fear) in a just God is inconsequential. He rejects the belief that breaking oaths (religious, legal, or political) could bring about a more peaceful and just society. "It is beyond all question, that in a policed city, *even a bad religion is better than none*."[146] The better question, for Voltaire, is which is more dangerous, atheism or *fanaticism*, which he says is "a thousand times more mischievous"[147]? After working through the ups and downs of theism, atheism, and fanaticism, he concludes:

> What are the inferences from all this? That *atheism is a most pernicious monster* in sovereign princes, and likewise in statesmen, however harmless their life be, because…if it be not so mischievous as fanaticism, it is almost ever destructive of virtue.[148]

In 1768, his convictions against atheism bared their Voltairean teeth in his seething "Epistle to the Author of the Book *The Three Impostors*."[149] The epistle, really a poem, refers to the 1719 work *Treatise of the Three Impostors*,[150] which attacks the Abrahamic faiths by accusing Moses, Jesus, and Muhammad of being "cheats," their religions hoaxes, and their followers dupes. *The Three Impostors* was brutal—a contemptuous, slanderous, and intentionally blasphemous assault that wreaked of the same sectarian intolerance Voltaire despised. It offended his own brand of theism, and he saw *The Three Impostors* as a pretense, composed by anonymous radicals whose atheism actually undermined the spirit of the Enlightenment. The light they purported to offer the world was darkness indeed, a sham that warranted his best rebuttal.

These highlights from the "Epistle" will give you a sense of how he deconstructed the deconstructors:

Insipid writer, you pretend to draw for your readers
The portraits of your [three] impostors;
How is it that, witlessly, you have become the fourth?...
Criticize the servant, but respect the master.
God should not suffer for the stupidity of the priest:
Let us recognize this God, although he is poorly served....

If the heavens, stripped of his noble imprint,
Could ever cease to attest to his being,
If God did not exist, it would be necessary to invent him....

But you, faulty logician, whose sad foolishness
Dares to reassure them in the path of crime,
What fruit do you expect to reap from your fine arguments?...

I know these awful monuments [sectarian religion] better than you;
I have unmasked them with my pen for the past fifty years.
But, as the fearsome enemy of this fanaticism,
I have also celebrated God when the devil was vanquished.
I always distinguished between religion
And the misery bred of superstition....
I have told the disputants, hounding one another:
"Cease, impertinent ones, cease, unfortunate ones;

Foolish children of God, cherish yourselves in your brothers,
And stop biting one another for absurd chimeras."[151]

"If God did not exist, it would be necessary to invent him."

And what God might Voltaire conceive sans revelation or religion, rooted solely in science and reason? We find Voltaire's own "confession of faith" described in his dictionary's chapter on "Theism." In my view, this suffices as Voltaire's self-flattering description:

> The doing of good, there is his service; being submissive to God, there is his doctrine.[152]

A SUBLIME ANTICHRIST

Why would I sacrifice a chapter to include among our "sleepers" the fiend that Dennis Diderot complimented as the "sublime, honorable and dear Anti-Christ"?[153] Why expose readers to this enemy of faith, who wrote to King Frederick II of Prussia, "Ours [Catholicism] is assuredly the most ridiculous, the most absurd and the most bloody [religion] which has ever infected this world"?[154] Because:

+ Voltaire's deconstruction was second to none in its influence. More than anyone else, he articulated, popularized, and stimulated the Enlightenment movement and its lasting impact. The great deconstructionists since him, cynics from Friedrich Nietzsche to Ricky Gervais, stand on his shoulders. If you're going to deconstruct today, pay attention.

+ Voltaire's deconstruction of religious fanaticism (in any faith) remains relevant. Wherever people who say they love God continue to practice sectarian hatred, justify intolerance, and perpetrate violence, his prophetic indictments stand. He calls us to wake up and repent because, when we don't, we create atheists.

+ Voltaire's deconstruction of Christianity continues to be poignant. When we consider the incorrigible dissension across Jesus's fractured church, Voltaire's call to (1) own our history of violence and (2) rise above our politicized divisions sounds like the biblical prophets and apostles. He dreamed of a world where the walls of hostility crumble and we unite with our global neighbors as children of one God, who is the supreme Good. Where Christianity clings to its fractious demons, then we have become antichrist.

+ Voltaire's deconstruction of atheism is just as poignant. How many people today jump from bad and intolerant religion into toxic and intolerant atheism? How many who bail on Christianity retain the fundamentalist and fractious spirit? How many who despise the hypocrisy of Christianity embrace a progressivism that turns up its nose at forgiveness and closes off paths to redemption as "complicity with injustice"? How enlightened are these cultured despisers, really? Voltaire has a word for them too.

+ Finally, Voltaire's populist activism is a mixed bag. He was as compromised as his opponents. He was dishonest, cruel, and privileged. But he proved himself to be more than an armchair critic. His activism was relentless, costly, and, at times, noble. The Calas case was only the first of many occasions where his advocacy for tolerance extended to people whose faith he found abhorrent. He persisted in fighting on their behalf because he was true to his own faith—that tolerance includes defending the freedom of conscience in the Other, even while curtailing their fanaticism and warning us (conservatives and progressives) away from ours.

13

UNVEILING THE DARKNESS AS DARKNESS: FRIEDRICH NIETZSCHE, PART 1

"Who shall be the lord of the earth?"
—Friedrich Nietzsche, *Thus Spake Zarathustra*[155]

If anyone competes with Voltaire's exacting deconstruction of Christian faith, it has to be Friedrich Nietzsche, the German godfather of postmodernism. Voltaire had a profound influence on Nietzsche. Nietzsche dedicated the book *Human, All Too Human: A Book for Free Spirits* to Voltaire on the hundredth anniversary of Voltaire's death.

> At the moment of *Human, All Too Human*, it is indeed in "Voltaire" that Nietzsche sees "himself" the most, almost as his double. He recognizes essentially a certain accent, a certain timbre of his voice, a certain tone which he did not yet know to be "his" and which puts him in kinship with Voltaire: the tone of a cold, hard and mocking intelligence, the very tone of a "critical" spirit which rends up like a ploughshare, rends itself up, sets to work on the question whilst calling itself into question; the tone of a scalpel-wielder, icy and pitiless.[156]

But, in fact, Nietzsche's blade cuts much deeper than his predecessor's. For whereas Voltaire carves up the superstition, hypocrisy, and intolerance of French Catholicism—slicing away Christianity while defending theism, humanism, and morality—Nietzsche seems set on amputating it all. While Voltaire saw the Lisbon earthquake as a tragedy arousing him to grief, empathy, and anger, Nietzsche identifies an earthquake on the Isle of Ischia in 1883[157]—coinciding with the completion of his epic poem *Thus Spake Zarathustra*—as a portent of himself. Nietzsche expects his "transvaluation of all values"[158] to be the earthquake, the dynamite, the tremors that upend everything for future generations, "reversing all meaning, the consequence of a struggle (*Kampf*) led by Nietzsche against millennia of lies."[159]

So, with Nietzsche, heads up. This is going to get dark. Nietzsche's deconstruction exposes the darkness as darkness—and sometimes intensifies it. Fear not: we're going somewhere with it—into the Light that shines in the darkness and overcomes it. But first, it requires sharing some world history that is ugly, where only the cross will save us.

This chapter follows the perilous trek of deconstruction (1) from the brittle faith of Christendom (2) through the tragedy of the human condition (3) to the loss of meaning or something far worse, and, finally, (4) into the inexplicable Light that shines through God's wounds and your own.

HUMANITY IN FREEFALL?

Remember 2022? That was a rough year for a lot of folks. So was 2020–21, though. Oh, and 2019 was hard for me, too. Although not nearly as bad as 2018. Assessing this whole era realistically, it's fair to say our civilization is in crisis—or should I say collective freefall?

The four horsemen of the apocalypse are out of the barn (again).

+ *The earth protests:* we're well into actual environmental crises on multiple fronts. "Heat domes," forest fires, "atmospheric rivers," and historic flooding shattered records (and communities) in my city and across the groaning globe.

+ *The plague spreads:* we suffered an actual pandemic with a profound body count and escalating anger as the world polarized over vaccination and masking protocols.

+ *The nations rage:* we are experiencing wars and rumors of wars, while at least three empires do what empires always do. We've also seen a resurgence of the ugliest nationalism and the most authoritarian national ambitions since the Second World War.

+ *Faith is on fire:* as The Great Deconstruction continues, Christianity is simultaneously being evacuated, reframed, or radicalized. Since the year 1990, the percentage of American adults who identify as "Christians" has dropped from 86 percent (1990) to 80 percent (2000) to 63 percent, while the rise of religious "nones" (unaffiliated) ballooned from 7 percent to 29 percent over that same stretch.[160] Fewer people identify as Christian, but even those who do are actually attending religious services less and less.[161] And while many people continue to affirm some construct of "Jesus," if we check the substance, he'd generally be unrecognizable to the disciples who knew him.

In an ominous post, my friend Archbishop Lazar opined:

The plagues listed in the Book of Revelation will come to pass, not by God's action against man but because of man's own avarice and callousness.

…We are seeing the beginning of an extremely tragic era [in] man's history—or rather another stage in a tragic era that began decades ago.…

This is really a matter of societal suicide by means of self-indulgence and sheer arrogance. Human beings are themselves the living Bowls of Wrath mentioned in the Apocalypse—the Book of Revelation.[162]

Gloomy, for sure. Yet to our sleeping prophets, none of this would be surprising. And, mercifully, for some, not entirely hopeless. Let's rewind over a century ago to give ear to Nietzsche's "prophecy of two centuries," written between November 1887 and March 1888. I have put additional commentary of my own in brackets.

NIETZSCHE'S PROPHECY

Of what is great one must either be silent or speak with greatness. With greatness—that means cynically and with innocence.

What I relate is the history of the next two centuries. [Thus, Nietzsche is a voice from both our past—1888—and our future—2088, because, as I expressed earlier, prophecy is but a shadow cast back from the future.] I describe what is coming, what can no longer come differently: the advent of *nihilism*. [Nihilism: the philosophy that life has no meaning.] This history can be related even now; for necessity itself is at work here. This future speaks even now in a hundred signs, this destiny announces itself everywhere; for this music of the future all ears are cocked even now. For some time now, our whole European culture [and now we would say Western, perhaps even global, culture] has been moving as toward a catastrophe, with a tortured tension that is growing from decade to decade: restlessly, violently, headlong, like a river that wants to reach the end, that no longer reflects, that is afraid to reflect.[163]

Nietzsche's prophecy is not only about *world* history (still unfolding, still unraveling). It also describes the hazardous course of *personal and social deconstruction*—handy to know if we're just halfway through the minefield in its current cycle. He predicts the path upon which nineteenth-century postmodern progressivism will continue to evolve. Given the historic series of collapses beginning with the "Great War" (1914–1918), we ought to inquire as to what pitfalls yet lie ahead.

Nietzsche lays out two centuries of development in these familiar stages:

STAGE 1: THE FAILURE OF CHRISTENDOM: BRITTLE MEANING

What is Christendom? Earlier, I briefly defined *Christendom* as "a Christian-dominant state or culture." We used to define Christendom as the marriage of church and state, where Christianity was a state-sanctioned and state-regulated religion. In Christendom, the "official" church was either in control over, or was controlled by, its relationship to governing powers—whether an emperor, a king, a parliament, or a local magistrate. The faith of the king (e.g., Protestant or Catholic) determined the faith *de jour* of the people, and infant baptism was synonymous with citizenship.

But Christendom would push its boundaries further than that. Today, we would regard Christendom as a *cultural assumption* even in liberal democracies that claim separation of church and state. Christendom exists among any faith group that imagines they live in a nation or culture that was historically Christian, continues to be Christian, or should be Christianized again. Often, that idea extends to a sense of dominion, privilege, and victimhood (if they sense their dominion slipping away). The spirit of Christendom can permeate cultural mindsets even after they have long abandoned the lordship of Christ or substantial Christian practice. Christendom, in the end, becomes Christless civil religion, thinly disguised with a plastic fish on its tailgate. The "Jesus brand" is pasted onto the real vehicle: political or social will to power.

Friedrich Nietzsche, Fyodor Dostoevsky, Søren Kierkegaard, and (too late) Dietrich Bonhoeffer saw how *brittle* that form of faith had become! They directed their scalding criticism of the church at its lapse into a bland social club of "cheap grace." The gospel of Christendom was oblivious to the divine presence and allergic to the *Jesus Way* of cruciform faith.

Cheap grace marries whatever moralist masquerade is popular at the moment, whether prudish or promiscuous, conservative or liberal—whatever is most "sexy" or least demanding at the time.

Poor Nietzsche was the son of a Lutheran minister who died when heartbroken Freddy was just a boy. He was raised in a moralistic home with his widowed mother, grandmother, two aunts, and a sister (hence, his misogyny). At first, he sought to follow his father's vocation as a minister but shifted from theological studies to philosophy as he lost his faith.

We can't verify the first source of his infamous "God is dead" rhetoric, but I can imagine Nietzsche adopting and adapting it from a Lutheran hymnal[164] as the congregation sang about the death of God in Christ on Good Friday. Yes, "God is dead"—there on the cross, crucified by us and for us. And I can imagine Nietzsche muttering to himself, "Damn right he is!"

THE GREAT DISILLUSIONMENT

In Nietzsche's work *The Gay Science*, a mad prophet appears in the town square and, in a dramatic prophetic act, shatters a lantern on the cobblestone. Perhaps he is mimicking Jeremiah when he smashed the jar at the Potsherd's Gate (Jeremiah 19) or Christ when he overthrew the tables in the outer courts of the temple (Matthew 21:12–13). The madman laments:

> God is dead! God remains dead! And we have killed him! [This is his indictment of what Christendom has done to God, to the felt presence of the Spirit in our midst, through our cheap grace, our moralism, and lack of participation.] How shall we console ourselves, the murderers of all murderers! The holiest and the mightiest thing the world has ever possessed has bled to death under our knives: who will

wipe this blood from us? With what water could we clean ourselves? What festivals of atonement, what holy games will we have to invent for ourselves? Is the magnitude of this deed not too great for us? Do we not ourselves have to become gods merely to appear worthy of it?[165]

So, The Great Disillusionment was already in motion—the clay feet of Christendom were crumbling. And now, the crumbling proceeds to toppling, just as Nietzsche foresaw. The spiritual damage of fact-less, faithless narcissism—the leaven of celebrity hucksters and priestly abusers—has penetrated and permeated the moldy loaf. Throw in the politicization of the church, and what's the aftermath? A *post-Jesus Christendom* that has given us spiritual food poisoning.

The credible witness of Christianity appears irreparable for decades to come—possibly forever—probably for the good. A dismal prognosis, but we need to lance the boil *before* we can be healed.

And yet…I rejoice to see a robust minority whose boldness and rare discernment have quietly grown as a bright light just outside the threshold of this calamity—a kind reminder that the "tent of meeting outside the camp"[166] was never completely vacant.

BRUTAL OR BRITTLE?

Biblical fundamentalism can be debunked by a college freshman, but the beauty of Christ can withstand the most formidable attack Nietzsche can muster."
—Brian Zahnd[167]

While Nietzsche's critique of Christendom confronted its metaphysical and moral failings, I believe he failed to strike at the heart of Christian faith. Sure, one can decimate the false faith of a corrupt or irrelevant institution. But he neglected the deepest vulnerability of *any* faith, including his own.

Specifically, Nietzsche failed to address adequately the problem that Voltaire, Dostoevsky, and, later, Weil and Albert Camus had the courage to underscore: the problem of *"the surd"* (Weil) or *absurd*. That is, pure, unredeemed, and irrational tragedy. Especially the suffering and death of children.

Voltaire rejected the voluntaristic god who does whatever he wills, including directly causing wars, tsunamis, and the death of innocents. Dostoevsky's

"Ivan" in *The Brothers Karamazov* defies the god who idly witnesses brutal war crimes against children, even if he were to redeem them in the end. Even Camus's Dr. Rieux, in his novel *The Plague*, an atheist physician who attends a child dying in torment, is silenced. There is no *rational theodicy* for absurd affliction.

As for Nietzsche, he resorts to simply denying that the problem of evil even exists. There is no problem because there is no evil—suffering and tragedy are beyond good and evil. He regards the very concept of evil as dangerous, invented by the powerless and weak out of their own resentment. He regards Judaism and Christianity as dangerous to human vitality and potential by making suffering sacred. He counters that what we've described as *evil* or *tragic* is all just part of life's drama, to be *nobly* and *heroically* accepted.[168] That perspective is all well and good in Homer's mythology or for a privileged intellectual. But it is all too fragile when Jewish children are herded into gas chambers by Nietzsche's confused fans (short for *fanatics*). In the end, Nietzsche's own "evil-skepticism" would prove far more fragile and dangerous as his mental health shriveled away.

STAGE 2: THE RISE AND FAILURE OF MODERNITY: INADEQUATE MEANING

Still, Nietzsche saw and foresaw what follows on the heels of the Great Disenchantment. He was no cheerleader for liberal modernity. He understood its inadequacy as a meaning-making movement—its central values were borrowed capital from Christianity, and when that was spent, what then? This worried him.

He saw through modernity's reaction against God. It wasn't just antichurch or post-Christendom. Modernity could not see that it was not merely rejecting some divine being—it was recoiling at Reality itself, setting itself up for something worse.

The modernists are still with us, not yet up to speed with Nietzsche's insights. These bright and reasonable minds (think of the New Atheists) still believe that if we could just evolve beyond this stupid, superstitious faith (even the Enlightenment theism of Voltaire), humanity would be much better for it. If we could just find our way to a rationalist, materialist consensus, we would transcend *all* the conflicts *always* rooted in religion, and humanity would achieve light, peace, and freedom. It's as if they had skipped class when "History of the Twentieth Century 101" came around. They've forgotten why the postmodernists since Nietzsche graded modernity with an F.[169]

What history revealed—what Nietzsche saw—was that, having abandoned Christendom's brittle faith, the fathers of modernity failed to provide adequate resources to create meaning. Modern rationalism, scientific materialism, and social engineering aren't up to dealing with the BIG questions of love, grief, faith, or death. The eighteenth-century bourgeois liberals could not provide an honest and adequate answer to the human condition, and their children knew it.[170]

What happens when we discover that recycling the Enlightenment as deconstruction cannot generate an answer to the question of meaning?[171] Nietzsche tells us. When these movements are exposed as bankrupt, the result is stage three....

STAGE 3: THE RISE AND FAILURE OF NIHILISM: NO MEANING

We go from...

1. *Christendom* (brittle meaning)
2. to *Modernity* (inadequate meaning)
3. to *Nihilism* (no meaning)

Nietzsche was *not* a nihilist. Don't shoot the messenger. He was the doomsday prophet warning us of nihilism. Nihilism refers to the radical disillusionment and cynicism that comes when post-Christian modernity offers no meaning—when the promises of deconstruction turn out to be a lie. That discovery, as Nietzsche foresaw and as we have witnessed (think Hitlerism), causes people to become hardened, leading them to violent and destructive behavior.

It's not just that "God dies," it's that every system and structure that we created and identified with reality dies with God. When we escape one cage, we race into a new, gilded cage, but when the gild wears off, we find out it's still a cage. Or we trade one boat for another only to realize that boats themselves are useless against the storm. And so, we conclude there is no meaning and throw up our hands.

Again, understand that Nietzsche was *not* a nihilist.

The modernist solution wouldn't work any better than Christendom did—and Nietzsche saw it. He knew we aren't designed to believe that our existence, that our lives, have no meaning. People are, by nature, meaning-makers—we search for meaning, we long for meaning. So, despite the disillusionment, the cynicism, and the deconstruction that follows betrayal by the Christian hierarchy and the liberal elites, it may surprise you that we don't (*can't*) end up having many nihilists. While nihilism is certainly a destructive way of seeing the world, it's not the most dominant philosophy. After nihilism, what then?

We'd better find out. We're finding out. Once the current round of deconstruction runs out of steam and leaves us empty, what then? Nietzsche tells us.

STAGE 4: THE FAILURE OF "TRUE WORLD" IDEOLOGY

We're human. We can't believe in *nothing*. We can't believe that life is *meaningless*. Thus, when we experience this life as deeply tragic, movements always arise that offer a way out—an alternate reality.

Nietzsche called these movements "true world" ideologies. Whether it's the Christian heaven, the Buddhist atman, or political utopia, they make their appeal by offering the following:

+ Belonging (from alienation)
+ Meaning (from mundane, accidental lives)
+ Safety (from vulnerability)
+ Self-esteem and worth (not just, "I'm an accident")

With religion debunked, those who offer utopia in the temporal realm (whether it's the Bolshevik revolutionaries or the QAnon conspirators) always conceive a plan: all we need to do to get to utopia is... [surprise!] *deconstruct!* Deconstruct the church, then the government, and then society and the family—burn it to the ground. *After* that, utopia! Well, *after* the necessary carnage. Until carnage becomes the point.

THE PROMISED LAND IS NEVER REALLY HERE

Nietzsche's critique is that all these models fall short because the promised land *is never really here*. It's always up there, over there, or down the road.

"True world" ideologies say, "There is an ideal world, and an ideal you. But the ideal world doesn't match your real world or your experience of yourself. But we have it. It's here behind our back. You can have it if you join us. Yes, you're discombobulated—but we'll connect the dots for you."

Nietzsche's worry was that if the choice is between *nihilism* (no meaning) and the promise of a *true world* for me to escape to, then we'll opt for *any* movement that offers belonging, meaning, safety, self-esteem, and worth...

we'll take it. And we did. The twentieth century ignited in wave after wave of ideological possession marked by bloodshed.

IDEOLOGICAL POSSESSION: TWENTIETH-CENTURY BLOODBATH

As Nietzsche predicted, Christendom decayed, modernity proved inadequate, nihilism left us empty, and so ideological possession revealed itself "in all its glory"—or, rather, *gory!*

"If we could just get rid of all that awful religion. Imagine! Heaven on earth!" But...

First, there can be no Christian "what-about-ism" here—no "Yes, but they..." finger-pointing that avoids the beam of religious violence in our eye by pointing to the flaws of our opponents. Christians, Muslims, Jews, Hindus, Buddhists, and others perpetrate war and oppression to this day. Modernity's radical skeptics defended religious tolerance even while Protestants and Catholics were still drenching the land in blood. Gratefully, the Enlightenment *did* manage to put the brakes on religious crusades in Europe, where the church failed to do so.

But Nietzsche—no friend of the church—wondered this: once we've rid ourselves of religious insanity, what will we get? Peace on earth, good will to all? He didn't think so. He was right. Behold what we reaped:

+ Millions of souls trafficked as the transatlantic slave trade expanded under *enlightened* entrepreneurs (naysayers notwithstanding)[172]

+ Two World Wars

+ Nazism: twelve million concentration camp deaths, of which six million were Jews

+ Stalinism: ten million Ukrainians in Stalin's Soviet state deliberately starved to death. And how many millions (including my wife's Opa) were sent to their deaths in the Gulag?

+ Mao's Marxist revolution: eighty million unnatural deaths, including starvation in "The Big Leap Forward"[173]

+ Pol Pot's Cambodian genocide: two million more died under his regime[174]

+ The bomb (only one nation has ever used it in battle)

+ The Cold War and its proxy wars across Africa, Asia, and Central and South America.

Nietzsche foresaw such outcomes. *"God is dead. We killed him. And now we're god. Watch the bloodbath."* Nietzsche predicted an even greater darkness unleashed in the world, and he was right: those who offered an *escape* from the human condition, only to worsen it. The *deconstruction* contracted into a singularity, then erupted as a great and more terrible *destruction*. Not only would post-theist theories renege on their promise, but, in less than a century, the anti-faith utopian projects would eclipse the body count of every religious genocide in history combined!

TRUE WORLD, TRUE SELF

Today, my hope is that our deconstruction (personal and social) would shed layers of the false self that obstructs us from being our best selves in a just society. Nietzsche's two-hundred-year-old prophecy is a gift that exposes the volatile shadow side of that hope. What do I hear him saying about us? About me?

First, we'd better be VERY careful when we talk about the truth. The prophets of authenticity rightly laud our being faithful to our *true selves*. But Freddy cautions me: finding my *true self* or "my true identity" must not be a bid to escape the reality of struggle, of hard-lived human experience. He condemns any *true self* that is just another *"true world false self."* Who am I? I am NOT just an imaginary saint, "hidden with Christ in heavenly realms"[175] without context or roots "here below," with no existence in the real world, with no righteousness in practice. Beware that the *true self* is not just a negation of who I am as I face the trials of the human condition here and now. The *true self* is not an imputed fantasy—it's the existential process of becoming human.

My true self is also not an otherworldly, pristine spirit borrowing my body. To be fully human includes my wounds, doesn't it? Or were Christ's wounds excluded from his true self—or from his life as incarnate human flesh? No, our wounds (personal and corporate) are real, and they are now. Any notion, any faith, any ideology that makes no place for the human condition will only feed our sense of separation, alienation, and shame. It will fail the test of meaning for our existence.

Nietzsche knew this: in the face of affliction, disillusioned utopians will fall into soul-sucking resentment (or *ressentiment*)—a hateful desire for revenge among the downtrodden that can lead to slave revolts and bloody revolutions.[176] If deconstruction can succeed in killing God (again) and razing the church, then what?

We resent existence itself. We wave a defiant fist at the air.

And then what? We might say, "I'm done. I'm outta here."

And then what?

This is Nietzsche's dark gift. He makes us play our deconstruction all the way out—as he did. All the way to the very bottom of the abyss. No denial, no escape, no imaginary utopia here or elsewhere.

And then what?

Nietzsche exhorts us: it's time we stopped trying to flee the reality of our real struggle in THIS world into the safety of some happily-ever-after "true world" up there or over there. It's time to stop damaging our sense of agency with an *elsewhere* kingdom or *"elsewhen"* utopia. In his own broken way, he called us to face our anxiety and heed our calling as life-affirming image-bearers of the divine—for ourselves and (I would add) our children. There's a name for this: *Existentialism*.

14

TRY YOUR FAITH:
EXISTENTIALIST COURAGE

"Existentialism is the affirmation of man's
absolute freedom in an absurd universe."
—George Grant[177]

"Life scares us.... Freedom scares us. In a world that is so conditioned by
addictions and virtual experiences it frightens us to be free."
—Pope Francis[178]

Thus far, our memos on the seven historic sleepers have included the apophatic agnostics and Socrates (via Plato), who led us out of the shadows of delusion, then our beloved "frenemies," Voltaire and Nietzsche—those great "haters" who would save us from ourselves. Now we segue to three great prophets of Existentialism, although it's also fair to regard Nietzsche as an Existentialist. What, you might ask, is Existentialism? Or at least, how am I using the term in this book?

EXISTENTIONALISM'S KEY VOICES

Existentialism is more of a movement than a philosophy per se. Its foundational voices emerge in the nineteenth century:

- Søren Kierkegaard (Danish): the father of Existentialism
- Fyodor Dostoevsky (Russian): the greatest novelist of all time
- Friedrich Nietzsche (German): the father of postmodernism

In the twentieth century, atop a long and eclectic list, I would include such key names as these:

- Martin Heidegger (German): *Being and Time*
- Simone de Beauvoir (French): feminist herald
- Albert Camus (Algerian/French): father of absurdism
- Jean-Paul Sartre (French): "Existence precedes essence"
- Viktor Frankl (Austrian): *Man's Search for Meaning*

KEY THEMES

Despite their many personal, cultural, and ideological differences—hostilities, often as not—those we label *Existentialists* (in retrospect) share some distinctive, overlapping themes and concerns, even if their answers vary. Among their major categories, I would include the following:

- **Existence.** Existence—*your* existence—matters, and it shouldn't be assumed. Whether there is a divine essence (God) or not, a human nature or not, we don't start there. We start with and are stuck in the real lives we've been thrown into. Within that struggle, we find and make meaning, and, for some, that's where we find God.

- **Meaning.** What gives our lives meaning? The existential quest for meaning moves us beyond nihilism (meaninglessness) and the absurd. What makes life worth living? Whether meaning is received or created in close encounters with God, humanity, suffering, or death, these great thinkers (including Nietzsche) rejected nihilistic despair.

- **Absurdity.** When they speak of the *surd* or the *absurd*, the existentialists are confronting life's tragedies, the problem of evil, and the angst-anguish of life before, and in the face of, death. They reject rationalist and religious theodicies and ask (fearlessly or in fear and trembling), "What's the point? Why not suicide? Why be good? What is good?" Existentialists don't ask these questions rhetorically. They make them their life pursuit.

- **Individual Freedom and Responsibility.** In asking these questions (answers or not), they distrust any appeal to a political system, social ideology, religious tradition, or technological trend that allows us to sidestep our terrifying personal freedom and responsibility. The status quo, the crowd, the mob, the collective—that's the demonized herd of Gadarene swine rushing headlong to their deaths.[179] Rather, we'll stand alone before God, accountable for every bad-faith choice—because we have real agency in this world, no matter what befalls us.

+ **Authenticity (Courage).** In this predicament, we take a leap of faith, we become human, we willingly embrace life on its terms, and we learn the transforming power of co-suffering love. Again, our truest self is *not* an abstract, perfectionist ideal in some alternative heavenly plane of existence. Rather, our true self is the life we live here and now—authentically and courageously—and, for Christians, this means living as those baptized in self-giving, cruciform love.

CRITIQUES

I can sound pretty enthusiastic about Existentialism. I am. I am an Existentialist. Orthodox Christians generally are. But if the Existentialists have taught me anything, it's that even Existentialism needs to be deconstructed—it's the very last movement that would resist critical thinking. They would all agree that defending deconstruction from deconstruction is ironic, ill-advised, and, frankly, mediocre. Existentialism ruthlessly critiques itself because a movement with ideas so rich is risky, and, like any philosophy, its masters or their disciples may lead us astray. What I watch for:

+ **Radical individualism >> alienation.** Their rightful reaction to lockstep alignment with the mindless herd has a shadow side. The centrality and responsibility of the individual (especially in Kierkegaard) set in motion a trajectory that became its own cultural disease: radical individualism that calls deconstructionists out of community into isolation and alienation—conditions that have devolved in an unprecedented mental, emotional, and social health crisis.

+ **Radical voluntarism >> each makes our own rules >> morality of pure will.** "Voluntarism" refers to the primacy and triumph of the will. At its very best, this looks like courage—making hard choices to do hard things when the path disappears into the fog. It means accepting what is and acting in good faith. Its shadow side says, "No one gets to tell you how to live—neither the government, nor the church, nor your family…not even

God. Decide for yourself what is right and wrong, and maybe there is no good or evil. There's not even such a thing as human nature. It's really for you to decide. Do what you will, be what you will."

+ **Radical freedom >> self-made values >> self-will >> will-to-power.** Existentialists talk a lot about freedom, which is a fairly Christian idea. "We've been released from bondage to religious laws and man-made traditions. Don't let anyone put that yoke back on your shoulders. 'It is for freedom that Christ set you free.'"[180] But there's a pseudo-freedom afoot within the atheist wing of Existentialism that equates freedom with generating your own values, according to the passions of self-will. And where self-will rules, it inevitably *lashes out*—worse, it *rules over* those whose freedom hinders ours.

CHRISTIAN EXISTENTIALISM

Nevertheless, I maintain a certain *Christian approach* to Existentialism. In the next several chapters, I will draw together and adapt key elements from four of the great thinkers/writers of the nineteenth and twentieth centuries. We'll more closely zero in on:

+ **Friedrich Nietzsche:** No, that's not a typo. And no, he wasn't a Christian. But Nietzsche laid down a gauntlet for serious Christians who wanted to test whether their faith was genuine, so we'll proceed to our second encounter with him before hearing the Christian existentialists.

+ **Søren Kierkegaard:** Kierkegaard lived a troubled life, but he was a brilliant philosopher and inspired provocateur, able to write from various points of view under many pseudonyms.

+ **Fyodor Dostoevsky:** This Russian Orthodox novelist is famous for books such as *The Brothers Karamazov* and *Crime and Punishment*. He was keenly aware of the torments of human despair. And he was unafraid of laying out a devastating case against faith through his characters. His responses were surprising, as we'll see.

+ **Simone Weil:** Her again! Yes, in fact, I've asked my favorite "sleeper" to grace this section with the final word because she brings us into the same abyss that swallowed Nietzsche, but there, in the "absence" of "God-forsakenness," she found—and showed me—the cross that is *decreation* par excellence.

15

CON-TESTING FAITH:
FRIEDRICH NIETZSCHE, PART 2

From late 2010 through 2012, still licking the wounds of burnout, I immersed myself in doctoral studies through Bangor University, Wales. My supervisor there, Dr. Lucy Huskinson, is a world-class Friedrich Nietzsche scholar. The focus of my studies was Canadian political philosopher George P. Grant, who engaged Nietzsche in every book he published. That is how I found myself neck-deep in books by the man who is infamous for the (out of context) statement, "God is dead."

Huskinson's book *Introduction to Nietzsche* assesses and affirms the value of engaging Nietzsche's thought for Christianity. She prepares readers who hope to dip into Nietzsche by avoiding reductionist caricatures that naively paint this great philosopher as either the devil incarnate or some sort of closet Christian. She maximizes what we might learn from Nietzsche by reminding us to not simply react to his needling but also observe and diagnose our own instinctive responses.

Her final chapter in that book, "Testing Faith: Redeeming Christians from Themselves," provides a great contribution to an urgent need of the day. In it, Huskinson sees Nietzsche's primary target audience as Christians, provoking them to test the strength of their faith. By opening ourselves to Christianity's harshest critic and facing his deepest questioning, our faith is "salted with fire," but "salt is good" and ought to be internalized.[181] After Nietzsche's furnace, will any faith remain? He was doubtful.

Let's start with Nietzsche's "God is dead" test, then proceed to *testing his test* for its criteria and assumptions, not to avoid the test but to stoke it and shape it for those Nietzsche calls "the most serious Christians"—with one such Christian in mind. Yes, her again: Simone Weil.

INTO THE WILDERNESS

Huskinson writes,

Our human life, Nietzsche says, is something to celebrate and own, and this includes its every struggle and pain. Nietzsche calls us out of the waiting room and "into the wilderness" to confront our suffering and, as we saw earlier, to test ourselves and to force us into learning how to become spiritually stronger and self-sufficient....

...[The death of God] provides superb test conditions to assess the strength of a Christian's faith. Nietzsche describes the test of Christian faith as *"the needful sacrifice."*[182]

In Nietzsche's words,

These serious, excellent, upright, deeply sensitive people who are still Christians from the very heart: they owe it to themselves to try for once the experiment of living for some length of time without Christianity, they owe it to *their faith* in this way for once to sojourn "in the wilderness"—if only to win for themselves the right to a voice on the question whether Christianity is necessary.[183]

To review, Nietzsche's test includes a context, a condition, and several possible consequences.

CONTEXT OF THE TEST: A WILDERNESS SOJOURN

According to Nietzsche, the necessary *context* of this test must be a wilderness trial, a confrontation with the "disgust and horror" of life.[184] Nietzsche knew this wilderness, having suffered the trauma of war and its wounds on his body and psyche. He knew the excruciation of experiencing a fatherless childhood, spurned love, betrayal, and isolation.

That Nietzsche should prescribe this context for the refiner's fire is appropriate because affliction (what Simone Weil calls *"malheur"*—non-redemptive suffering) quickly exposes those aspects of faith that are less than faith or pseudo-faith: benign mental assent to doctrinal creeds, inherited religious rituals, flaccid moralism, or a host of fantastical "god" projections of our own making.

However, the *context* of Nietzsche's test suffers two serious (though not insurmountable) limitations. First, he describes the wilderness sojourn as if this were an experimental suffering that is chosen or willed. Second, he assumes that, in such a wilderness, we can either voluntarily embrace or relinquish faith. But to what degree is affliction or faith a matter of the will?

Nietzsche had not volunteered for his own exposure to heartbreaking affliction. Nor does most of humanity for whom the wilderness is not so much a chosen sojourn as an inescapable state of debilitating and demoralizing tragedy and/or injustice. Some imaginary capacity for romantic, mythical heroism may work in classical Greek tragedy—but in the darkness of historical slave galleys or modern genocide, necessity's cruelty separates faith from thought experiments. In the context of the Hebrews' exile or Hitler's ovens, faith may be present or absent, but the suffering itself and whatever faith remains in its wake is not so much chosen or relinquished as given/received or lost/taken.

To be fair, Nietzsche didn't write for the poor of the poor in the third world or industrial-age factories. He rightly challenges the nominal faith of the bourgeois herd that merely believe that they believe. That their faith might amount to merely playing, pretending, and delusion was of great concern to Nietzsche, not least because that form of Christianity unchecked is oppressive, repressive, and ultimately breeds injustice—a worry shared by his contemporary Søren Kierkegaard. Both philosophers sought to initiate a purge of this pitiful and petty (but altogether dangerous) religiosity.

Yet how does a class of comfortable, oblivious churchgoers—in Nietzsche's Europe or Bible-Belt America—*choose* a wilderness that exceeds mere simulation? Are we to suppose that the well-to-do could manufacture a sufficient crucible for themselves? One can imagine the insignificant pseudo-trials that Nietzsche's target crowd might compose for themselves. Would these provide the authentic context required for the test? Upon reflection, we might conclude that "wilderness" sojourns are typically too difficult (for the destitute) or too easy (for the privileged) to effectively serve as a forge for faith.

However, Simone Weil is one example of how the advantaged can pass through the fire without being disingenuous. As the daughter of wealthy, secularized French Jews, Weil chose to immerse herself in the sufferings of the poor and live among the afflicted. Her life suggests three motives that create a potentially valid context of suffering for Nietzsche's challenge:

1. One can voluntarily descend into the darkness of the fray for an *ideological conviction*, as Weil's anti-fascism compelled her to enlist in the Spanish Civil War.

2. One can voluntarily *stand in solidarity* as an advocate among an oppressed people group that suffers involuntarily, as we see in Weil's year in the factory and long-term involvement with the French labor movement.

3. When confronted with *life-and-death danger* where flight is an option—as with the Nazi occupation of France—one can stay and face into the storm, though Charles de Gaulle stymied Weil's attempts to do so.

Still, even if one could use Weil's motivations to embark on a wilderness pilgrimage, how or why would setting aside faith provide a valid trial for faith's veracity? Isn't our faith tested by how it stands up under pressure, rather than how we stand up without it? Nietzsche did not think so. This leads us to his prescribed condition: the "God is dead" test.

CONDITION OF THE TEST: LIVING WITHOUT CHRISTIANITY

Presumably, if one can live for a time *as if* God is dead, one might discover whether their Christian faith is genuine or necessary. ("Let it go, and if it comes back to you....") Of course, the *condition* of the test is rather loaded with assumptions and begs certain questions.

How does one for whom Christianity is "serious" and "from the heart" decide to "live without Christianity"? What must this abandonment of faith include or entail in real life?

Ritually, we might easily imagine withdrawing from religious services and gatherings and ceasing the practice of Scripture reading and prayer for an extended period of time. A prolonged fast from venues and meetings that reinforce indoctrination and religious habits could be of great benefit to those who need to face the world outside their artificial religious bubbles. But, for serious, from-the-heart Christians, these elements comprise only externals that spiritual imposters can mimic without faith.

Socially, Nietzsche might expect the Christian to lay aside Christian fellowship for a time and to relate as friends only to agnostics and atheists.

Where this is possible, it is perhaps also necessary in terms of detoxification from the language and groupthink of the herd. But that leaves us with questions about friends and family members. How does abandoning them "prove" my faith?

Yes, Jesus did say, "If any of you come to me…and don't hate your father and your mother, your wife and your children, your brothers and your sisters—yes, and even your own life!—you can't be my disciple" (Luke 14:26). But Jesus's call is from family to faith, not from family and faith to…what? I suppose Nietzsche's wanderings from city to city do present relocation as a viable option, if the goal is to facilitate desocialization from Christian ghettos.

Ethically, does Nietzsche also require faith examinees to cast aside their Christian ethics and morals? Are we to refrain from love and forgiveness, from patience and kindness, from humility and goodness? I believe these are qualities common to humanity, and not specifically Christian mores. But not so for Nietzsche. He identified these traditional virtues as peculiar to the slave mindset of Christianity. Nietzsche is not calling Christians into liberal secular humanism. Rather, he invites them to freedom from a moralistic slave ethic to something bolder, amoral, or even immoral—something more "life-affirming" but less loving.

This aspect of the test would be problematic for those Christians (like me) who believe the Jesus Way of the Gospels *is* prescriptive of an abundant life rather than the stuffy Victorian pietism of Nietzsche's experience. Perhaps Christianity was always meant to move beyond the Tree of Knowledge of Good and Evil (i.e., withering moralism)—back to the Tree of Life. Then, laying down moralistic religiosity *is faith* and is as truly "Christian" as it is Nietzschean. We ought to be in sync with Nietzsche's life-affirming instigations.

Finally, at the level of *belief* or *faith*, Nietzsche would have the serious Christian attempt to lay down Christian belief per se—not just assent to creeds and dogma, but the very *belief* that God exists. This seems simple enough to one who has already lost their faith. Nietzsche abandoned his faith because it was no longer *believable* to him. He may not have realized how involuntary his anti-conversion was. He came to see things in a new way—he had a *metanoia*—a change of heart and mind that left him *unable* to believe. Asking him to live for a time as if God *does* exist may have worked as a test of his atheism, but could he have genuinely self-generated sufficient faith to make the test authentic? The same difficulty (or impossibility?) exists in reverse for the convinced believer.

In the West, Christianity has often emphasized a commitment or decision. We *choose* to trust in the word and person of God in Christ. And, yes, there is something to faith as a response of the will. But for Weil—as for Christians, Platonists, Hindus, or Buddhists—the further one travels East in thought, the more faith is an awakening, an enlightenment, an encounter. Revelation generates faith. We are "born from above" (John 3:3, 7)—"not born from blood, or from fleshly desire, or from the intention of a man, but from God" (John 1:13).

In Simone Weil's Christian Platonism, *faith is the experience of a heart illumined by love.* We "see the light." To lay aside faith on purpose would be like closing one's eyes in hopes of extinguishing the sun. Or, at least, eliminating one's memory of it. Not so simple.

Brian Zahnd told me about a time when he sought to appropriate the "God is dead" test—quite a risk for an active church leader if tried in earnest. He described his mental shift from "God is" to "God is not." What remained unchanged was the doubt itself. He merely converted from a believer with doubts about faith to an unbeliever who doubted his doubt. Such are the limits of converting by choice.

Still, in following Nietzsche's advice, the serious Christian *might* arouse lingering doubts that would lead to practical agnosticism or full-fledged unbelief. They might honestly ponder, for instance, the real contradictions posed by the existence of a good God and the afflictions people suffer in the world. For Simone Weil, this meant refusing to rationalize her way to a palatable theodicy. She said a firm no to spinning worldly evils into a greater providential good. Like Nietzsche, she embraced necessity (*amor fati*) and essentially said of the universe, warts and all, "*It is what it is.*" But rather than negating faith, when Weil gazes into the darkness, she *finds* faith (or it finds her) in the cross. Again, for Weil, the crucifixion of Jesus represents the sole intersection of ultimate goodness and affliction—the cruciform bridge across the eternal chasm between God and the world.

Further, Weil chose strategies of "attentive waiting" in which she fasted from Christian practice, projections, pursuit, or prayer. She wanted to avoid creating a god of her own projection OR in the Church's image. When she finally and reluctantly began to pray, she restricted herself to the "Our Father" in *Koine* Greek and refused baptism into church membership. Her motto was that if you tried to pursue God, you would create a projection. But she also discovered that if you preferred the truth over God, you would inevitably run into Christ...and she did. In the end, the cross of Christ revealed itself at the center of her wilderness and generated faith in an era of trauma.

CONSEQUENCES OF THE TEST...AND WHAT IS BEING TESTED?

If the serious Christian does successfully enter the wilderness and lay aside Christianity for a time, Nietzsche sees a number of possible outcomes. Let us review them as Huskinson lays them out:

> Nietzsche is in effect calling Christians to assess both the value and limits of their faith by sacrificing it in order to see whether it is strong enough to return. Such a sacrifice can occur only in the solitude of wilderness—which is to say, when the person is confronted with the suffering and horror of life. The test is to see whether the person can joyfully affirm his or her suffering as part of a blessed life (and wish its eternal recurrence); or, by contrast, either wish for his or her escape from it (by seeking comfort in a compassionate God) or feel the need to belittle it (by regarding it as a means to a higher end, such as divine retribution).
>
> If Christians can endure the former, then they have successfully lived without recourse to their God and can subsequently pass judgment on whether Christianity is necessary for the living of their life. If they still maintain it is indeed necessary, their faith will subsequently be reborn in strengthened form as a genuine or "more serious" faith. If it is not strong enough to return, they are released from an unnecessary restraint on the living of their lives.[185]

We can summarize the potential consequences of our faith test as follows:

1. Some might have the courage to joyfully endure and affirm suffering (without recourse to faith) as part of life, in which case (he thinks) God is proven unnecessary.

2. Some will be unable to endure affliction in their own strength, wishing only to fly back to God for consolation and reprieve (see Paul in 2 Cor 1:1–9).

3. Some will minimize suffering by looking beyond it or making sense of it through some redemptive/retributive outcome (e.g., Paul in 2 Cor 4:17 or Jesus in Heb 12:2).

4. A very few may endure the suffering and earn the right to judge faith as still necessary, in which case faith may return in a purer and stronger form.

Again, I perceive cracks in the foundation of Nietzsche's test as it stands. First, Nietzsche is establishing a double bind. After experiencing the wilderness trial, (a) if I find I *didn't* need my faith in God, it proves that Christianity was an unnecessary crutch, and it can be discarded. But (b) if I find I *did* need God, it proves my Christianity is still nothing more than a crutch and *should* be discarded as escapist (not life-affirming). Presumably, the serious Christians will not *need* their faith but will nevertheless deem it necessary (but why?) and be free *not* to discard it. In other words, the faith worth keeping after affliction was unnecessary in affliction! Confused yet? Your furrowed brows are a sign of spiritual health.

Still…I may misinterpret Nietzsche here, but it is exceedingly important *not* to miss his fair concerns regarding Christian faith.

First, if our faith drives us into *denial* or *triumphalism*, rather than taking up the cross that Christ has offered, it is toxic.

Second, if our faith uses God to *flee* from life as it is into a Christian ghetto or gnostic super-spirituality, rather than affirming and living life as Christ did, it is worse than useless.

Assenting to these points, a few other aspects are problematic. First, I wonder if Nietzsche's test of faith is more correctly a test of faithlessness. That is, isn't it rather a test of one's capacity to live *without* faith? Or, more positively, is this really a test of one's ego strength or soul strength apart from faith, simply a Zarathustrian sorting of the sheep from the goats? The righteous are those who embrace fate without faith. The unrighteous are those who must resort to faith in an imagined cosmic manager in order to function.

The hidden and unproven assumptions include the following:

1. Nietzsche assumes that *the ability or inability to sustain and embrace life without faith falsifies faith.* But does it? We may or may not have the personal courage or "soul strength" to face suffering. Some people endure great suffering with courage to the bitter end. Others cannot. But then, what is being tested? The necessity of faith? Or simply one's will power?

2. Nietzsche assumes *faith's veracity is tested by its usefulness.* But is it? Is faith entirely utilitarian? Or is the truth or reality of faith's *object* (God) what

is critically important? If faith in a lie "works" somehow, does the usefulness of that faith justify trusting in the lie, like some universal placebo effect? Or may my faith, however weak and prone I am to vacillate, be well founded because the anchor of truth holds even when I do not?

3. Nietzsche assumes *faith is falsified by one's need to run to God for comfort.* Is it? Isn't fleeing into the arms of God or leaning on his strength when ours fails, by definition, the central point of faith? The human will, when tested to the limits, comes to a terminus, after which we either fall into the arms of God or into the madness of the abyss. Short of that, we have not ventured far enough into the wilderness. We may not *need* faith to that point because life is still coddling us.

Friedrich Nietzsche and Simone Weil stand opposed in terms of atheism versus Christian faith. But they share some major commonalities. Both embrace suffering within their broader affirmation of life. They were equally committed to a stoic doctrine of *amor fati* (love of fate—*not* fatalism). Both looked into the abyss. Weil saw a crucified man. What did Nietzsche see?

Ultimately, both Weil and Nietzsche also became martyrs of their own willful convictions. It is unfair to presume how much Nietzsche's final illness can be attributed to his philosophy. In Weil's case, her desire for the decreation of her will looks rather self-absorbed and was ultimately fatal. In the end, Weil has no use for Nietzsche, but I am sure he would have seen Weil as one of his rare but "serious Christians."

THE PRODIGAL TEST

I teach a course entitled "Quest for Meaning: Readings in Existentialism" at St. Stephen's University (New Brunswick),[186] where I offer this chapter up for discussion. One astute student, Heather, found Nietzsche especially helpful in her deconstruction. She suggested a parallel between Jesus's parable of the prodigal and Nietzsche's challenge. Heather noted that the father did not hinder—or even object to—the younger son's departure. Indeed, he funded it! What seems to the reader like shameful disrespect or rebellion is, from the father's perspective, a calculated risk in his own goodness. In the words of my recovery sponsor, "God gives us the dignity of finding our own bottom." Once that happens, we might truly come home in a way that the elder brother apparently never did.

God does not coerce obedience—divine Love consents even to our way-wardness, however foolish or dangerous. Granted, the Scriptures include an abundance of dire warnings about the consequences of wandering away. Again, we have accounts of Jeremiah and Jesus weeping over their prodigal people. They see the collateral damage. But they also let us go, and they pray for our *willing* return—which is the only faith that counts. In the end, *authentic* faith—*serious* faith—requires a free choice, not an ultimatum. No gun-to-the-head threat of eternal torment will suffice. The Father will not abide a hostage video confession.

We may feel the urge to follow Nietzsche out the door to "sow our wild oats" for a time. Heather recalled the Amish and Old Mennonite traditions where the community releases their teens for a season into the wilderness of worldly experiences before they decide whether to be baptized and remain with the colony.[187] As with the prodigal son, it's a calculated risk because some choose to leave forever. What if God's most terrifying words are, "You may go"?

If staying amounts to slaving away or fear of punishment, our resentment will grow—toward our Father and our brothers and sisters—just as we see in the elder son. Could it be that the most resentful ex-church deconstructionists (you know them) were never afforded that freedom? Were they compelled to stay by fear tactics and control from bully pulpits? Or are they the elder brother who finally said "Enough!" and broke free with their resentment still intact? Human hearts are too complex for any of us to judge. Far better if we examine where our churches have departed from the freedom and open door of the Father's house into controlling practices that generate resentment.

I have obviously questioned the advisability of Nietzsche's test as it stands. But I believe both Nietzsche and Weil made a strong case for the need to examine ourselves in these days of anemic faith among the Christian herd. Are we willing to hear Nietzsche's concerns, or shall we recoil in defensive-ness? To hear Nietzsche *at all* is to risk the crucible of examination. So, I commend Nietzsche to those who would grill their faith and their resentment to know themselves more deeply. But for a more prudent approach in con-*test*-ing faith, I believe we'll find Kierkegaard is the wiser and, in some ways, more reliable and brutal inquisitor.

16

THE GRAND PROVOCATEUR: SØREN KIERKEGAARD

> "People leave Christianity not because the church didn't teach about Jesus but because the church didn't live like Jesus."
> —Mason Mennenga[188]

Søren Kierkegaard (1813–55) was Denmark's greatest philosopher, and he is often regarded as the true father of Existentialism. His prolific works, written under many pseudonyms, include philosophy, theology, psychology, literature, and fiction. Among an array of genres, he employed hundreds of parables in his arsenal of deconstruction.

Kierkegaard was a master provocateur whose social and spiritual critiques of Danish society and European Christendom were every bit as scathing as Nietzsche's, but with the opposite agenda. He wielded the sharp edge of his literary scalpel (or sword) not to slay Christian faith but to purge and renew it—to make it authentic and relevant, a matter of individual faith and not just a club to join or herd to follow. His agenda was not to slay Christianity but to see it resurrected.

Volumes exist on Kierkegaard and his "good faith" Existentialism, and others have laid out his life and thought more thoroughly and beautifully than

I can.[189] For this chapter, after giving such a large stage to Nietzsche, I intend to focus on two major and related points of contact.

First, like Nietzsche, Søren Kierkegaard directed his disdain for mediocrity at the church of his day. The "herd" or "crowd" in his crosshairs was Christendom. Second, rather than testing one's faith by *setting it aside* (à la Nietzsche), Kierkegaard suggested that those who identify with Christianity ought to test their faith by actually *trying* it for once. Christians, he felt, should take the risk of making the authentic choice to *become* Christian. The correlations and contrasts between Nietzsche's deconstruction and Kierkegaard's deconstruction will become clear as we examine Kierkegaard's principal provocations, drawn from over two dozen of his books and articles. Gratefully, Charles Moore has collected selections from these sources in a must-read compendium, *Provocations*,[190] by my friends at Plough Publishing.

THE NEED FOR GOD

Kierkegaard's first principle is a mirror opposite of Nietzsche's view of faith. While Nietzsche regarded the need for God as a life-negating, soul-sucking weakness that bound Christians to spiritual slavery and generated *ressentiment*, Kierkegaard was convinced that our need for God was nothing to be ashamed of. In fact, he insisted that "*to need God is* nothing to be ashamed of but is *perfection itself.*"[191] Whereas Nietzsche holds Christians in contempt for their pathetic need of God, Kierkegaard can think of nothing sadder than the one who lives out their days without ever discovering their need.

For Kierkegaard, the most vibrant faith is measured by a decisive commitment to *absolute dependence.*[192] He holds the curious faith of pew-sitters as suspect. Only in the decisive act of stepping out (as Abraham did), in complete dependence on God is our faith truly tested. To have perfect faith is to live in such a way that *we need God.*

But God's invitation extends beyond the heroes of the faith we read about in Hebrews 11. Christ sees all those whose need derives from affliction. To those in need, he issues the invitation, "Come to me, all you who are weary and burdened" (Matthew 11:28 NIV). In Kierkegaard's poetic words,

> This invitation stands at the crossroad, where temporal and earthly suffering has planted its cross, and there it beckons, "Come here, all you poor and miserable, you who must slave in poverty to eke out an

existence with nothing more than a toilsome future. Come here, all you despised and discarded ones, whose existence no one cares about, not even as much as for a domestic animal, that has more value! All you sick, lame, deaf, blind, crippled, insane come here!" The invitation blasts away all distinctions in order to gather everybody together.[193]

This passage dovetails with the drunken speech of Marmeladov in Dostoevsky's *Crime and Punishment*, when he sees his own wretchedness and how it drove his daughter to sell herself to feed her starving siblings. In an epiphany of grace, he projects these beautiful words into the mouth of Christ at the final judgment:

> He will judge and will forgive all, the good and the evil, the wise and the meek.... And when He has done with all of them, then He will summon us. "You too come forth," He will say, "Come forth ye drunkards, come forth, ye weak ones, come forth, ye children of shame!" And we shall all come forth, without shame, and shall stand before him. And He will say unto us, "Ye are swine, made in the Image of the Beast and with his mark; but come ye also!" And the wise ones and those of understanding will say, "Oh Lord, why dost Thou receive these men?" And He will say, "This is why I receive them, oh ye wise, this is why I receive them, oh ye of understanding, that *not one of them believed himself to be worthy* of this." And He will hold out His hands to us and we shall fall down before him...and we shall weep...and we shall understand all things! Then we shall understand all!...and all will understand.... Lord, Thy kingdom come![194]

For Dostoevsky, as for Kierkegaard, knowing our desperate need for mercy qualifies us for grace and defines perfect faith. The tax collector in Christ's parable cries out, "God, be merciful to me, sinner that I am" (Luke 18:13). In Jesus's judgment, "He was the one who went back to his house vindicated by God" (v. 14).

By contrast, how hard it will be for mediocre mainstream church members—what Kierkegaard calls "the crowd."

THE CROWD VERSUS THE INDIVIDUAL

For Kierkegaard, nothing is as dangerous as following *the crowd* and believing that you're following Jesus. He sees the crowd as a place where we hide, where we conceal how empty our existence is—a spiritual tranquilizer where we divert faith in God to the trustworthiness of the masses.[195] Kierkegaard can think of nothing so loathsome to God as running with the herd.[196]

The *individual*, on the other hand—the *single and solidarity individual*—stands before God. The individual cannot hide in the herd or resort to "But my pastor told me," "I was just following orders," or "Hey, everyone was doing it." Kierkegaard claims:

> Every call from God is always addressed to one person, the single individual. Precisely in this lies the difficulty and the examination, that the one who is called must stand alone, walk alone, alone with God.... "The single individual"—with this category the cause of Christ stands or falls.[197]

It's easy enough to indict Kierkegaard as the father of radical individualism and accuse him of a lone-ranger mentality—he is the archetypal "island" of Paul Simon's song "I Am a Rock." But Stephen Backhouse notes that Kierkegaard hated herds so much precisely because he recognized them as a malignant or false form of sociality. The mob is impersonal and inhuman. Real social relations can only happen between real people. His focus on becoming an *individual* is not because he is antisocial but, in fact, the opposite.[198] So, let's do our best to hear his heart.

The *individual* is the locus of faith that is:

+ *Responsible*: Kierkegaard makes eye contact with us, pulls us from the crowd, and says, "Each of us must answer to God for ourselves—for how we live our lives."

+ *Relational*: He invites the individual beyond ritual acts, religious meetings, and doctrinal confessions into a personal relationship with the living God.

+ *Subjective*: He establishes this relationship as an inward experience—existential communion with God in the heart or innermost being of every individual. Christ *in* you *is* the hope of glory,[199] not your church membership or Christian culture!

CHRISTENDOM: A "DEADLY COUNTERFEIT"

Kierkegaard believed nothing is as dangerous to authentic faith than what he called "the established church" or "Christendom"—to him, it was a deadly counterfeit. He condemned his Danish brethren for "playing at Christianity" within the systems of cultural Christendom, a game far more treacherous than any historic heresy or schism.[200] Heresy, heterodoxy, atheism, secularism—these have never crushed, and will never crush, Christian faith. Rather, the more deadly poison is a saccharine cultural substitute for authentic faith—"cordial drivel, mediocrity served up sweet."[201] Kierkegaard wrote, "The apostasy from Christianity will not come about by everybody openly renouncing Christianity; no, but slyly, cunningly, by everybody assuming the name of being Christian."[202]

The enemies of Christ will never "martyr away" true Christian faith. We need never worry about that. But in an anemic and hypocritical church— there our faith dwindles and drains away, whether from the *be-leavers* who feel the aching spiritual vacuum or from those who are oblivious to it and just numb out.

The problem is compounded when the church doesn't *look* or *sound weak*! Kierkegaard worried about "the church triumphant"[203] that fills large halls, proclaims the victory of the kingdom of God, and postures as the army of God that has arrived and overcome. He didn't know the half of it—perhaps we do. "The church triumphant," he sneers, "is a sham" that has "taken the church of Christ in vain."[204] He sees the true church (he calls it "the church militant") as *not* having arrived—it is forever *becoming*, forever *changing*, continually "drawn to Christ in humble obedience" in anticipation of the coming kingdom. "As soon as Christ's Church makes a deal with this world, Christianity is abolished."[205]

Yet, for Kierkegaard, the deeper issue is not so much that the church presents as victorious but that its pastors are afraid of making plain the requirements of Christian discipleship. They are falsifying the gospel to pacify the people with a status quo-religious performance. Why are the leaders so afraid to tell the truth? He thinks it's because people would "shudder to see at what distance from it we are living."[206] And if they did? What's the worry? That they will exit the church? Or demand that it change? You can see how poignant and prophetic Kierkegaard is to this hour. And how provocative he intends to be:

> Strictly speaking, it is not I who am ringing the alarm bell; I am starting the fire in order to smoke out illusions and knavish tricks; it is a police raid, and a Christian police raid, for, according to the New Testament, Christianity is incendiarism.[207]

I sometimes worry that deconstruction becomes a euphemism for spiritual arson. So did Dostoevsky, as we'll see in the chapter to follow. But Kierkegaard isn't worried. He owns it. And he sees his work as contiguous with the incendiary witness of Christ, the apostles, and the nature of New Testament Christianity. No doubt, he would identify and smoke out many of our "knavish tricks" that pass for Christianity today. I imagine he'd target our spiritual addiction to the entertainment industry, consumerism, civil religion, politicization, and spectrum ideology.[208]

BECOMING CHRISTIAN

Contra both Nietzsche and Christendom, Søren Kierkegaard proposes that we test our faith by actually *trying it*—we must *become* Christians. A simple test of the church crowd's character suggested to him that the crowd was an impediment to *becoming* Christian. Why? Because, he said, only the individual can become a Christian.[209] You can't be "born Christian" by inclusion through birth into a Christian family or baptism into the/a Christian church. What then is a "Christian"?

A Christian is a follower, not a fan: Christ was looking for *disciples*—not "adherents" to Jesus's teaching, "admirers" of his celebrity, or even "worshippers" of his deity. His call was to followers of a *life!* Jesus came to *save* the world, not *instruct* it. And that salvation includes following the pattern of his footprints—joining Christ on the Jesus Way.[210] "Take up your cross and follow me" is not a dogmatic belief system. It's the application of Jesus's whole life to the life of the whole church—simply put, it is to be like Christ, from his baptism to his resurrection.[211]

Kierkegaard was huge on *"the imitation of Christ,"* which, for him, meant "following the example, being willing to witness for the truth and against untruth, and to do so without seeking any support whatsoever from any external power, neither attaching oneself to any power nor forming a party."[212] I suspect old Søren would not be so pleased with our current partisan/denominational power factions, which have multiplied exponentially since his time. Nevertheless, he prays for us still, "You yourself were the way and the life—and you require only followers. If we have dozed off into this infatuation, wake us up, rescue us from this error of wanting to adoringly admire you instead of wanting to follow you and be like you."[213]

Christian faith is a decisive act, not a belief system: Kierkegaard argues that the one and only proof of faith that Christ validated was obedience to

Christ:[214] "Anyone who *chooses to do the will* of God will find out whether my teaching comes from God or whether I speak on my own" (John 7:17 NIV).[215]

For Kierkegaard, the order of operations is critical: first the action-situation, then the decision of faith. First the venture, then the proof.[216] Good intentions and resolutions are useless fictions. What matters is the choice—and not just any choice:

> Christ must be the way, the truth, and the life for you, only then does he become everything to you. Christ must be all or nothing for you. But only when his mighty voice speaks to you and says, "I will be everything to you," will he be everything for you.... Nothing, neither the most trifling nor the most important thing, must stand between you and Christ. No, the commitment must be unconditional. So must it be, but at the same time remember that Christ is grace, that it is to grace that you can so commit yourself.[217]

Note the important caveat at the end of this statement. Kierkegaard remembers Luther's *grace alone* motto—that we're not saved by our decisive action but by the grace of Jesus Christ. But, he says, it is grace that calls us and empowers us to follow. His point is that the object of faith is a Person, not a doctrine: God incarnate in this particular human, the Rabbi from Nazareth.[218] And faith itself is the life of one who has heard and acted on the Rabbi's call to follow—not as one has decided but *in the way* that Jesus himself modeled and taught in, for example, his Sermon on the Mount.[219]

AUTHENTIC CHRISTIANITY

Like all the Existentialists, but second to none of them, Kierkegaard demands authenticity marked by discipleship rather than fandom. What are the major identifiers of such a life? They don't sound all that foreign or provocative: *love, freedom,* and *grace*. Don't we all preach that? I hope so. But Kierkegaard wants us to mean it. Mean what? Let's see…

LOVE

First, Kierkegaard wrote that God's love is like a deep spring, hidden and mysterious—still waters that murmur and ripple, waiting to be discovered. God's love is like a gentle stream, secretly flowing and beckoning us to love in the way God loves. Our God-relationship forms and shapes our love—constitutes what love is—and always leads us to God. Any diversion from our love for God is an illusion or self-deception.[220]

Listen, he's not speaking as a pastor who's putting the brakes on deconstruction to keep you coming to his church. Kierkegaard is practicing focused deconstruction on false loves and obstacles to an existential knowledge of God—hindrances he had identified *in* the church.

Next, he identifies Christian faith with the command *"You shall love your neighbor as yourself"* (Mark 12:31), which he defines as *unconditional love for all people*.[221] "Unconditional love" has become a cliché these days, but Kierkegaard's account echoes these words of Christ:

> [12] "When you give a lunch or a supper," he said, "don't invite your friends or your family or relatives, or your rich neighbours. They might ask you back again, and you'd be repaid. [13] When you give a feast, invite the poor, the crippled, the lame and the blind. [14] God will bless you, because they have no way to repay you! You will be repaid at the resurrection of the righteous."   (Luke 14:12–14)

Kierkegaard understands this to mean that for *neighbor love* to be unconditional, it cannot be preferential, as are romantic love or friendship. Such love must be self-renouncing and directed without favoritism to one's neighbor as an equal, as an act of obedience to Christ's *"you shall."* Trust in the *"you shall,"* he says.[222] He pushes this equality of neighbor love even to one's enemy, without exception.[223] And not *despite* their imperfections with a mind to their potential—no, we love them as they are now, today, right in front of us.[224]

FREEDOM

You'll remember that Existentialism is obsessed with absolute freedom—whether *in* Christ or *from* Christ. Here we find Kierkegaard both in sync with and at loggerheads with Nietzsche once again. They agree that Christian moralism and the institutional church are opponents of life-affirming freedom.[225] They also agree that our ethics must transcend moral absolutes and binary laws (metaphorically, the Tree of Knowledge of Good and Evil), and instead be guided by dynamic, life-affirming impulses. But what are these impulses? This is where the two men fundamentally disagree.

Having concluded that Christianity is life-denying, Nietzsche personifies creative, willful, life-affirming freedom with the Greek god of wine and music, Dionysus. In his book *The Birth of Tragedy Out of the Spirit of Music* (1872),[226] he represents the Dionysian spirit with a kind of frenzied self-forgetting that transcends rationality. He calls us to give free rein to the impulses of our deeper passions, to lose ourselves in ecstatic frenzy. We will discover the meaning of our existence there—not in religious restraint or scientific facts but in the experience of life as art.

Kierkegaard's freedom is of another order altogether. While he agrees that the Christian religion and Enlightenment rationalism cannot deliver the goods of existential meaning, human flourishing, or true freedom, he believes that obedience to the impulses of our passions is *not* freedom—it is the worst form of slavery. Any addict in recovery can confirm this reality from painful experience. Kierkegaard says, "Unconditional freedom, freedom which equally well chooses the good or the evil, is nothing but an abrogation of freedom…. and emphasizing freedom of choice as such means the sure loss of freedom."[227]

Kierkegaard did not believe that the freedom we seek is found by forever keeping our choices open. That's not freedom—that's imprisonment in vacillation. True freedom is the fruit of freely and decisively choosing "the one thing needful,"[228] which he identifies with binding ourselves to the one Source of true freedom, Jesus Christ. "Freedom is the choice whose truth is that there can be no question of any choice."[229] Here, Kierkegaard is firmly in the tradition of Paul: "It is for freedom that Christ has set us free. Stand firm, then, and do not let yourselves be burdened again by a yoke of slavery" (Galatians 5:1 NIV).

Kierkegaard's "freedom" includes the important adjective *voluntary*. Our faith, our obedience, our love, and even our suffering or persecution must be voluntary if we would regard them as Christlike—a sacrificial offering is always voluntary. Yes, we may lose everything through misfortune or calamity…

> But if I voluntarily give up everything, choose danger and difficulties, this is something entirely different. When this happens, it is impossible to avoid the trial that comes with carrying Jesus' cross. This is what Christian suffering means, and it is a whole scale deeper than ordinary human adversity.[230]

Thus, counterintuitively, binding ourselves to Christ, we find freedom, so that even the apostles' chains and the martyrs' pyre become signs of a deeper freedom than Nietzsche's wildest ecstasy.

GRACE

Here is a common scenario: after a lifetime of oppressive religion, an individual breaks free from the herd. Christ liberates them from bondage to the legalistic demands of their controlling churches. They learn that we live under the great expanse of grace, not the constrictions of the law. The enormous yoke of striving is lifted from their shoulders, and, for the first time, they feel they can breathe again. Big sigh!

But then they read Kierkegaard—they feel his intensity, they hear his demands, they cringe at his cross. All filtered through the not-yet-healed wounds of their religious PTSD. It sounds like he's setting us up for another round of religious striving. He understands this and responds.

First, he clarifies: *striving can never earn our salvation*. He makes this point as strongly as any of the "grace teachers" do today:

> The mystery of grace consists in the fact that the most strenuous human effort is still fool's play, a wasted inconvenience, a ridiculous gesture, if it should be an attempt to earn salvation—and still to push on just like one who soberly and seriously believes that by his efforts he could earn salvation.[231]

Second, he motivates: *grace is empowering*. The grace of the Holy Spirit fills us to achieve what the law never could. Grace transforms us from the inside out. God's "thou shall/shall not" commands are not like the legalistic demands of the Pharisee party, where I try to lift my head with my eyebrows. No! They are extensions of God's commands in Genesis 1–2 ("'Let there be light!' And there was light!") as God continues his work of creation in each individual ("'Let there be love!' And there is love!"). Grace continues to generate or give birth to cruciform love that far exceeds the righteousness of the Pharisees.[232] It's not just a cosmetic change of behavior. It's the inner transformation of a human heart that mobilizes courage and frees us to follow.

Third, he rebukes: *the grace that exempts action (faith) is a farce*. Kierkegaard observes, anticipates, and condemns any grace teaching that says, "Since we are all saved by grace anyway, why should I exert myself? Let's keep clear of any kind of effort because it's all grace anyway."[233] He regards such grace as stupefying inaction, a paralyzing mockery. A grace that says, "No, you don't need to take up your cross and follow" is meaningless and unchristian. It's also a repudiation of Jesus's own words in the following verses and other passages:

[17] Don't suppose that I came to destroy the law or the prophets. I didn't come to destroy them; I came to fulfil them! [18] I'm telling you the truth: until heaven and earth disappear, not one stroke, not one dot, is going to disappear from the law, until it's all come true. [19] So anyone who relaxes a single one of these commandments, even the little ones, and teaches that to people, will be called least in the kingdom of heaven. But anyone who does them and teaches them will be called great in the kingdom of heaven.   (Matthew 5:17–19)

Kierkegaard would simply have no time for the theological gymnastics that relegate Jesus's central message to the old covenant, as some people insist because, they say, Jesus spoke it *before* the cross (just *no!*). When those who identify as "grace people" consider Jesus's own words to be too "religious," then they have misunderstood the indivisible union of empowering grace and the command, "Take up your cross and follow me." Kierkegaard integrates these words of Christ with grace, like so:

God's requirement is and remains the same, and altered, perhaps even sharpened under grace. The difference is this: under the law my salvation is linked to the condition of filling its requirement. Under grace I am freed from this concern—but God's requirement remains.[234]

Provocative? Yes. Even maddening. If not, we've not really heard him—or Jesus either.

PROVOCATIONS

Having read the collection of Kierkegaard's writings in *Provocations*, I can see the genius of the title of that book. Kierkegaard provokes *everyone*. He ruthlessly deconstructs a whole era (modernity), an entire society (Western civilization), and an entire religion (Christendom as he knew it).

He gets the deconstructionists nodding—then turns his gaze on them. He provokes deconstruction itself and assails the fashionable doubt of skeptics, triggering their fragility and defensiveness. Brian Zahnd reminds me of him—the moment he became a darling of the progressives, Zahnd started poking. He noted the irony of progressives who manifest their own brand of fundamentalism. The backlash came fast and furious (literally)—poignant proof confirming Zahnd's point to a T.

What makes Kierkegaard a giant of deconstruction is the impartiality of his provocations alongside his unadulterated (by Christianity) faith in Christ. Christians who are interested in deconstruction will find that Kierkegaard's crucible spares no one and nothing. He'll even submit your construct of Jesus *and* your doubts about him to the flames. What remains thereafter? For him, three points should suffice.

1. CHRIST IS THE PARADOXICAL, SCANDALOUS GOD-MAN

For Kierkegaard, the hypostatic union of God and humanity in the incarnation of Jesus Christ is *anything but* a doctrinal platitude of the institutional church. The notion of the God-man is *not* a relic of Constantinian Christianity that dissolves in deconstruction. Rather, no greater paradox exists and no scandal is more inconceivable than the "compounding of God and a socially insignificant man."[235]

Kierkegaard's complaint is that the church has domesticated the scandal out of the gospel by retroactively reducing Jesus's humanity to worldly greatness or expunging his life of anything that made it a true stumbling block.

> Aha! This is why today's Christianity is nonsense. All the danger is taken away. No, Jesus Christ is the sign of offense and the object of faith. Only in eternity is he in his glory. Here on earth, he must never be presented in any other way than in his social insignificance—so that everyone can be offended or believe.[236]

I can measure the degree to which my Christianity has diluted the gospel by how these words of Jesus are either incomprehensible to me or offensive: *"Anyone who falls on this stone will be smashed to pieces, and anyone it falls on will be crushed"* (Matthew 21:44). This type of language should be thrilling to every serious deconstructionist. Yet it's just there that so many shrink away.

2. RELATIONSHIP IS DECISIVE

Kierkegaard surely mourns, "How long?" with the martyrs under the altar[237] when he hears "personal relationship"—a phrase I suspect he coined—diminished to a twentieth-century evangelical banality. God's language of "covenant" puts it even more strongly: relationship with Christ is a marriage to a living Person. Here we see Kierkegaard's deconstruction in sharp contrast to Nietzsche's. Nietzsche urged Christians to divorce themselves from every social network or belief system wearing the Jesus label—and from Christ himself. But Kierkegaard saw deconstruction as a blazing fire that consumes everything within our lives (and *within* our religious systems) opposed to that divine marriage. The distinction is entirely relational. Nietzsche's Jesus is a bad idea. Kierkegaard's Jesus is a divine husband. If you managed decades of churchgoing but never got to Kierkegaard's Jesus—*ouch!*—then I hope Nietzsche's deconstruction is a necessary step back that creates the possibility for the next step forward.

Kierkegaard's "personal relationship" or Christ's "new marriage" begins with a serious realization of our need for the *person*—not the idea, not the doctrine—of Christ. To experience the relationship is to undergo transformation (radical reconstruction), which might be the real reason we recoil:

> Christianity is not so much related to transforming the intellect— but to transforming the world. But this transformation is the most painful of all operations, comparable to a vivisection. And because it is so appalling, to become a Christian was changed long ago. Now it is only a matter of remodeling the intellect.[238]

Kierkegaard doesn't sound like he leaves much room for those struggling with genuine doubt. No, he doesn't. Indeed, he provokes even the doubter.

3. DOUBT IS REBELLION!

I know: not *all* doubt is rebellion. Don't worry, I'll offer a rejoinder to Kierkegaard's assertion. But first we have to hear him. We're not here to recruit Kierkegaard as an ally. We're visiting his parlor for a deconstruction. Here's the claim:

> ...arguments against Christianity arise from doubt. This is a complete misunderstanding. The arguments against Christianity arise out of rebellion, out of a reluctance to obey. The battle against objections is but shadowboxing, because it is intellectual combat with doubt instead of ethical combat against mutiny.[239]

Love him or hate him, Kierkegaard is an engaging wordsmith—*by design*. He keeps us interested enough to demand of him, "How can you say that?" and then he tells us. First, he returns to his definition of faith as an act of trust that precedes knowing. The leap of faith first, then the ground under your feet (think *Indiana Jones and the Last Crusade*). If faith is decisive action, what is doubt? Do you see what he's doing?

By *acting*, your life will come into collision with *existence*, and [only] then you will know the reality of grace. Nowadays, we have turned the whole thing around. Christianity has become a worldview. Thus, before I get involved, I must first justify it. Good night to Christianity! Now doubt has surely conquered.[240]

I can think of other shades and sources of doubt, but the doubt Kierkegaard describes is a continuation of his deconstruction of modern Christian rationalism, of "worldview Christianity" that is inactive (i.e., faithless). And faithless Christianity generates doubts. Reasons never resolve the doubt; they only feed it. The only solution is the radical faith of active discipleship—the imitation of Jesus.

I mentioned other sources of doubt. For me, these include traumatic experiences, human suffering, parental worries, and endless distractions in an overwhelming world. But if I'm honest....

I remember one of those occasions when I was feeling super-stuck and unable to hear God's voice. One of my mentors' sons invited me to his home, where he and his wife prayed for me. After a time of listening, two messages emerged, both reflective of Kierkegaard. The sense I had was that crucifixion involves nails in both hands. I could see myself on a cross, one hand nailed down, representing my sin—confessed and forgiven. But the other hand flailed, representing "self" (as in self-will). Surrendering our lives to Christ involves forgiveness, for sure, but it also involves heeding his call to follow, to faith in action.

What this kindly couple heard from God in prayer was a simple question: "What is the last thing that Jesus asked you to do that you haven't yet done—or aren't willing to do?" I quickly saw that I was stuck because I wouldn't move. My faith was stalled because I had stopped following. Kierkegaard is less diplomatic:

The objections to Christianity may be dismissed with one single comment: do these objections come from someone who has carried out the commands of Christ? If not, all his objections are nonsense. Christ continually declares that we must do what he says—and then we will know that it is truth.[241]

Let me rush to say that this is not *all* that Kierkegaard says about doubt, nor does he say it to everyone. This sort of rhetoric is for the religious slacker whose doubts grow in the infertile soil of apathetic cultural Christendom. He's trying to jar sleepers awake—similar to the jolting messages of Jesus to the seven churches in Revelation 2–3.

But he also has a heart for the weary ones, the poor in spirit who see their need and who pray for mercy. Jesus never rebukes them. To the humble, says Kierkegaard, Christ is pure compassion.

I said I would offer a rejoinder: *not all doubt is rebellion*. In fact, I see a healthy and necessary doubt at work in the deconstruction Kierkegaard initiated. In my case, my doubts about divine retribution and eternal conscious torment *drew me* to Christ rather than away from him. Doubts can be bulldozers rather than boulders, the *via negativa* that removes obstacles to lead us home.

So, while Kierkegaard rightly sees rebellion as a common root of doubt, his grand deconstruction of modernist Christendom likewise provokes doubt. Not in God, and not as a counter to faith, but to expose all that has made Christianity mediocre. Kierkegaard is provoking authenticity, not apostasy. Brian McLaren's word—*perplexity*—captures the best of this idea. It's about honesty, curiosity, and critical (but not rationalist) thinking.

For McLaren, doubt, in this sense, isn't an enemy of faith (for those of "good faith"). Rather than being a negative experience or something sinful, perplexity becomes a vehicle that carries us into the next season:

> Doubt need not be the death of faith. It can be, instead, the birth of
> a new kind of faith, a faith beyond beliefs, a faith that expresses itself
> in love, a deepening and expanding faith that can save your life and
> save the world.[242]

In just two sentences, McLaren's explanation is as good a summary of Kierkegaard's gospel as I have seen. But Kierkegaard would never have allowed me to tie off his lifework so prettily. He was a profound struggler. He was compelling and sad, as brokenhearted as Nietzsche was. Both men were prodigal sons of privileged pietism. Both failed to distinguish the enormous difference between the *solitary individual* and *personhood grown in communion*.[243] Kierkegaard is irritated, like so many prophets who know the cost of discipleship. And he's likewise a faithful deconstructionist, sickened by mediocrity.

I think he wants a final word. It comes in the form of two questions to those who, in deconstruction, resort to dispensing with faith in Jesus: "Do you want to leave too?"[244] and "Where are you going?"

Not merely in the realm of commerce but in the world of ideas as well our age is organizing a regular clearance sale. Everything is to be had at such a bargain that it is questionable whether in the end there is anybody who will want to bid. Every speculative price-fixer,... every Privatdocent, tutor, and student, every crofter and cottar in philosophy, is not content with doubting everything but goes further. Perhaps it would be untimely and ill-timed to ask them where they are going, but surely it is courteous and unobtrusive to regard it as certain that they have doubted everything, since otherwise it would be a queer thing for them to be going further....

In our time, nobody is content to stop with faith but wants to go further. It would perhaps be rash to ask where these people are going, but.... In those old days it was different, then faith was a task for a whole lifetime, because it was assumed that dexterity in faith is not acquired in a few days or weeks.[245]

17

POSSESSED:
FYODOR DOSTOEVSKY, PART 1

I believe Russian author Fyodor Dostoevsky (1821–81) is the greatest novelist in history. His towering works include *Crime and Punishment* (1866), *The Idiot* (1869), *The Possessed* (1872), and *The Brothers Karamazov* (1880). Dostoevsky's psychological profiles and cultural critiques reveal a penetrating, prophetic heart, forged in his own existential crises. As with our other sleeping prophets, I cannot do his lifework justice, but I can draw your attention to a few major themes relevant to deconstruction. They include the following:

+ **Possession:** Dostoevsky uses the Gospel story of the Gadarene demoniac to parse the social upheaval and ideological possession that his Russia was experiencing (*and that we are experiencing in our world today*). Here, his insights eclipse Nietzsche's prophecy at its best.

+ **Affliction:** With brutal honesty, Dostoevsky wades into the greatest challenge to authentic faith: the problem of suffering and evil, especially the suffering of innocents. He treads where angels and even Voltaire and Nietzsche dared not go.

+ **Transformation:** Dostoevsky shows how the fever of the conscience-as-judge and the power of co-suffering love conspire to awaken transformation in a human soul. He anticipates Freud's work in psychoanalysis and arguably proves to be the wiser of the two.

In the course of the next several chapters, we will explore each of these themes and how they deepen our understanding of the depths of deconstruction and the hope of reconstruction.

IDEOLOGICAL POSSESSION

]There exists no greater or more painful anxiety for a man who has
freed himself from all religious bias, than how he shall soonest find a
new object or idea to worship.

—Fyodor Dostoevsky, *The Brothers Karamazov*[246]

Although I had long been familiar with the biblical account of the
Gadarene demoniac that Dostoevsky uses as an illustration of ideological possession, my understanding of this story has broadened since my introduction
to Eastern Orthodoxy. One adjustment I've had to make on my journey into
liturgical contexts is the preaching schedule. My Baptist roots did not follow
a set pattern of Scripture readings, and in my ten years with the Mennonites,
the lectionary rolled through a four-year cycle. But for our Orthodox siblings,
the norm is for Gospel readings to repeat themselves annually. So, our Sunday
homily revisits the same text on the same calendar week every year.

The upside of this practice is that it follows a deliberate rhythm rather
than the whims and hobbyhorses of independent preachers. Texts are selected
to compose a yearlong drama of redemption—a protracted Passion play of
sorts. The downside is that, with only fifty-two weeks in a year, many beautiful Gospel passages are never preached during a Sunday service. The even
bigger downside—a downright annoyance for those who've been preaching
for, say, three or four *decades*—is that, somehow, the story of the Gadarene
demoniac(s)[247] edges its way in *twice* every year (and a third time for special
occasions). You can understand why, having preached that text over eighty
times (!), Vladika Lazar is happy to defer it to me when possible. The conversation goes this way:

"Irénée [my Eastern Orthodox name], would you give the sermon next
Sunday?"

"Gadarene demoniac?" I ask, cringing.

"Yes," he blushes—the only time I see Vladika looking sheepish.

How did that recurrence happen? We don't seem to know. Why did it
happen? Perhaps because we *need* to hear the story—and to hear it *often*. And
instead of brooding over Christ's alleged SPCA violation with the herd of hogs,
we might better give heed to how the story speaks to our herd instincts (à la
Kierkegaard). This stark warning against ideological possession became crystal
clear to me when I read Dostoevsky's novel *The Possessed* (also titled *Demons* or

The Devils). This literary classic, set in nineteenth-century Russia, opens with a poem by Aleksandr Pushkin and Luke's account of the demoniac story:

> Strike me dead, the track has vanished,
> Well, what now? We've lost the way,
> Demons have bewitched our horses,
> Led us in the wilds astray.
>
> What a number! Whither drift they?
> What's the mournful dirge they sing?
> Do they hail a witch's marriage
> Or a goblin's burying?
>
> A. Pushkin[248]

> And there was one herd of many swine feeding on this mountain; and they besought him that he would suffer them to enter into them. And he suffered them.
>
> Then went the devils out of the man and entered into the swine; and the herd ran violently down a steep place into the lake and were choked.
>
> When they that fed them saw what was done, they fled, and went and told it in the city and in the country.
>
> Then they went out to see what was done; and came to Jesus and found the man, out of whom the devils were departed, sitting at the feet of Jesus, clothed and in his right mind; and they were afraid.
>
> —Luke, ch. viii. 32-37[249]

FOUR DYNAMIC ACTS

Fyodor Dostoevsky's archetypal reading of this story is so poignant—so ingenious—I daresay I may feel *compelled* to preach it every six months until my departure from this world. How does Dostoevsky employ the gospel narrative as a revelation for his times?

First, he sees the story in four dynamic acts:

1. **The Gadarene man**, demonized and dehumanized.

2. **The demonic presence**, leaving the Gadarene man and entering the herd.

3. **The herd of pigs**, possessed and violently rushing to their self-destruction.

4. **The former demoniac**, healed and restored to his right mind, ready to follow Christ.

CAST OF CHARACTERS

Next, Dostoevsky assigns characters to each of these four stages of the parable. Each character represents an era or ideology in his historical context.

Stepan Verkhovensky—the groundless Idealist: A wonderfully comical character, this melodramatic Romantic is a pseudo-intellectual who can dream of universal happiness while losing one of his serfs in a champagne-impaired card game. Stepan represents the waning liberalism of the 1840s. In the story, he is dependent on the patronage of a widow landowner, **Varvara Petrovna**, a generous if unforgiving noblewoman who represents the compromised religion of classist Russia in its precarious twilight years.

I see in these two characters and their odd relationship the Gadarene demoniac: precious in himself but also the "house" where the demons are birthed.

Nikolai Stavrogin—the insidious nihilist: Stavrogin is the son of Varvara, and, as a child, he was a student of Stepan. *The Possessed* pictures his nihilism as an expression of the "legion of demons" exorcised from the demoniac. His very existence derives from his violent reaction to shallow liberal idealism and culturally compromised imperial religion. The result is a cocky, creepy man who sees himself *beyond good and evil*, as revealed in a disturbing confession in a chapter censored from the published book.

Pyotr Verkhovensky—the revolutionary: Pyotr is the estranged son of Stepan and had only met him a few times. He is enamored with Stavrogin's nihilist ideas and wants to press them into action through murder and unhinged revolution. Metaphorically, as an enthusiast who can stir his group into a frenzy, he represents the herd of swine that, once demonized, rush violently into the sea. **Alexei Kirollov** is likewise possessed by Stavrogin's nihilism but, in his case, plans to offer himself as a sacrifice to the cause through suicide, somehow seeing his death as the death of God and the deification of human self-will. He will be the *man-God* (antithetical to Christ the *God-man*) in his own eyes. Dostoevsky's dire prophecies, embodied in these characters, were fulfilled as the nihilism of the 1860s inevitably led to the Bolshevik Revolution of 1917 and three bloody decades of the Siberian gulags.

Ivan Shatov—the Restored: Ivan, the son of Vavara's deceased valet, had also been a student of Stepan. Like Pyotr, he at first becomes an acolyte of the nihilist Stavrogin. But, as life unfolds, he denounces Stavrogin, renounces his amoral ideology, and becomes a deeply convinced Christ-follower. It is said that his speeches echo Dostoevsky's own convictions. In this sense, he is like the Gadarene man after his deliverance and, Dostoevsky hopes (in vain), the future of Russia after the demonized herd has come to its end.

The great journalist and satirist Malcolm Muggeridge says of *The Possessed*:

> Dostoevsky's theme is that the subversive ideas of the age were entering into people's minds, as the devils were entering into the Gadarene swine, which similarly destroyed them.
>
> What Dostoevsky understood with such wonderful clarity is that the romantic notions of old Verkhovensky are the inevitable prelude to the devilish ones of his son Pyotr and that both derive from the man who might be regarded as the patron saint of [Geneva], Jean-Jacques Rousseau, who insisted that men can only be free when they do what they like. And that doing what they like is conducive to their individual, collective happiness, peace, and security. Exactly the opposite, Dostoevsky says, is the case. When men are dominated by their own desires, they fall into the most terrible of all servitudes. Young Verkhovensky [Pyotr] is simply old Verkhovensky [Stepan] writ large. The old one is serious and foolish; the young one is frivolous and merciless. And after them both comes inexorably the Gadarene rush over the cliff.[250]

Muggeridge isn't merely inferring these ideas from between the lines. Dostoevsky articulates them in a dialogue between old Stepan and Sofya (whose name means "wisdom") Matveyevna, a kindly itinerant Gospel salesperson. Stepan, having seen the fruitlessness of his life, is awakening to the truth even as he drifts in and out of a fevered delirium.

> "Now read me another passage…. About the pigs," [Stepan] said suddenly.
>
> "What?" asked Sofya Matveyevna, very much alarmed.

"About the pigs...that's there too...*ces cochons* [these pigs].[251] I remember the devils entered into swine and they all were drowned. You must read me that; I'll tell you why afterwards. I want to remember it word for word. I want it word for word."[252]

After Sofya reads Stepan the passage, Stepan gives us Dostoevsky's punch line (spoiler alert):

"My friend," said Stepan Trofimovitch in great excitement, "...that wonderful and...extraordinary passage has been a stumbling-block to me all my life...so much so that I remembered those verses from childhood. Now an idea has occurred to me; [a comparison]. A great number of ideas keep coming into my mind now. You see, that's exactly like our Russia, those devils that come out of the sick man and enter into the swine. They are all the sores, all the foul contagions, all the impurities, all the devils great and small that have multiplied in that great invalid, our beloved Russia, in the course of ages and ages. [Yes, this Russia that I always loved]. But a great idea and a great Will will encompass it from on high, as with that lunatic possessed of devils...and all those devils will come forth, all the impurity, all the rottenness that was putrefying on the surface...and they will beg of themselves to enter into swine; and indeed maybe they have entered into them already! They are we, we and those...and Petrusha and [the others with him]...and I perhaps at the head of them, and we shall cast ourselves down, possessed and raving, from the rocks into the sea, and we shall all be drowned—and a good thing too, for that is all we are fit for. But the sick man will be healed and "will sit at the feet of Jesus," and all will look upon him with astonishment.... My dear, [you will understand after], but now it excites me very much.... [You will understand after. We will understand together].[253]

I've composed the following table to summarize how Dostoevsky's *The Possessed* uses the gospel story as an archetype of which Russian history is just one example. What haunts me is how his visions are all the more transparent today.

Biblical Story	*The Possessed* Characters	History of Russia	Archetype
The Gadarene demoniac	Stepan Verkhovensky	Old Russia's religious classism and post-Christian liberalism	*Faith and Culture Debased* E.g., by the liberal ideal of "freedom" as *self-will*.
The demons	Nikolai Stavrogin	Nihilism	*Demonic Ideology* E.g., the idolatry of absolute deconstruction. Neo-nihilism.
The herd of swine	Pyotr Verkhovensky	Bolshevik Revolution, National Socialism	*Destructive Revolt* E.g., disillusionment with deconstruction lashes out in destructive extremist *isms* (from authoritarian right-wing nationalism to left-wing totalitarianism)
The healed man	Ivan Shatov	Dostoevsky's hope: faith transformed via co-suffering love.	*Recovered Faith* E.g., the minority report of the Jesus Way embodied, complete with the cross.

A CENTURY ON FIRE

Dostoevsky's contribution to our moment is that, like Nietzsche, he prophesies how treacherous the trajectory of cultural deconstruction would become in his time. The path he sees and foresees is necessary, inevitable, and terribly perilous. His analysis of cultural movements is more specific than Nietzsche's and ultimately expands to describe a domino effect, including:

1. compromised Christianity and bourgeois Enlightenment liberalism (together, the demoniac)

2. unsustainable nihilism (the demons)

3. utopian progressivism (the demons enter the herd)

4. incendiary revolution (the demonized herd charges)

5. totalitarian control (the herd drowns)

For Dostoevsky—and for us—the tragic fuse is sparked when liberal and progressive idealists become so disillusioned with their failed utopian hopes and so possessed by the smell of smoke and blood that destruction becomes an end in itself. Deconstruction devolves into cultural arson. When protests and pamphlets and lobbying fail to bring about the justice we demanded, someone lights a fire. So, while Kierkegaard writes that Christianity is incendiary, for Dostoevsky, the real arsonists are those progressives whose torches are ignited by disillusionment. Liberal utopian overreach is exposed as just another useless crusty wineskin. It's a very volatile moment when any social revolution realizes that its dreams are doomed but continues the revolution for its own sake. Dostoevsky describes that moment in *The Possessed*, beginning with a great section of the town being lit up by vandals:

> A great fire at night always has a thrilling and exhilarating effect. This is what explains the attraction of fireworks.... A real conflagration is a very different matter. Then the horror and a certain sense of personal danger, together with the exhilarating effect of a fire at night, produce on the spectator (though of course not in the householder whose goods are being burnt) *a certain concussion of the brain and, as it were, a challenge to those destructive instincts which, alas, lie hidden in every heart, even that of the mildest and most domestic little clerk.... This sinister sensation is almost always fascinating. "I really don't know whether one can look at a fire without a certain pleasure."* [254]

Dostoevsky then turns to the possessed souls who have set the fires, whose minds are aflame with demons for whom deconstruction is destruction.

> *"It's all incendiarism! It's nihilism! If anything is burning, it's nihilism!"* I heard [Governor Lembke] almost with horror; *and though there was nothing to be surprised at, yet actual madness, when one sees it, always gives one a shock....*
>
> *"...The fire is in the minds of men and not in the roofs of houses. Pull him down and give it up! Better give it up, much better! Let it put itself out. Aie, who is crying now? An old woman! It's an old woman shouting. Why have they forgotten the old woman?"* [255]

Dostoevsky's worries became a hellish reality in his lifetime and for the century that followed.[256] Indeed, the Pyotr character was inspired by a real-life radical revolutionary, Sergey Nechayev, who composed his *Revolutionary Catechism* in 1869. Here's a chilling sample of Nechayev's interpretation of progressive deconstruction (points 3–6 of "The Duties of the Revolutionary Toward Himself"):

> 3. The revolutionary…knows only one science: the science of destruction…. The object is perpetually the same: the surest and quickest way of destroying the whole filthy order.

> 4. The revolutionary…despises and hates the existing social morality in all its manifestations….

> 5. The revolutionary is a dedicated man, merciless toward the State and toward the educated classes; and he can expect no mercy from them. Between him and them there exists, declared or concealed, a relentless and irreconcilable war to the death….

> 6. Tyrannical toward himself, he must be tyrannical toward others. All the gentle and enervating sentiments of kinship, love, friendship, gratitude, and even honor, must be suppressed in him and give place to the cold and single-minded passion for revolution…. Night and day he must have but one thought, one aim—merciless destruction. Striving cold-bloodedly and indefatigably toward this end, he must be prepared to destroy himself and to destroy with his own hands everything that stands in the path of the revolution.[257]

DECONSTRUCTION OR IDEOLOGICAL INFECTION?

Sergey Nechayev was extreme. He was violent (a murderer) and incited violence. Is it fair to compare his manifesto with *deconstruction?* OR could we better identify his ideas as an ideological infection? It's one thing for a deluded Russian student to print off-the-latch pamphlets. But, despite Dostoevsky's watchtower warnings, that same caustic insanity became the central platform and practice of the Soviet Empire and its ruling demoniac, Joseph Stalin. The herd that drowned in that stampede numbered in the millions. Before the end of their reign of terror, they trampled to death a good many innocents (my Eden's Opa included) en route to their watery graves.

Luckily, nothing like that could happen in our liberal democracies, right? It's a good thing our history isn't sullied by violence, malice, and xenophobia, hmm? No disillusionment, rage, or vitriol in our herds, is there? At least our conservatives conserve peace and our progressives never turn to cruelty, right? When we say, "Burn it all down," we never mean it literally, do we? It's just a metaphor, after all. Thankfully, our news cycles don't feature tiki-torch marches, enraged militias building private arsenals, or political "prophets" murmuring about a second civil war.... It's not like anyone has stormed state or national capitol buildings and erected gallows, is it? We're just quietly, happily deconstructing, aren't we? /s (My daughter-in-law Colette taught me to add "/s" if my sarcasm is in doubt).

Deconstruction and peacemaking are hard to pair. But Dostoevsky wishes they weren't. He was *not* at all campaigning against deconstruction. But, unlike us, he discerned a distinction between deconstruction and ideological possession. His novels deconstructed toxic ideas and demonic means before they became actual genocide. He hoped and wrote and spoke for better ways forward, offering an exit ramp to the coming carnage.

At times, Dostoevsky's solution sounds *way* too nationalistic, an appeal for revival in the soul of his Russia—always an incredibly dangerous proposition. Today, nationalism fuels the violent cult of Putin and his possessed Orthodox sycophants. But, again, if we listen carefully, Dostoevsky hopes for better. In his 1880 speech celebrating the poet Aleksandr Pushkin, he proffers a counterintuitive nationalism that suggests every nation has unique redemptive gifts that, given freely, might unite the world. He argues that Russia's great gift to the world is the spirit of a selfless, universal brotherhood that he has seen in village serfs and monastery elders speckled across the land:

> To become a true Russian, to become fully Russian (and you should remember this), means only to become the brother of all men, to become, if you will, *a universal man*.... Our destiny is universality, won not by the sword, but by the strength of brotherhood and our fraternal aspiration to reunite mankind....
>
> ...At last it may be that Russia pronounces the final Word of the great general harmony, of the final brotherly communion of all nations in accordance with the law of the gospel of Christ!
>
> I know, I know too well, that my words may appear ecstatic, exaggerated and fantastic. Let them be so, I do not repent having uttered them.... "...Are we predestined among mankind to utter the new word?"...

...I see its traces in our history, our men of genius, in the artistic genius of Pushkin. Let our country be poor, but this poor land "Christ traversed with blessing, in the garb of a serf." Why then should we not contain His final word? Was not He Himself born in a manger?[258]

Dostoevsky's dream was a gospel invitation—perhaps, like Jesus, he spoke past the legion of unclean spirits to humanize his demonized nation by asking, "What is your name? Do you remember? Are you still in there? I know you are." Christ calls to us today in the same way. To become a true American, Canadian, Russian, Ukrainian, (insert your nation), etc., is to be exorcised of enmity and to become truly human in the likeness of the true Human, Jesus Christ. This One loves everyone as his own dear brothers and sisters, and, in his incarnation, he erased the borders of enmity to unite hostile peoples into "one new human."[259]

Now that would involve some deconstruction! Neither Marxist nor capitalist revolutions have accomplished this (or even wanted to). But maybe like so?

[14] [King Jesus] is our peace, you see.... He has pulled down the barrier, the dividing wall, that turns us into enemies of each other. He has done this in his flesh....

[15] ...The point of doing all this was to create, in him, one new human being out of the two [or about 195 (nations)!], so making peace. [16] God was reconciling both of us to himself in a single body, through the cross, by killing the enmity in him.   (Eph 2:14, 16)

Dostoevsky was no idiot. He knew the human condition better than... probably *anyone* since Jesus. He knew the darkness that lurks in the hearts of men (see *Crime and Punishment, The Possessed,* or *Notes from the Underground*!). He knew that mass exorcisms were well beyond our authority. Our experience with deconstructing nations is akin to that of the frustrated disciples trying to help the demonized child who kept convulsing and throwing himself into the fire.[260] Isn't that exactly what we keep doing?

But such children are not mere metaphors. Real children in this world—in breathtaking numbers—throughout the entirety of their short lives, are afflicted beyond what we could imagine or endure. For Dostoevsky, this was an even greater challenge to faith—the greatest, in fact—and he had the integrity to undergo it.

18

AFFLICTION—FULL STOP: FYODOR DOSTOEVSKY, PART 2

"When I thought I had reached the bottom, a knock came from below."
—Stanislav Jerzy Lec[261]

In my introduction to Dostoevsky in the previous chapter, I referred to the Russian novelist's courageous engagement with *affliction* and his profound awareness of human psychology. His keen insights into ideological possession extend to the angst of the individual, so he was truly a founding father of Existentialism. His own wrestles with personal demons—including facing a firing squad before a last-second reprieve, epileptic seizures, and a chronic gambling addiction—gave him the experience and intuition to craft the inner torment of characters in need of redemption.

In this chapter, we'll look at deconstruction through the lens of absurd affliction, the accusing conscience, and the way of transformation: co-suffering love.

ABSURD AFFLICTION

Earlier, I described affliction, in a technical sense, as a narrower concept than suffering. Suffering in this life is inevitable, and when we accept life on life's terms, even the suffering can become an occasion for growth, wisdom, and meaning. We may learn from suffering, developing resilience and becoming wounded healers. Suffering can have a purifying effect—hence, "the refiner's fire" of Malachi's vision,[262] through which we come to gleam like precious metals.

When I speak of *affliction*, however, I am referring to tragedies and evils that have no redemptive value in this life for the victim. Affliction is impervious to rationalizations and exposes every theodicy as blasphemous. We've seen Voltaire's revulsion against every attempt to justify affliction as somehow part of a greater good or ineffable plan. Folks like Dostoevsky, Camus, and Weil were among those rare, brave souls willing to look affliction in the eye and not break their stare or shrink back in despair. Their worldview did not abide denial—any account of God or humanity that needs to sweep affliction under the rug is worthless. Affliction, in this sense, is the most powerful and, oddly, purist form of deconstruction.

When authors such as Dostoevsky, Camus, and Elie Wiesel wrote about affliction, their first instinct was to describe the suffering and death of children in gruesome detail. I think of the Afghan children who have been maimed or killed from airstrikes over the years[263] or the Ukraine children who were raped and murdered by soldiers in 2022.[264] Such visceral images topple privileged and sentimental constructs of life and reality.

I will recount three examples from these authors, with this trigger warning: I cannot unsee their descriptions, nor can I cordon off my heart from the realization that the scenes they drew came from real-life occurrences. If you have experienced severe trauma and/or have a sensitive heart, please skip to the next main heading. I don't mean to be gratuitous, but if the Great Deconstruction wants to put humanity or God or faith on trial, the affliction of children is Exhibit A.

1. Dostoevsky's Ivan. In *The Brothers Karamazov*, Ivan, a young atheist, presents his case against God to his brother, Alyosha, who is a novice in the nearby Orthodox monastery. His argument against God is the cruelty of humanity:

> "People talk sometimes of bestial cruelty, but that's a great injustice and insult to the beasts; a beast can never be so cruel as a man, so artistically cruel.... These Turks took a pleasure in torturing children, too; cutting the unborn child from the mother's womb, and

tossing babies up in the air and catching them on the points of their bayonets before their mothers' eyes. Doing it before the mothers' eyes was what gave zest to the amusement...."

"Brother, what are you driving at?" asked Alyosha.

"I think if the devil doesn't exist, but man has created him, he has created him in his own image and likeness."[265]

Ivan continues his tirade for pages, with unimaginable tales of human wickedness, perpetrated against children, that Dostoevsky borrows from all-too-recent historical events. He presents atheism's case against faith—not that there is no God but that, if one child must suffer a torturous death, such a God is unworthy of worship, no matter what miracle of redemption brings about a final harmony:

> Oh, Alyosha, I am not blaspheming!... You see, Alyosha, perhaps it really may happen that...I, too,...may cry aloud with the rest, looking at the mother embracing the child's torturer, "Thou art just, O Lord!" but I don't want to cry aloud then.... It's not worth the tears of that one tortured child who beat itself on the breast with its little fist and prayed in its stinking outhouse, with its unexpiated tears to "dear, kind God"! It's not worth it, because those tears are unatoned for. They must be atoned for, or there can be no harmony. But how?... If the sufferings of children go to swell the sum of sufferings which was necessary to pay for truth, then I protest that the truth is not worth such a price.... And so I hasten to give back my entrance ticket.... And that I am doing. It's not God that I don't accept, Alyosha, only I most respectfully return him the ticket.[266]

I believe the most important thing that Dostoevsky ever wrote was what he *didn't* write next, after allowing the full force of Ivan's assault—or rather, *lament*. Alyosha offers no rationale for suffering, no theodicy to justify divine consent, not even the hope of redemption in the age to come. His three responses are brief and on point:

+ *"Rebellion,"* he murmurs as his first instinct. That would be Kierkegaard's first guess. Rebellion is often the real issue, even as a just protest against religion. Ivan counters. No, it's not that.

+ *The cross.* The cross of Christ is Alyosha's only theology of suffering, and rightly so: "But there is a Being and He can forgive everything, all and for all, because *He gave His innocent blood for all and everything.* You have forgotten him...."[267] Ivan offers no rebuttal to the cross. No, he hadn't forgotten, and he even wonders why Alyosha hadn't mentioned Jesus earlier. Instead of a counterargument, Ivan launches into his lengthy tale, entitled "The Grand Inquisitor," in which a Catholic inquisitor jails Jesus and castigates his folly for resisting Satan's wilderness temptations. He then justifies why the church needed to give in to those same temptations, especially condemning Christ for the unbearable freedom with which he had burdened humanity. Ivan's lengthy speech concludes with Jesus silently kissing his accuser, who storms out but leaves the door open so Jesus can depart in peace.

+ *The kiss.* As Alyosha's final response, he mimics Jesus's answer of silence, then gently kisses his brother. Ivan sees the plagiarism in his act but asks for one more kiss, and they depart as friends. Alyosha—i.e., Dostoevsky—knows when to shut up and listen, belaying the obsessive need to win an argument about God's existence or goodness. No useless "evidence that demands a verdict." Instead, only gentle affection. I wish I had known this thirty years ago.

2. Albert Camus's *The Plague* (1947). Albert Camus describes an epidemic in Oran, Algeria, in which the entire city is quarantined. The story is an allegory for the virus of Hitler's National Socialism and the various responses of the populace to that ideological infection—whether denial, despair, flight, or fight. The central hero is a Dr. Rieux, a humanist and agnostic. He does not believe God sent the plague, nor does he expect God to save them from it. But Rieux recognizes that no matter what happens, the task is to be human—and to remain human—in the face of absurd affliction. In Camus's story, the cruelty is never attributed to God or to evil men (except by a priest), but to a ruthless disease and its effects on a particular child.

> The doctor squeezed hard on the bar of the bed where the child was groaning. He didn't take his eyes off the little patient who suddenly stiffened....
>
> ...[He] had never stared directly, for so long, at the agony of an innocent.
>
> Just then the child, as if he had been bitten in the stomach, bent again with a spindly groan. He remained contracted like that for several long seconds, shaken with chills and convulsive trembling,

as if his frail carcass bent under the furious winds of the plague and cracked under the repeated gusts of fever. Once the squall had passed, he unwound a little, and the fever seemed to draw back and leave him panting on a humid, poisoned shore where rest already resembled death. When the burning tide came over him once again, for the third time, and lifted him a little, the child cowered, retreating to the depths of the bed in terror of the flame that was burning him, shaking his head wildly and throwing off his covers. Fat tears seeped from beneath his swollen eyelids, beginning to run down his leaden face, and after the bout, exhausted, stiffening his bony legs and his arms whose flesh had melted away in forty-eight hours, the child in the devastated bed assumed the pose of a grotesque crucifixion.[268]

"The pose of a grotesque crucifixion." Should Camus's choice of imagery for the torturous death of an innocent surprise us, even coming from an agnostic? That phrase, that picture…. When he (or Dr. Rieux) refuses to avert his eyes from the absurd affliction of a tormented child, his terminus is the cross. Is this the death of God for Camus? Or it is a revelation that the cruciform God (self-giving, co-suffering Love) is, finally, the universe's only response—nothing else, nothing less, is appropriate or adequate.

Where is God? God is in that child. God-in-Christ is that child. This is the Mystery. Which brings us to our final citations in the series.

3. Elie Wiesel's *Night*. Wiesel describes affliction and death in Nazi-occupied Poland. The narrator, Eliezer, recalls his first night in a death camp:

> Never shall I forget that night, the first night in camp, which has turned my life into one long night, seven times cursed and seven times sealed. Never shall I forget that smoke. Never shall I forget the little faces of the children, whose bodies I saw turned into wreaths of smoke beneath a silent blue sky.

> Never shall I forget those flames which consumed my faith forever.

> Never shall I forget that nocturnal silence which deprived me, for all eternity, of the desire to live. Never shall I forget those moments which murdered my God and my soul and turned my dreams to dust. Never shall I forget these things, even if I am condemned to live as long as God Himself. Never.[269]

Do you see why so much that passes for deconstruction today feels shallow by comparison? But maybe you're well aware that you aren't just "playing." Maybe you relate to Wiesel's description. Maybe you've suffered your own holocaust, your own unanswered prayers for a reprieve that never came. This is affliction. Eliezer asks, "*Why did I pray? What a strange question. Why did I live? Why did I breathe?*"[270]

Where is God? It is an awful and crucial question. We *must* go there. Wiesel's *Night* certainly does:

> A child has been caught collaborating in resistance against the Nazis and sentenced to hang. Alas, his body is not heavy enough to break his neck. His slow strangulation is the death of faith.
>
> "Where is God? Where is He?" someone behind me asked....
>
> For more than half an hour [the child in the noose] stayed there, struggling between life and death, dying in slow agony under our eyes. And we had to look him full in the face. He was still alive when I passed in front of him. His tongue was still red, his eyes were not yet glazed.
>
> Behind me, I heard the same man asking:
>
> "Where is God now?"
>
> And I heard a voice within me answer him:
>
> "Where is He? Here He is—He is hanging here on this gallows."[271]

WHERE IS GOD?

He IS hanging. HERE. On THIS gallows.

I think I just got it. Absurd affliction puts the "full stop" on God. On faith. On meaning and existence. Why live? Why breathe? We cannot—must never—merely reform our toxic idol-images of God or resuscitate our feeble faith. We cannot slap a bandage on the cancer of lost meaning or repair a pointless existence. Once deconstruction sets in in earnest, it is only *finished* (*tetelestai*) when we behold the crucified God who IS hanging, who is hanging HERE, on THIS gallows. The gallows we've built for him, that humanity builds for all of God's children, that we build for ourselves. Divine Love is hanging HERE, in *this*, in *our* affliction. The meaning of the incarnation is that Christ unites (present tense) himself to human existence and co-suffers the human condition. He undergoes all its tortures and diseases and deaths. He *is* hanging *here* on *these gallows*, making *this* world—*your* life—his cross.

Or he is nowhere.

If you ever decide to sacrifice your faith, don't waste your apostasy on the hubris of new atheism or the hypocrisy of Christians like me or the hollow allure of a bazillion shiny things. Let's at least agree to join Ivan Karamazov and Dr. Rieux and Eliezer in a horror worth despairing over—the crucifixion of God in the affliction of every child soul. *Here* is the abyss wherein the cross stands and the world swirls.

God—full stop. Finished. *Tetelestai.*

And yet...then there is this paradox, this antinomy, this miracle: "*It is finished*" means *it is begun.*

My friend Jonathan Martin once said,

> "He descended into hell..." and he keeps on going there, because we do. "Even the darkness is light to you..." So he keeps bringing heaven into the hell you make and the flames you thought would consume become the flames of Pentecost that transform you, into something new."[272]

THE CROSS OF CO-SUFFERING LOVE

I am sure this chapter was horrible for you to read. I'm sorry. It was worse to compose. But for those children who live and die in affliction tonight, are we not obligated by our humanity (if not our faith) to stop switching the channel, to at least attend and bear witness? Does not the crucified God demand that our "*Where are you?*" move beyond a desperate (or cynical) rhetorical question into a sincere inquiry, one that remembers to consider the cross? Dostoevsky knew the way—*one* way, the *only* way—by which anguished souls might be healed and transformed: the way of *co-suffering love.*

Dostoevsky's works had a profound influence on the twentieth century's premier Russian theologian, Sergius Bulgakov. Bulgakov felt the sting of affliction and the agony of abandonment—in real life, not as fiction: he suffered the death of his four-year-old son. His testament to his little boy and the way he met the crucified and co-suffering God in his dark valley are breath to my spirit after all this sadness, a glimmer of light to conclude this chapter:

My holy one, at the sanctuary of your remains, beside your pure body, my fair one, my radiant boy, I found out *how* God speaks, I understood what "God spoke" means! In a new and never-before-known clairvoyance of heart, along with the torment of the cross heavenly joy came down into it, and with the darkness of divine abandonment, God reigned in my soul. My heart was opened to the pain and torment of people—hearts until then strange and hence closed were exposed before it with their pain and grief. For the only time in my life I understood what it means *to love* not with a human, self-loving, and mercenary love, but with that divine love with which Christ loves us. It was as if the curtain separating me from others fell and all the gloom, bitterness, offense, animosity, and suffering in their hearts was revealed to me. And in ineffable rapture, frenzy, self-forgetfulness I said then—you will remember this, my fair one—I said: *God spoke to me*, and then hearing you I simply added that *you spoke to me too*.... To forget *this* and to doubt *after this* means for me to die spiritually. One can lose one's treasure, be frightened before its defense, but even unworthily cast aside and lost, it is a treasure all the same.[273]

19

ATHEISM, DECREATION, AND THE ABSENCE OF GOD: SIMONE WEIL

"There are two atheisms of which one is a purification of the notion of God."
—Simone Weil[274]

"Atheism can be like salt for religion. It is negative theology posited in the most absolute way. Most of the time, psychologically speaking, atheism represents a disappointment with the narrowness and limitations of a certain concept of God."
—Hans Urs von Balthasar[275]

We will return to Dostoevsky to round out this section on the wisdom of the great sleepers. But, first, as we discuss the paradox and mystery of *communion in absence*, I yield the floor to Simone Weil—patron saint of the afflicted. Her own chapter at last! We met her earlier in the chapters on Plato and Nietzsche, but this reprise on deconstruction comes to a head with her negative theology of "decreation" and "Christian atheism." By way of reminder, this brief description from the preface to her *Notebooks* hints at her vocation and importance:

> Simone Weil: French philosopher, activist, and religious searcher, whose death [from tuberculosis] in 1943 was hastened by starvation....

Weil has earned a reputation as one of the most original thinkers of her era. T.S. Eliot described her as "a woman of genius, of a kind of genius akin to that of the saints." Albert Camus called her "the only great spirit of our time."[276]

This modern saint and mystic was a deconstructionist to a fault—first, in terms of our constructs of God, and then, even more radically, in her earnest desire to *decreate* the egoistic will.

With regard to God, she described a version of atheism that is essential to authentic faith. You'll probably recognize affinities with our earlier discussion on the apophatic theology of the early church. Weil says, in her enigmatic way,

> A case of contradictories which are true. God exists: God does not exist. Where is the problem? I am quite sure that there is a God in the sense that I am quite sure my love is not illusory. I am quite sure that there is not a God in the sense that I am quite sure nothing real can be anything like what I am able to conceive when I pronounce this word. But that which I cannot conceive is not an illusion.[277]

Weil referred to this phenomenon as "religious atheism." Her Canadian devotee, George P. Grant, labeled it "Christian agnosticism." Today, we might dare to call it *deconstruction,* but Weil would agree only insofar as (1) the disciple's false conceptions of God are ruthlessly purged and (2) they continue to be expunged of self-will, while also (3) being relentless in their pursuit of the Truth. Weil rightly saw the necessity of a pruning in which our illusions about God are *dis*-illusioned and the fruitless branches of *faux* faith are cut off and consumed in the fire. Deconstruction is not strong enough a term for this kind of self-emptying. The apostle Paul called it *kenosis*[278]—Weil's term was *decreation.*[279]

Weil scholar Susan Taubes explains,

> Atheism, which used to be a charge leveled against skeptics, unbelievers, or simply the indifferent, has come to mean a *religious* experience of the death of God....
>
> The thesis of religious atheism has been most boldly formulated by Simone Weil: the existence of God may be denied without denying God's reality.[280]

Granted, Weil does philosophize about God's "non-existent reality," but deeper than any head games were her direct encounters with human affliction (à la Dostoevsky, Camus, and Wiesel in the previous chapter). For Weil, this is the great dilemma: she remains unshakeable in her conviction that God is perfect, immutable Love. And yet, she is faced with *affliction*, which she defines here:

> In the realm of suffering, affliction is a thing apart, specific, irreducible. It is wholly different than simple suffering. Affliction grips the soul and marks it to the depths with a mark belonging only to itself: the mark of slavery.[281]

The contradiction between goodness and affliction tears at her soul:

> I feel an ever-increasing sense of devastation, ceaselessly and increasingly torn, both in my intellect and in the centre of my heart, at my inability to think with truth at the same time about *the affliction of men, the perfection of God, and the link between the two.*[282]

Not one for abstractions, Weil cites specific scenarios where the connection seems impossible:

> A man whose whole family had died under torture, and who had himself been tortured for a long time in a concentration camp; or a sixteenth-century Indian, the sole survivor after the total extermination of his people. Such men if they had previously believed in the mercy of God would either believe in it no longer, or else they would conceive of it quite differently from before....
>
> I must move towards an abiding conception of the divine mercy, a conception which does not change whatever event destiny may send upon me and which can be communicated to no matter what human being.[283]

Weil sees the problem of evil, of affliction and goodness, of God's absence and presence in our suffering, as a real contradiction. To her, the genuine impasse cannot be solved rationally, and she especially refuses any theodicy that makes God arbitrary. Nevertheless, she clings to the truth of God's unwavering mercy. There's only one Way, one Truth, one Life that warrants her attention. She focuses on the *intersection*—the simultaneous presence—of human affliction *and* divine goodness at the strangest moment in the history of the cosmos: Christ's "cry of dereliction" from the cross, "My God, my

God, why have you forsaken me?" (Matthew 27:46 NRSV, NIV). When God experiences God's absence—when God becomes an "atheist"!

How can Weil—how can we—simultaneously conceive of the absence of God in affliction and the presence of God in mercy? We can't. We can only *behold* Christ's anguish and *be held* by divine Love, *both at once*, in the crucifixion.

CRUCIFIXION, ABANDONMENT, ABSENCE

As I wrote earlier, George P. Grant was a Canadian political philosopher and devotee of Simone Weil. He witnessed the tragic deaths of hundreds of civilians in his care during Hitler's London bombings. So he understood Weil's dilemma directly. His experience of affliction also led him to embrace her vision of the cross, which likely saved his sanity. In a conversation with David Cayley, he explains:

> Whatever Christianity may be, it cannot get away from the cru-cifixion.... One sees here the just man being most hideously put to death, and this means to me that in Christianity there is always not only the presence of God but also the absence of God. I would say that this is central to Christianity.... I want to be very careful because the very substance of what I have thought about anything would go if I couldn't believe in the absence of God....
>
> God is love means that God is...loving right now. For love to be perfect to Simone Weil it has to cross an infinite distance [between goodness and affliction].... That is what the crucifixion meant to her: on the cross Christ expresses his love for his enemies, he expresses his desolation, the cry of dereliction in which he feels cut off from God's transcendence, and yet he crosses that infinite distance.... She is essentially a theologian of the cross....
>
> The fact that we see here below the affliction of human beings has been the deepest traditional argument against God's being. How can you look at this world and say it comes from love?
>
> I would say the crucifixion is the supreme act of justice on Christ's part—not that he was crucified but that he submits to the crucifix-ion. It's a supreme act of justice to love one's enemies.[284]

To come full circle, this revelation of the cross—those outstretched, nail-pierced hands that span (present-tense, continuous) the distance between affliction and mercy, absence and presence—was central to my own salvation in 2008–09. The co-suffering Love that both cried out with me *and* heard my cry of abandonment found me in my self-construed abyss. I can't explain it *into* you—I can only testify that this was my experience.

But let's not take my word for it alone. I've asked a friend to share his own gut-wrenching story of *decreation* and encounter. If we're to fathom the depths of Weil's truth to the dregs of human misery, this anonymous, modern-day "centurion," tormented by the blood on his own hands, surely speaks the truth in this stream-of-consiousness confession.

CENTURION IN RECOVERY: MORAL INJURY, THE CROSS, AND SIMONE WEIL

"My release from the military was shortly followed by rumblings of a virus in China that was threatening to become a global pandemic, and within a few months, the coronavirus pandemic was upon us.

"For the first time, I began to critically examine my life in the military, and not just the actions of my superiors, who I felt had betrayed us, but my own actions, my own ideals, and everything that I had once believed in. What followed was an agonizing unveiling of myself that to this day is still painful to talk about. I began to think about all the decisions I had made, my callous indifference to the suffering that I was helping to create, my willingness to do whatever the mission demanded, even when I knew the cost and who would end up bearing it.

"I often wondered how the Roman soldiers slaughtered thousands in the name of the empire and still kept their humanity, only to realize that I was just like them, and they didn't keep their humanity, just like me. My heart was hard, I did not care, and I did my duty to my country, just like the Roman soldiers who slaughtered Gauls by the thousands.

"I began to think of my friends who had died, either in combat or from mental wounds that would not heal, about my own mental wounds, and I dropped even deeper into anguish and stayed in this pit for what felt like eternity. My entire world was shattered, and everything I thought I stood for felt like a farce; there was no happy ending, there were no silver linings; there was only suffering and the suffering that I created. I felt as though my moral compass had been smashed, my conscience torn into pieces and unable to be reassembled.

"I remember during this time coming across a short essay by Tadeusz Borowski called 'Auschwitz Our Home,' where he wrote about seeing the world from the perspective of a slave for the first time as he was imprisoned at Auschwitz. He wrote:

> We work beneath the earth and above it, under a roof and in the rain, with the spade, the pickaxe, and the crowbar. We carry huge sacks of cement, lay bricks, put down rails, spread gravel, trample the earth…. We are laying the foundation for some new, monstrous civilization. Only now do I realize what price was paid for building the ancient civilizations. The Egyptian pyramids, the temples, and Greek statues—what a hideous crime they were! How much blood must have poured on to the Roman roads, the bulwarks, and the city walls. Antiquity—the tremendous concentration camp where the slave was branded on the forehead by his master and crucified for trying to escape!
>
> Roman law! Yes, today too there is a law….
>
> If the Germans win the war, what will the world know about us? They will erect huge buildings, highways, factories, soaring monuments. Our hands will be placed under every brick, and our backs will carry the steel rails and the slabs of concrete. They will kill off our families, our sick, our aged. They will murder our children.
>
> And we shall be forgotten, drowned out by the voices of the poets, the jurists, the philosophers, the priests. They will produce their own beauty, virtue, and truth. They will produce religion.[285]

"I heard what Borowski was saying with a sincere clarity, and I heard him saying it to me, he the slave, and I the Roman centurion supervising his detention, ready to crucify him if he tried to escape. I tried to deny what was clearly the truth, and some days I succeeded, but most days I could not, and I began to contemplate suicide. In the brief moments when I felt mental clarity, I reached out to friends to make sure I didn't have access to firearms, pills, or the ability to drive my car in case the periods of anguish and suicidal ideation became strong enough to push me to act.

"During all this time, from when I lost my faith until the present, I had still kept up my study of Christianity. I could concede that it was significant in the lives of many people, and I could happily say that people derived genuine meaning and purpose from it; but despite all of my attempts, I was just an atheist with an obsession-focused Christianity. It was just a collection of facts, beliefs, and theories that meant no more to me than the facts, theories, and beliefs associated with *Star Trek*. I did not understand and could not understand how or why I should believe any of it.

"In this period of anguish and despair, I was diagnosed with a condition commonly called 'moral injury,' the most fitting description of what I was feeling. The moral injury was so deep that I felt my conscience was irreparable and unable to be recovered. I hated who I was and what I had done, and I was so disgusted with who I had become that I felt I needed to be dealt with like a mass-murdering criminal. But people would find out that I used to serve and would thank me for my service. I knew deep down that someone had to pay for my actions, and, despite what Christians believed, Jesus was just a guy who died on a cross two thousand years ago. He could not pay a damn thing; he was dead. The pain manifested itself in many ways: I would vomit, develop migraines, have random panic attacks, and randomly break down in tears or swell with fits of rage.

"As time passed, I began to feel more and more desperate and started grasping for anything that could pull me out of the dark pit into which I had thrown myself. I decided to reread the Synoptic Gospels for the umpteenth time, hoping that maybe I would see something that I had not seen before, and, unfortunately, I did.

"I got to the Sermon on the Mount. Some say that Jesus's teachings in the sermon are advocating for nonviolent resistance to the Roman occupation. Rereading it in this light gave new weight to these words because I knew that, had I lived in those days, I would have been one of the Romans they were resisting.

"The words themselves are not biting; they are, in almost every way, loving and inviting, but I couldn't see them that way. I saw the subtext, resistance to occupation, and could only see myself as the enemy that Jesus's followers were defying. I knew all about the brutality of Roman soldiers in Judea; I knew the history; I had read the primary sources; and I saw myself as one of them—not as a follower of Jesus.

"As I read, I felt even more and more alienated and descended further into affliction. I finally got to the Passion narratives and read about the soldiers who beat, mocked, and crucified a man who did nothing to them. They tortured him, they gambled for his clothes, they laughed as he died. I saw them for what they were—men who killed Jesus without a trace of compassion or remorse—and I was one of them.

"I had never identified with the Roman soldiers in the Gospels, either those mentioned explicitly or those alluded to through context, but now I could do nothing else. Over the next few days or weeks, I continued to ruminate on my newfound perspective. I began, *against my will*, to imagine myself at the foot of the cross, watching as he died, watching as his disciples wept, and not caring, not feeling any remorse, simply standing there knowing that I was doing my duty to secure and protect Rome at whatever the cost, no matter how ugly it might look. I would have executed the Son of God, and I would have felt right in doing so. In moments of lucidity, I would try to reason with myself, to find a way to understand that I wasn't like them, that I wouldn't have done what they did, but I knew it wasn't true; I had ample evidence to the contrary.

"Eventually, the periods of affliction became so severe that I started to dissociate and shift between mental states from embodied pain to disembodied terror where I could do nothing other than see myself as Jesus's executioner. During this time, I kept listening to a song on repeat for days titled "Jesus Wept" by Demon Hunter. They sing,

> I'm why
> Bloodshed...
> I'm why Jesus wept[286]

"I felt the words '*I'm why Jesus wept*' in quite a literal way. I was the reason for his agony at Gethsemane, I was the one coming for him, I would be the one to beat him, I would be the one to torture him, my hands would pierce his, my words would mock him, my spear would kill him, and I, with callous indifference, would have stood guard, having executed another insurrectionist who threatened the order, rule, and power of Rome.

"In one of these bouts of anguish, while listening to the song, I heard the words—words that I had read hundreds of times—'*Father, forgive them, they know not what they do.*'[287] Perhaps 'hear' is the wrong word, but I knew the words were being said. And I understood that Jesus did not just weep because I was coming to torture and kill him. He wept for me, knowing what I was, knowing what I would become.

"I, however, refused to hear him. These were the alleged words of a dead man two thousand years ago. They meant nothing; they could do nothing. Jesus was dead. His followers, perhaps in a fit of mental hysteria like the one I was going through, became convinced he was raised from the dead. But dead men do not come back from death, and the hands of the Roman soldiers—my hands—killed them. After the first time I heard those words, I keep hearing them, or maybe experiencing them. Each time I would kill him, I would hear him say it again: *'Father, forgive them, they know not what they do.'*

"As time passed, I began to ask myself, 'What if, what if this isn't all just bullshit, what if somehow there is something to this?' And in my desperation to get out of the hell that I was putting myself through, I allowed myself to put aside skepticism and pay attention to whatever it was I felt and let it be what it would be.

"Finally, one day, after seeing myself stab the side of Christ once again, I felt myself, like the soldier at the cross in the Gospel of Luke, saying, *'Surely this man was the son of God.'*[288] And I felt compelled to repeat the Jesus prayer, *'Jesus Christ, son of God, have mercy on me, a sinner.'*

"And he did. I accepted forgiveness and felt for the first time that there was a small light in the darkness, and I began to move toward it.

"I was, and still am, intensely skeptical, especially of my own mind at the point of extreme pain and desperation; and if I am pressed on it, I would probably describe it as a mental breaking point where what was left of my fragmented conscience grasped for anything it could, and *found something*.

"It was about then that I began to read Simone Weil. I felt, for the first time, that I had encountered someone I could actually understand. I began to see in her aspects of myself. Like me, I believe she was autistic. Her writings, the way she reenvisions the abstract socio-emotional concepts baked into Christianity as real, incarnated phenomenon, the insight that the essence of true love is attention—it so clearly flows from an autistic mind. Her focus, her obsession, her awkwardness, her way of seeing the world and making lateral connections between disparate abstract concepts and then rooting them so eloquently in the concrete and tangible notion of justice is something that I think could have only come from an autistic.

"I had, for the first time in my life, found a person who could speak about Christianity in my own mother tongue, in the only language I really know, without the reliance on any cognitive faculties that are outside of my ability to grasp. What were once abstract, esoteric, and ancient beliefs in a set of historical events were transformed into an incarnated reality that I could touch, feel, and experience. The depths of her compassion, her strict need for order, for justice, and for things to be made right in the world in the face of injustice were urges and desires that I could find in myself, no matter how broken I felt; what I saw in her, I could find in me.

"I allowed myself, in the presence of her writings, to simply give myself over to attention, and to follow through on her insights. I remember reading her insights from when she was in Portugal, watching the wives of fishermen singing hymns before their husbands went to sea, when she said that Christianity was the religion of slaves, and that she, like other slaves, could not help belonging to it.

"I thought again of the Roman slaves and how I felt as a Roman soldier, and, in those moments of attention, I put down my sword, took off my armor, and decided to join them, whatever the cost. I began to see the world from their perspective, not as the Roman soldier overlooking Tadeusz Borowski as he and his fellow slaves labored to build monuments to injustice. I began to see that the way of Jesus is not esoteric, magical belief but radical solidarity with the oppressed and a commitment that justice be done for these people in the name of love.

"Through Weil's writing, I slowly started to be able to digest Christianity, not as a series of facts but as a path. I dived even deeper into Weil and found that the more I read, the more of the Christian tradition I was able to decode. She was like the decryption key to a steganographic message hidden within the Christian tradition. It felt as though I were a foreigner living in another land and hearing for the first time in thirty years someone speak to me in my mother tongue. Things finally started to make a little bit of sense. After a year of anguish and despair, I felt the pain lifting."

A LIFELONG JOURNEY OF TRANSFORMATION

If the last two chapters teach us anything, Dostoevsky, Weil, and my centurion friend echo the apostolic conviction that *salvation* is not an abstract transaction where I secure eternal life if I pray the right prayer, confess the right creed, or cross the right threshold of behavior. Not that our prayers, beliefs, or deeds are pointless. After all, the New Testament—Jesus Christ most of all—invites the world to repentance, faith, and a life reordered around his Way.

But rather than reducing salvation to a doctrinal concept or final destiny, Dostoevsky and Weil show us how *salvation includes a lifelong journey of transformation from the inside out.* Salvation is not a way to avoid affliction or abandonment but the very place where we meet the crucified God. As Weil expressed:

> It is in the affliction itself that the mercy of God shines—in the depths, at the center of our inconsolable grief. If, while persevering in love, we fall to the point where the soul cannot restrain the cry, "My God, why have you abandoned me,"—if one remains at this point without ceasing to love, we finish by touching something that is not affliction, that is not joy—that is the central essence, essential, pure, beyond the senses, common to joy and to suffering. It is the very love of God.
>
> We know then that joy is the sweetness of contact with the love of God; that affliction is the wound of this same contact when it is painful; and that only the contact itself matters, not the manner of contact....
>
> I would want to be able to testify to this with gratitude.[289]

We come to experience the "way of the cross" as the means of grace, as God's presence even in our affliction—through fevers, tears, and, most of all, Christ's co-suffering love. Ah, *co-suffering love*—that synonym for empathy, compassion, and solidarity that Archbishop Lazar taught me nearly two decades ago. How best to explain it? Here we invite Dostoevsky back for his third and final contribution.

20

FEVERS, TEARS, AND CO-SUFFERING LOVE: FYODOR DOSTOEVSKY, PART 3

SALVATION DECONSTRUCTED

Expanding on our theme from the end of the previous chapter, I invite you to think about salvation as the story of your life rather than as a single before-and-after landmark where you claim, "I got saved." *Justification* is not a "get-out-of-hell-free" card or a ticket into paradise after we die. Rather, by faith, we *participate* in the grace of the Father, Son, and Spirit—in their *saving process*. We are *being* transfigured into the image of Christ. Again, this transformation does not commence *after* we're "saved." It IS the salvation project—the new life of those who are "*being* saved."[290] Our salvation is embedded in, and unfurls through, the struggles of our real-life existence.

Dostoevsky presents our journey to the cross and beyond as both grace (because the Lord is gracious) and a colossal struggle (because we wrestle). Salvation IS the *via dolorosa*—not just the first or the last step of the journey, but the whole path, our struggle, our life. Seeing salvation as a *becoming* is hard for Western minds, which often demand to know who is "in" and who is "out," when I'm "in" and when I'm "out," whether I'm secure or whether I can "lose it." In our insecurity, we lust for certitude about when and how and for whom the hell-for-heaven deal is closed.

I propose we set aside that obsession long enough to try on Dostoevsky's existentialist Orthodoxy, where our existence (our real life, every day of it) is the way home to the Father's house. Your life is *not* about killing time in a world you're "just passing through." Rather, your salvation is an epic, cross-bearing ascent, further up and further in with Christ. The Good Shepherd is leading us beyond the world's moth-and-rust-eaten, self-absorbed value systems into fullness of life—here, now, and forever. He's constructing in us the eternal life of love, joy, peace, beauty, truth, and justice. And that, my friend—your *LIFE* in Christ—*IS* your salvation journey.

Yes, we experience major turning points and landmarks along the way, but Dostoevsky reveals how divine grace fashions our salvation story far before we respond and guides us forward even when we're still deeply convinced of our own darkness.

Renovating a life takes a lifetime and more, especially if the Spirit's ambitions for us extend far beyond sin management. *Salvation* restructures the entire system of underlying wounds, thoughts, beliefs, feelings, and behaviors that drive us. That will require a *conversion* that many cheap-grace "converts" skip over and many deconstructionists leave half-baked.

Dostoevsky's novels are a deep probe into the inner workings of our struggle, of our transformation, of our salvation—which are all of one piece. Do I make God's completely free grace sound like an incredibly costly venture? Fair enough. Think of Jesus's word in Luke 14:

> [26] If anyone comes to me and does not hate father and mother, wife and children, brothers and sisters—yes, even their own life—such a person cannot be my disciple. [27] And whoever does not carry their cross and follow me cannot be my disciple.

> [2] Suppose one of you wants to build a tower. Won't you first sit down and estimate the cost to see if you have enough money to complete it? [29] For if you lay the foundation and are not able to finish it, everyone who sees it will ridicule you, [30] saying, "This person began to build and wasn't able to finish."

> [31] Or suppose a king is about to go to war against another king. Won't he first sit down and consider whether he is able with ten thousand men to oppose the one coming against him with twenty thousand? [32] If he is not able, he will send a delegation while the other is still a long

way off and will ask for terms of peace. [33] In the same way, those of you who do not give up everything you have cannot be my disciples.

[34] Salt is good, but if it loses its saltiness, how can it be made salty again? [35] It is fit neither for the soil nor for the manure pile; it is thrown out.

Whoever has ears to hear, let them hear.   (Luke 14:26–35 NIV)

Nothing in that speech smacks of "easy-believism." Jesus describes salvation in terms of cost and struggle—a calculated risk, even. So, yes, we weigh the cost of taking up our cross to follow Jesus. But Dostoevsky's stories also describe the salvation journey *not* so much as something we calculate or deliberate but more like an arduous experience we *undergo*—again, something that happens *to us* inside the very lives and relationships that serve as God's many *means of grace*.

GOD IS THE GRACE, LIFE IS THE MEANS

Take very careful note: we must not mistake God as the *cause* of the *means* by which God *saves* us. To use a particular example, if a drunk driver hits someone, and the harm they cause leads them to rethink their life, God didn't cause the drunkenness, the accident, or the harm. But, by grace, the tragic circumstances may be the *means* by which they turn their life around.

Now, let's say the driver left someone seriously disabled, confined to a wheelchair for the rest of their life. The driver's guilt might torment and imprison them for decades. And their victim may experience both excruciating physical pain *and* emotional pain. The result may be a life stolen by both the drunk driver and that person's own smoldering bitterness.

What does *salvation* look like for these men? I am switching to the term *men* instead of using the generic *them* because this is not actually a hypothetical situation. I'm sharing a true story. Stephen, the victim of the DUI, came to see that his broken spiritual condition was every bit as paralyzing as his physical suffering. Somehow, inexplicably, he came to realize that he had to forgive the man who had done this to him—for his own sake and for the sake of the Other. He began to see that, somehow, he held the man's salvation (his transformation, his freedom, his life) in his own crippled hands! *Not* as the *cause* of his salvation, but as the *means* of God's grace through his own self-liberating agency.

Stephen was able to arrange a flight (with his mother) to cross the country and meet the drunk driver—who was debilitated by unresolved shame—to communicate an excruciating victim-impact statement *and* a word of abso-lution that was only Stephen's to grant. Stephen's courageous tears became a corrosive agent, devouring the chains that bound both men to the trauma of that event. This is the way of the cross, the path of salvation, the means of grace I'm talking about. This is how Dostoevsky thinks and writes about salvation, for the truth of Stephen's story is true on a grand scale: God is the grace, while life (and even our suffering in it) is the means.

Think about it in this way: God did not crucify Jesus. *We* did that. The cru-cifixion of the Son of God was a hideous murder and humanity's greatest act of wickedness. And yet, in language reminiscent of my friend C. Baxter Kruger, God entered the abyss of our great darkness and penetrated its depths with redeeming light.[291] I often distinguish the crucifixion (what we did to God) from the cross (what, in the midst of crucifixion, God-in-Christ did for us). I want to emphasize again that God never *causes* evil—not ever—but, as our redeeming genius, Christ transfigures our affliction into the *means* of his grace for our salvation.

So, while God is *not* the author of suffering or sickness, accusation or con-demnation, assaults or overdoses, darkness, dread, or despair, we may encoun-ter Christ and his messengers of grace in those places.

For the rest of this chapter, I want to illustrate the following *two means of grace*—"*fevers*" (of the accusing conscience) *and* "*tears*" (of empathy or co-suf-fering love)—from Dostoevsky's stories because they describe existential sal-vation so well.

"FEVERS" AND THE ACCUSING CONSCIENCE

I'm very grateful to those kind souls who undertook the labor of love to produce free, online English translations of Dostoevsky's major masterpiec-es.[292] Being able to do global searches of his writings puts us at an enormous advantage, especially if we want to follow key terms and themes. For example, in a quick search of every occurrence of the words *fever* or *feverish* across his main works, I found the following:

- *Notes from the Underground* (1864): 9 occurrences
- *Crime and Punishment* (1866): 52
- *The Idiot* (1869): 43
- *The Possessed* (or *Demons* or *The Devils*) (1872): 33
- *The Brothers Karamazov* (1880): 43

That's 180 occurrences in five books!

What is it with Dostoevsky and fevers? When read in context, the fevers are almost always manifestations of severe emotional stress, and then predominantly an experience of guilt—that is, a raging internal battle with an accusing conscience. Here are three samples from *Notes from the Underground*:

> I was so harassed, so exhausted, that I would have cut my throat to put an end to it. I was in a fever; my hair, soaked with perspiration, stuck to my forehead and temples.[293]

> To borrow from Anton Antonitch seemed to me monstrous and shameful. I did not sleep for two or three nights. Indeed, I did not sleep well at that time, I was in a fever; I had a vague sinking at my heart or else a sudden throbbing, throbbing, throbbing!... That night I was ill again, feverish and delirious.[294]

> My heart sank. I knew, too, perfectly well even then, that I was monstrously exaggerating the facts. But how could I help it? I could not control myself and was already shaking with fever.[295]

There is an intense conjunction of *fevers* and the *conscience* in *Crime and Punishment*. Even as the perpetrator Raskolnikov is plotting a murder, his conscience smites him with a nightmare, warning him away just as God had warned Cain:[296]

> "Thank God, that was only a dream," he said, sitting down under a tree and drawing deep breaths. "But what is it? Is it some fever coming on? Such a hideous dream!"

> He felt utterly broken: darkness and confusion were in his soul. He rested his elbows on his knees and leaned his head on his hands.

> "Good God!" he cried, "can it be, can it be, that I shall really take an axe, that I shall strike her on the head, split her skull open...that I shall tread in the sticky warm blood, break the lock, steal and tremble; hide, all spattered in the blood...with the axe.... Good God, can it be?"

> He was shaking like a leaf as he said this.[297]

And again, after he had committed the terrible deed, here are three descriptions of his feverish struggle:

> He sat down on the sofa—and instantly recollected everything! All at once, in one flash, he recollected everything.

> For the first moment he thought he was going mad. A dreadful chill came over him; but the chill was from the fever that had begun long before in his sleep. Now he was suddenly taken with violent shivering, so that his teeth chattered and all his limbs were shaking.[298]

> "You've eaten nothing since yesterday, I warrant. You've been trudging about all day, and you're shaking with fever."[299]

> He was not completely unconscious, however, all the time he was ill; he was in a feverish state, sometimes delirious, sometimes half conscious.[300]

OUR INNER "PROPHET"

These fevers, accompanied by sleeplessness, loss of appetite, delirium, and sickness, are Dostoevsky's manifestations of the accusing conscience as investigator, prosecutor, or judge. The severity of the fever signals how resistant the character is to surrender. The fever sometimes breaks when the tortured soul accepts the verdict and gives in, repents, or confesses.

These days, the experience of guilt is so unwelcome in our world. Often that's because it's accompanied or displaced by toxic shame and no path to redemption. On the other hand, our sorry society has come to a point where every twinge of the conscience is considered pathological. "You're making me feel guilty" is treated as the worst possible offense.

But, for Dostoevsky, the conscience functions a lot like a God-given inner prophet who lives in every human being, resisting our arrogant urge to live "beyond good and evil." At its best, the conscience serves as a constant guide on the Jesus Way, pointing us to the Light and beckoning us away from darkness, denial, and bondage.

Remember what happened to David in this regard? He took Bathsheba, the wife of Uriah, impregnated her, then kept digging himself deeper into a hole until he even arranged for Uriah's death. What did God do? He sent the prophet Nathan to expose David's sin and invite him to repent. Something about that encounter connected the external prophet (Nathan) with a reawakening of David's inner prophet (his conscience). You can see that internal prophet hard at work within David through his *fevered* confession in Psalm 51.

Now, just as Nathan the prophet functioned as an external prophet to revive David's seared conscience, so too we see an external prophet in Dostoevsky's novel prompting Raskolnikov's surrender. One of my favorite characters in all of the great novelist's works is the magistrate and investigator Porfiry Petrovich—a master at criminal psychology. What I love about him is that even once he knows Raskolnikov is the murderer and has sufficient evidence to put him away, he continues to work at him. His goal is not to secure a quick conviction from Raskolnikov but to draw an honest confession out of him. For Porfiry, it's not about crime and the punishment of the perpetrator. Instead, through his interrogations, he acts as a priest and prophet to Raskolnikov's conscience, doing all he can to save the murderer's soul. It's not about prosecution or retribution—whatever pressure both the fevers and the magistrate apply are an appeal to a slumbering conscience: "Wake up!" They are a means to Raskolnikov's redemption.

A CAVEAT ON CONSCIENCE

For Dostoevsky, the conscience is like an infallible judge and benevolent prophet—even when employing fevers as a fiery ordeal to save us. But I feel that this is an oversimplification because even the conscience can become a prodigal son/daughter.

On the one hand, the conscience can become "seared" (1 Tim 4:2, various translations) like the younger son in the parable who eventually ignored his conscience altogether. In sociopaths, the inner prophet virtually seems to have been killed! Beware of ignoring God's inner prophet. Shunning its advice has never turned out well for me.

On the other hand, the conscience can also elevate itself as judge and accuser, just like the older brother did. It can speak condemning and belittling words to us when we stumble. It's as if the conscience on overdrive resigns as God's prophet of grace and hires on as the Accuser's voice instead. Talk about headhunting!

Has your conscience ever been so seared that you wind up slaving with the "pigs" (choose your vice)? Or has your conscience become so fastidious that it can't rise above condemnation? Well, the good news is that the Father welcomes both sons back home: one through a moment of clarity (the Holy Spirit) and the other through the pleading of the Father. As usual, the second invitation is a tougher sell.

Still, let's go with Dostoevsky this far: the conscience is a gift when it serves at the throne of grace and brings a prophetic invitation to leave our chains and head home to freedom. If it sneaks out of the room or crawls up onto the judgment seat, it needs a reminder to find its proper place in God's service, testifying, like all good prophets, of the good news of Jesus's radical forgiveness and unfailing love.

As for physical fevers, consult with a doctor and your conscience. Acetaminophen isn't always sufficient.

"TEARS" AND CO-SUFFERING LOVE

Sadly, the fevers that Dostoevsky's characters experience are rarely, if ever, sufficient to bring about their salvation or transformation. For all its prominence and ferocity, the fevered conscience may finally be rebuffed by a hardened heart. Salvation ultimately requires a deeper cleansing agent: the "tears" that represent "co-suffering love" or empathy.

One day, as my friend Ron Dart and I were chatting with Archbishop Lazar by the "holy well" at his monastery in Dewdney, British Columbia, he shared his conviction that Dostoevsky's great revelation was that "co-suffering love is the only power or force or strength that anybody can ever have for the healing of another human soul."[301]

Again and again in Dostoevsky, the soul in dreadful peril is rescued only through tears of empathy that pull them from the embers of deadly narcissism. When we see another's sin not as lawbreaking behavior but as the self-destructive effect of their affliction, our hearts may be stirred to shed tears the other person can no longer cry. Dostoevsky's tales demonstrate the saving power of co-suffering love that flows from eyes that see our suffering, that empathize, that draw near in solidarity. Lazar tells me that such empathy is the closest we get to being like Christ. Because is not the cross of Christ the apex of co-suffering love?

Of the many such episodes in every one of Dostoevsky's major novels, a few particular examples move me every time I read them, especially when the light of divine love radiates from those most afflicted themselves.

SONIA'S TEARS

In *Crime and Punishment*, the nihilist Raskolnikov waffles between madness over what he's done and icy detachment, which is the far greater threat to his soul. He continues hinting to Sonia, the child prostitute, until she can accept that it's true—that he is the murderer. Notice her reaction and how it affects the murderer's response:

She jumped up, seeming not to know what she was doing, and, wringing her hands, walked into the middle of the room; but quickly went back and sat down again beside him, her shoulder almost touching his. *All of a sudden she started as though she had been stabbed, uttered a cry and fell on her knees before him, she did not know why.*

"What have you done—what have you done to yourself?" she said in despair, and, jumping up, she flung herself on his neck, threw her arms round him, and held him tightly.

Raskolnikov drew back and looked at her with a mournful smile.

"You are a strange girl, Sonia—you kiss me and hug me when I tell you about that.... You don't think what you are doing."

"There is no one—no one in the whole world now so unhappy as you!" she cried in a frenzy, not hearing what he said, and she suddenly broke into violent hysterical weeping.

A feeling long unfamiliar to him flooded his heart and softened it at once. He did not struggle against it. Two tears started into his eyes and hung on his eyelashes.

"Then you won't leave me, Sonia?" he said, looking at her almost with hope.

"No, no, never, nowhere!" cried Sonia. *"I will follow you, I will follow you everywhere.* Oh, my God! Oh, how miserable I am!...Why, why didn't I know you before! Why didn't you come before! Oh, dear!"

"Here I have come."

"Yes, now! What's to be done now?...*Together, together!*" she repeated as it were unconsciously, and she hugged him again. "I'll follow you to Siberia!"[302]

After resisting so many fevers and interrogations, coldhearted Raskolnikov's healing begins at last. How so? Through Sonia's "passionate, agonizing sympathy for the unhappy man."[303] But do you also perceive the relentless love of the Good Shepherd, whose voice we hear in her words, "I will follow you, I will follow you everywhere," and "Together, together!...I'll follow you to Siberia"—even to hades, if necessary, as it so often is.

GRUSHENKA'S SCHEME

My other favorite example of the redeeming power of co-suffering empathy comes from *The Brothers Karamazov*. The scene is complex but well worth distilling. Alyosha, our young novice monk, has just lost his spiritual father, Elder Zossima. But instead of miracles attending Zossima's death (a sign of sainthood), the monastery is shocked by the putrid stench of Zossima's unusually rapid decomposition. Jealous accusers immediately slander his character. The scandal so wounds Alyosha's faith that he's ready to throw his innocence away in the arms of Grushenka, a headstrong beauty who, together with Rakitin, a conniving acquaintance, conspires to seduce Alyosha that very night. Rakitin's primary motive is a vengeful desire to see "the downfall of the righteous," and Alyosha's fall "from the saints to the sinners, over which he was already gloating in his imagination"[304] Rakitin lures Alyosha to Grushenka's home, where she is lying in wait (literally) to seduce him.

Grushenka, not really realizing why Alyosha is so downcast, pounces:

> "Let me sit on your knee, Alyosha, like this." She suddenly skipped forward and jumped, laughing, on his knee, like a nestling kitten, with her right arm about his neck. "I'll cheer you up, my pious boy. Yes, really, will you let me sit on your knee? You won't be angry? If you tell me, I'll get off?"[305]

The trap springs.... But, just then, a wonderful grace interrupts and obliterates the whole scheme:

> The great grief in [Alyosha's] heart swallowed up every sensation that might have been aroused, and, if only he could have thought clearly at that moment, he would have realized that he had now the strongest armor to protect him from every lust and temptation. Yet in spite of the vague irresponsiveness of his spiritual condition and the sorrow that overwhelmed him, he could not help wondering at a new and

strange sensation in his heart. This woman, this "dreadful" woman, had no terror for him now, none of that terror that had stirred in his soul at any passing thought of a woman. On the contrary, this woman, dreaded above all women, sitting now on his knee, holding him in her arms, aroused in him now a quite different, unexpected, peculiar feeling, a feeling of the intensest and purest interest without a trace of fear, of his former terror.[306]

Alyosha's moment of pure attention enables him to see through Grushenka's apparent wickedness to the truth of her broken heart, which has been betrayed by a lover to whom she has (despite appearances) remained faithful. The young monk's ability to see her faithfulness as forgiveness so surprises her that she spontaneously confesses, "It's true, Alyosha, I had sly designs on you before. For I am a horrid, violent creature. But at other times I've looked upon you, Alyosha, as my conscience. I've kept thinking 'how anyone like that must despise a nasty thing like me.'"[307]

The warm feelings become entirely mutual. Scolding Rakitin, Alyosha says,

> You had much better look at her—do you see how she has pity on me? I came here to find a wicked soul—I felt drawn to evil because I was base and evil myself, and I've found a true sister; I have found a treasure—a loving heart. She had pity on me just now.... [Grushenka], I am speaking of you. You've raised my soul from the depths."
>
> Alyosha's lips were quivering and he caught his breath.
>
> "She has saved you, it seems," laughed Rakitin spitefully. "And she meant to get you in her clutches, do you realize that?"[308]

Alyosha again rebukes Rakitin, who, by now, is going out of his mind at this unexpected U-turn:

> I didn't speak to you as a judge but as the lowest of the judged. What am I beside her? I came here seeking my ruin, and said to myself, "What does it matter?" in my cowardliness, but she, after five years in torment, as soon as anyone says a word from the heart to her—it makes her forget everything, forgive everything, in her tears![309]

Grushenka had never before heard anyone speak of her in this way—to this point, she had been betrayed, objectified, an object of lust, so much so that she could no longer see any good in herself. But Alyosha's compassion had become for her the means of redemption:

> "[Alyosha] is the first, the only one who has pitied me, that's what it is. Why did you not come before, you angel?" She fell on her knees before him as though in a sudden frenzy. "I've been waiting all my life for someone like you, I knew that someone like you would come and forgive me. I believed that, nasty as I am, someone would really love me, not only with a shameful love!"[310]

Delightfully, Dostoevsky summarizes the truth of the matter through his exasperated villain, Rakitin: "Well, so you've saved the sinner?" he laughed spitefully. "Have you turned the Magdalene into the true path? Driven out the seven devils, eh? So you see the miracles you were looking out for just now have come to pass!"[311]

And so, indeed, they had!

This is Dostoevsky's secret—and Moses's, Plato's, Kierkegaard's, and Weil's—the wisdom of the seven sleepers. Neither our beloved Jerusalem nor Athens, Petersburg nor Paris, Vancouver nor Washington—nor anywhere else in God's blessed world—will be saved by the grand ideological movements of their time or ours. Not by Marxism or capitalism, conservatism or progressivism; not even by The Great Deconstruction. Nor should we expect redemption to come via signs and wonders, saints or heroes. So much trust is routinely and consistently misplaced and disappointed.

Instead, wherever ordinary people—as unholy and afflicted as we are—open our hearts to see the pain beneath another's sin and shed a tear in humble solidarity, we become participants in God's grace, agents in their salvation and in our own as well. This is what we mean by *co-suffering love*. This is how Christ comes to us today. This is the beauty that saves the world—where, from the ashes of affliction, collapse, and deconstruction, the phoenix of our faith might inexplicably rise again.

PART III

PROVOCATIONS:
OUT OF THE EMBERS–
FAITH AFTER FREEFALL

21

REVENANTS: FAITH RESURRECTED

The *Great* Reformation: sixteenth century.

The *Great* Awakenings: eighteenth and nineteenth centuries.

And now, The *Great* Deconstruction: twenty-first century.

All *great*—including their great necessity, great perils, and great possibilities.

In the previous section, our seven sleepers showed us both the *necessity* and the *perils* of the current wave of deconstruction. Whether it leads to authentic spiritual rejuvenation or sweeping apostasy will depend on how each person or movement navigates the pressing questions of divine goodness and human affliction, both revealed in Christ. What I am certain of is that we cannot skirt the questions. I think Pope Francis showed courage in asking these questions forthrightly in his Epiphany homily for 2022:

> The journey of life and faith demands a deep desire and inner zeal. Sometimes we live in a spirit of a "parking lot"; we stay parked, without the impulse of desire that carries us forward. We do well to ask: where are we on our journey of faith? Have we been stuck all too long, nestled inside a conventional, external and formal religiosity that no longer warms our hearts and changes our lives? Do our words and our liturgies ignite in people's hearts a desire to move toward God, or are they a "dead language" that speaks only of itself and to itself? It is sad when a community of believers loses its desire and is content with

"maintenance" rather than allowing itself to be startled by Jesus and by the explosive and unsettling joy of the Gospel.[312]

For the pope and his namesake, Francis of Assisi, Christ and his gospel are startling, explosive, and unsettling—but, for them, these words are adjectives of joy! This is true—or can be—for all of God's people, both collectively (the church) and personally.

WE ARE "REVENANTS"

On January 5, 2022, author Russell Moore penned a chilling headline for *Christianity Today*: "The Capitol Attack Signaled a Post-Christian Church, Not Merely a Post-Christian Culture."[313] To speak of a *post-Christian church* is alarming, reminiscent of Christ's ominous warning to the church in Ephesus: "So remember the place from which you have fallen. Repent, and do the works you did at the beginning. If not—if you don't repent—I will come and remove your lampstand out of its place" (Rev 2:5). Judgment does, after all, begin with the household of God.[314] Surely, an objective, dispassionate assessment of much of the church today is that it has become mired in compromise and corrupted by politicization, and it is experiencing a freefall of influence—and rightly so. That's the narrative of embers and ashes, and it's not wrong. It's also not the final word.

Out of chaos, good news today: the great gift of the Jesus Way is *not* the church's ability to survive its own self-inflicted death. Rather, we marvel at how it can continually die and rise again.

In the midst of the storm, hope today: even in the great darkness of the church's imperial aspirations and its corrosive choices to become the idolatrous escort of state power—even after the deep disillusionment of The Great Deconstruction—inexplicably, a Light shines. A Voice from elsewhere speaks. A gift of faith that defies reason somehow persists.

Watch for it. Wait for it. Pray for it.

I am reminded of G. K. Chesterton's prescient words of a century ago, describing the church not as an all-powerful institution but as an alternative society that rises phoenix-like from its own ashes because, against *our* better judgment, Christ has never abandoned or divorced her. Nor does he simply patch her up. This is the One who was dead and is now alive[315]—the risen Son of Man who can even resurrect the rigid cadaver of a post-Christian church or civilization:

What is this incomparable energy which appears first in one walking the earth like a living judgment and this energy which can die with a dying civilization and yet force it to a resurrection from the dead…?

There is an answer: it is an answer to say that the energy is truly *from outside* the world…. All other societies die finally and with dignity. We die daily. We are always being born again with almost indecent obstetrics. It is hardly an exaggeration to say that there is in historic Christendom a sort of unnatural life: it could be explained as a supernatural life. It could be explained as an awful galvanic life working in what would have been a corpse. For our civilization *ought* to have died, by all parallels, by all sociological probability, in the Ragnorak of the end of Rome. That is the weird inspiration of our estate: you and I have no business to be here at all. *We are all revenants*; all living Christians are dead pagans walking about.[316]

"*Revenants*"—those who have returned from the dead. Not zombies but living wonders of Christ's power. Lazarus. Dorcas. Chesterton includes you and me too. Who knows, perhaps the church that has perished, been sealed away, and now "stinketh" could yet respond to Jesus's teary command, "Come forth!"[317]

So, what we called "church" has, once again, largely imploded—its hypocrisy laid bare, its motives exposed, a victim of the Kool-Aid it served and drank in exchange for the true Vine. Those who have fled the sinking ship frequently forget their complicity and continue to imbibe in the same contempt they condemned in their Mother. Selective amnesia, perhaps. The disillusioned may have emerged from a religious nightmare, but they can't perceive they're still twitching through the dream paralysis of ideological possession. Woke?[318] Oh no, my dear.

So whence this hope? Just watch. Wait. Pray…for what? Christendom has had a series of revolutions, and in each one of them, Christianity has "died." "*Christianity has died many times and risen again; for it had a God who knew the way out of the grave.*"[319]

On my rough days, if I read too much Kierkegaard, Nietzsche, Dostoevsky, or even my beloved Simone Weil, I can sometimes forget that the story of the church, the history of humankind, and life itself are more than mere tragedy. Yes, Dostoevsky insists that "beauty will save the world,"[320] but the existentialists' realism and pathos about human existence can leave me feeling morose.

Remember, my deconstruction included the trauma of burnout[321]—inside the life of a beautiful community of Jesus-followers. It was more than weariness. Cynicism, irritability, loss of idealism, and withdrawal set in. Monks and sages of old distilled this condition to the word *despondency*. I still slip into it when I forget Chesterton's insights.

So, after I've huffed out a half-dozen heavy sighs, Eden (always alert) asks, "What's that big sigh for?" If I read my sighs right, my body is trying to let go, to expel the stale wind and open my lungs for some good news. Not just for the church but for me personally. I need the good news. For myself.

Is anyone else overdue for some good news? For sources of inspiration and surprising joy? Okay, here goes....

FAITH FROM ELSEWHERE

After deconstruction, after freefall, out of the embers, what? *Inexplicable hope.* Over and again, I encounter faith in those who had lost their faith and resigned from seeking. It's hard to describe, but, when it happened in me, it felt like "faith from elsewhere," a *gift* of faith. The faith or faithfulness of Christ sprouted in the frozen soil of my heart, like snowdrops and crocuses poking through the snow, responding to the spring Sun that may yet overcome my long, horrid winter.

All I've written to this point is WRONG if we conclude that life is merely a tragedy spiraling into the darkness of nonbeing. Nietzsche was ultimately wrong because, fundamentally, his personal heartbreaks led him to renounce love itself, which IS the life force of human existence and the locus of meaning.

No, life is *not just* tragedy. At the heart of the human experience, something strange and wonderful is going on. Inside the pitch-black reality of Nietzsche's prophetic vision:

+ Inexplicable *light* shines in our darkness—and we didn't light it.
+ Inexplicable *hope* rises in very fragile people—and it's not so easy to squelch.
+ Inexplicable *faith* in God appears—when we've lost all reason to have it.
+ Inexplicable *love* shows up—so sacrificial that normal people in real life become saintly.
+ Inexplicable *goodness* emanates from people you don't even believe are "Christians."

This is awesome! After all that darkness, where does that light come from—transcending reason, evidence, nihilism, and despair? How is it getting brighter?

FAITH FROM WITHIN

Yes, it is a light *from* elsewhere, but it is shining *here*. From *within!* Abbot Lazar sometimes shares his personal journal entries with me and permits me to publish them. On this light that shines from within, I've not seen another reflection as beautiful as this one:

> There is a place deep within the heart of a person into which Satan cannot see, neither penetrate (for, he cannot enter into the Kingdom of God). And there, the troubled soul can find a peace which passes all understanding; there the wounds from the arrows of the evil-one can find balm and healing, and the arrows cannot penetrate there to wound one again. Here, one does not pray with words or even with actions, but one weeps and the teardrops themselves are prayer and confession and rejoicing and hope fulfilled.
>
> Here, there is already a communication between God and the soul which is outside the realm of the laws of nature. Here, every thought is known, and every movement of the heart is incense rising up, up to the Creator.
>
> Here, one finds the Holy Spirit and understands something of the potential of the soul which longs to cooperate with God's Grace, and perceives that only its sins form a barricade to that complete cooperation which it so earnestly desires.
>
> Here, one cannot remain, no matter how one longs to—longs even to die if, by that, it could remain in this deep place in the heart, being "this day in paradise with Me." And this, of course, is only a shadow of what is yet to come for those who persevere to the end.[322]

FAITH FROM WITHIN THE AFFLICTED

The revelation of Good News—through Scripture and the incarnation of Jesus—is that God is gracious and compassionate. This God hears the cries of our groanings and *comes down*. This God always descends to be found among the lowly in the low places. I want you to notice that nearly every *major* revelation of God in Scripture occurred not in the glory of the temple but in the darkness and dread of afflicted people. That's where the prophets show up, where God shows up, where Jesus shows up.

This God comes down and comes *from within* a people in bondage for four hundred years—and liberates an entire nation.

This God comes down and comes *from within* a parched people wandering through the wilderness, struggling to understand where they're going—and he serves living water to the thirsty.

This God comes down and comes *from within* the cave of Adullam—and he reveals himself to the fugitive David, delivering him from the hand of Saul.

This God comes down and comes *from within* those under siege who are singing lamentations but also "Great is Thy Faithfulness" in the midst of their devastation—and he answers their cries.

This God comes down and comes *from the prophets* in exile—and brings hope in a strange land, offering a vision of their redemption but also proclaiming the God who suffers with them and among them.

This God comes down and comes *from within* the occupied territories through the incarnation of Jesus, the Light of the World—and preaches freedom for the oppressed, even while they're still downtrodden.

Most of all, the Light who comes down also shines *from within* the wounds he bears on the cross for the salvation of all. The epicenter of human evil (our crucifixion of God's Son) becomes the cruciform throne upon which Christ is revealed as *Pantocrator* (Ruler of the Universe—a term used ten times in Scripture[323]).

Where does this God come from? From HERE! Not in an otherworldly elsewhere or utopian future. *From within* THIS world, in MY humanity, in the REAL human condition, MY falling-apart world. Out of the embers of my deconstruction!

And that's exactly where some of our sleeping friends come alongside us…HERE. Not elsewhere. Dostoevsky showed us that human transformation does not come through the great social movements and their ideological promises but through the power of co-suffering love, through the tears of a prostitute who can weep for a murderer to cleanse him of guilt.

Kierkegaard showed us that while you can't escape your suffering, if you take up *your* cross—*your* wounded life—and participate in the grace of God in the midst of suffering, that's where you'll find meaning.

Camus showed us the light of sacrificial love shining with goodness from within an agnostic doctor whose heart was oriented toward the Light of self-giving love, without even knowing or naming that Light as "Jesus."

Weil refused to rationalize away evil or tragedy. She just admitted the distance between goodness and affliction, then revealed how the cross spans the difference.

TAKE UP YOUR CROSS

After all that, where was the light? *Here*, in this world, in the darkness. It looks like a cross. It looks like a cruciform and wounded God. It looks like the people who, by necessity and tragedy and evils done against them, have been thrown out and thrown down at the foot of the cross. The light shines through those who've experienced assault and those who've wondered where God is in all of this. We heard it from Frankl: God is hanging there with you. From within *your* wounds, the light shines. The wounds of every bullet hole, every shrapnel wound, every sexual assault, every molestation of a child—all our wounds are drawn up into him and into his self-sacrificial love.

And then he says, "I want you to take up your cross now." The Jesus Way of the cross (cruciformity) is just this: "active, voluntary, self-offering love which is the life of God himself."[324] That's the light that shines *from within*, the life that rises from the embers of deconstruction. The faith that is...

+ wise but not clever.

+ deep but not ethereal.

+ engaged but not ideological.

Jesus says, "You are the salt of the earth, the city on the hill, and the light on the lampstand"[325]—meaning that we are to embody the grace of the Beatitudes:[326] poverty of spirit, mourning, meekness, hunger for righteousness, mercy, purity of heart, peacemaking, and even persecuted witnesses for his sake. We pray, "Let your kingdom come," meaning "reign in me, here today, from the inside out." We surrender our lives to his care, trusting in the grace of today.

For me, some days, faith is playful, and, in the words of Paul Young, I trust the ripples of grace. I watch how the light yoke of grace radiates out to who-knows-where. Other days, faith for me feels more like an hour-by-hour hanging in there for dear life. I ask Jesus for the serenity to accept what I cannot change—*about me, about you, about stuff.* I ask for the courage to change what I can (to let go of egoism and love whoever is in front of me), and I ask for the grace to walk me up Calvary hill, whatever that might mean today. Not really sage wisdom here, but it is my honest confession and survival guide to deconstruction.

INEXPLICABLE: COLLEEN'S STORY

Years ago, my friend Colleen experienced a "from the embers" miracle of the inexplicable light, faith, and courage from within. It is a deeply personal story, but she gave me permission to share it whenever I feel it might help someone. I feel like now is one of those times.

Colleen came to our community having a background of early childhood abuse. She functioned very well in her family, in her community, and in our church through the gift of dissociation. For decades, she was able to compartmentalize her agony (like so many child victims) in order to function in her marriage, raise a family, and participate as a fruitful and creative contributor to those in her life.

However, the walls of dissociation tend to wear thin—by design, I believe—so that, by the time she reached her forties, her emotional and physical health began to slip dramatically. Her anxiety increased into panic and agoraphobia. When she needed to drive into Vancouver, the attacks would hit as she crossed the main bridge into the city. Her decline took a toll on her marriage. At that point, she was desperate for help and began meeting with Eden and me for prayer. We taught her to meet with Jesus in the "safe place" of her heart, where she could be raw with him and exchange her lies for his truth and her burdens for his grace-gifts. Because of how vulnerable she felt, the process took some years. She would pray, "Why don't you just fix me?" and the gentle voice of Light *from within* would say, tenderly, "We're going as fast as you can."

We learned to begin sessions in her safest place—she used the imagery of a tree in a field. With the eyes of her heart, she imagined sitting in the shelter of that tree with Jesus *on her right*. That detail was tremendously important to her, especially in light of this passage in Acts 2:

> [25] I saw the Lord always before me,
>   for he is at my right hand so that I will not be shaken;
> [26] therefore my heart was glad, and my tongue rejoiced;
>   moreover, my flesh will live in hope.
> [27] For you will not abandon my soul to Hades
>   or let your Holy One experience corruption.
> [28] You have made known to me the ways of life;
>   you will make me full of gladness with your presence.
>
> (Acts 2:25–28 NRSV)

This messianic prophecy was true of Jesus, and it became true for Colleen as well. The tree was her safe place because Jesus was there. That image gave her the courage to continue facing her past and whatever hard work that required. The tree was always a place where she could retreat when things got too scary.

However, in personal prayer one day, she closed her eyes, went to the tree, and sat with Jesus—but out in the field ahead of them, she saw a pickup truck. She immediately opened her eyes and fled the scene. Over the next two weeks, every time she tried to pray, she would involuntarily return to that vision. Jesus would say, "We need to go there," but she would refuse and pop out of the experience. Finally, Colleen let us know what was happening.

"I recognize that pickup truck. It belonged to my dad. In the truck's box—that's where he raped me." The scene was so full of trauma, hurt, shame, and rage that she could not see herself going there. But now, Jesus promised he would go with her and gave her the courage to do so. Such experiences can cause abreactions and re-traumatize the victims of violence. I no longer believe they are always necessary, wise, or kind. But since Jesus spoke this word directly to her and promised to go with her, Colleen decided it was time. Our only job was to be safe witnesses.

Jesus joined her at the truck, and, mercifully, the very first thing he did was remove her father from the memory. He then began removing visual symbols of her pain from her body—he released her of the trauma, hurt, anger, and shame. When all of the extreme emotions disappeared (literally, she could not feel them anymore), I asked if anything else remained in the truck apart from her (as a little girl), gentle Jesus, and his pure light. She said that she saw a shadow (whatever that means), and Jesus sent that away, too, without any ado.

That day marked a dramatic turning point for her. Out of the embers of her past and its progressive encroachment on her daily life, she began to get her life back. To me, it's remarkable that God *came down and shone from within that place*. It wasn't a straightforward exit. The light shone in her very darkest, pitch-black, hideous memory. Jesus came to the little girl so that Colleen's dissociated "child parts" would not be abandoned but instead integrated into her true self. And here's the truly breathtaking part—even her hell became central to her safe place! Jesus could have demolished the truck and sent it to the wrecker or dumped it in a bottomless pit. But, for whatever reason, it became a part of her safe place! It became her cross, her bread and butter (or wine, if you please). *From there*, she developed supernatural courage and resilience. *From there*, she began traveling over that bridge into Vancouver several times a month to serve men *just like her dad* at a soup kitchen called Mission Possible. *From there*, she faced into the darkness with Jesus, and the light that shone began to radiate outward into all of her life.

Colleen and her husband faced into the painful places of their marriage, as well, and discovered the power of confession, forgiveness, redemption, and reconciliation (still going strong!). Not only did Colleen overcome agoraphobia, but she developed friendships at a local dragon-boat club, and her team ended up crossing the sea to the world championships, returning with hardware!

Eden and I witnessed the formation of a new woman—a new creation—the kind of new life that has arisen many times throughout world history. The light shines *from within* darkness—from the cross that we imagine is weakness! *Au contraire!*

NO COMPARABLE PLAN B

I hope we take our deconstruction so seriously that we're not just winging our way through something so powerful and precious. I hope you'll ponder as far as possible:

+ where it goes
+ where it can go
+ where it can go desperately wrong
+ where you could go if you don't flee from it

The type of deconstruction I know directly and have seen as an eyewitness is a call back to the cross. There's just no comparable Plan B. None that Moses, David, Isaiah, Jesus, or Colleen were interested in, anyway. Or if there is a Plan B, it probably looks too much like the previous century (or five) and *WAY* too much like the ideological blizzard of the twenty-first century so far.

Others have experienced the pain of the human condition far more than I—folks like Colleen, for sure, and probably you too. But I want you to hear that what you've endured, even in your bruising and wounding, is *real* and it's *welcome* (really) because it's exactly the place where the One who co-suffered your wounds is waiting to meet you.

In the next two chapters, I believe you'll see this truth revealed through some heroes of faith I once mistook for marginal or exceptional. Now their lives inspire me to seek a more Christlike faith. They are trustworthy guides who lead us home to the true and unfamiliar heart of the Jesus Way.

22

"LET US GO OUT TO HIM": THREE CRUCIFORM SISTERS

"Jesus too suffered outside the gate,
so that he might make the people holy with his own blood.
So, then, let's go out to him, outside the camp, bearing his shame."
—Hebrews 13:12–13

I concluded the last chapter with an idea that could help us move from the stuckness of deconstruction into the new life of reconstruction: What if the faith of those who seem marginal—those who suffer "outside the gate"—could serve as homing beacons to the heart of Christian faith? The author of Hebrews used this type of analogy to encourage fellow Jews who found themselves excluded from the temple and synagogues that they considered their spiritual center and home. But if the choice is between returning to what was once our secure place or abandoning Jesus, then far better to join Christ outside the city, where he was crucified. If the heartland of Christianity is the cross beyond the walls, then the disenfranchised who gather there may seem marginal to society, including the religious establishment and the ideological influencers. But, in truth, it's the downtrodden who've located the unvarnished gospel amid their own trials.

Once we see that reality, our quest for the kingdom of Christ and his righteousness (justice), à la Matthew 6:33, calls to us, "Let's go out to him, outside the camp"—and yes, perchance, "bearing his shame" with those who arrived ahead of us to kneel there.

And who are these models of cruciform faith who define the fulcrum of faith? Who are the candidates who join the Hebrews 11 hall of fame? So many saints to choose from! But in this chapter and the next, I will focus on a few individuals who have inspired me by their cruciform example, those whose integrity rebukes me to tears in the very best way. By that, I mean they invite me to courage rather than simply shaming me, even if I despair of emulating them. I can't be like them, yet they don't chase me off. Rather, they tell me, as I am, "*Let's go out to him*," and I weep at their welcome. I weep because, out of their embers (sometimes literal), Christ rises in me.

The exemplars I'll refer to are, first, three cruciform sisters from different eras—Ann Roza, Blandina, and Lydia—followed (in the next chapter) by the great Black[327] preacher, scholar, and activist Howard Thurman. Their stories and example carry such gravitas, such a solemn and sacred message, such a Christlike gospel, that they eclipse even our seven sleepers. I dare even say that the sleepers from part II (with the exception of Weil) are, by comparison, moons that reflect these Christ-transfigured suns! I may sound effusive, but you may find I don't exaggerate. The brevity of their stories is no indication of the depth of their souls, which seem to open up into the bottomless heart of God! First, our humble and humbling sisters.

SISTER ANN ROZA

It is the first week of March 2021. I am tracking news reports of unfolding events in a faraway city. The site is Myitkyina, capital of Kachin State in Myanmar. Crowds have filled the streets, protesting the coup that has deposed Aung San Suu Kyi's elected government. Militarized security forces have gathered for a crackdown, armed with tear gas and live ammunition. The day will end in bloodshed, just one more stage toward the ever-rising escalation of violence. Some sources will prematurely call this Myanmar's "Tiananmen moment."[328]

Amid the swirling chaos and inevitable clash, a senior nun dressed in a white tunic and dark veil kneels before a line of police near her cathedral, arms outstretched in a cruciform, pleading with junta members not to assault and arrest their compatriots. "If you want to do this, you'll have to come through me," says Sister Ann Roza Nu Tawng, also heavily armed, but with the unworldly weapons of prayer, courage, truth, and love.

Two officers fall to their knees, facing her to her left and her right, hands clasped in earnest, begging her to stand down or to understand their predicament.

"We are from here. We have to do this. Please stay away from here," they say.

Are they Buddhists? Or Christians? I can't tell. Sister Ann does not relent. Her outspread hands signify her conviction that she has already laid down her life—what then can they do to her? She fully expects to die this day. She doesn't. Instead, she becomes one of the public grieving witnesses whose voices echo around the globe on news feeds for the world to see.

In the aftermath, she reflects,

I saw police, military and water cannon following the protesters.

…they opened fire and started beating the protesters. I was shocked and I thought today is the day I will die. I decided to die. I was asking and begging them not to do it and I told them the protesters didn't commit any [crime]. I was crying like a mad person. I was like a mother hen protecting the chicks.[329]

Sister Ann's cruciform faith both embarrasses and inspires me.

She confronts the murky reflection of what attempts to pass as Christianity on my continent, exposing, for example, the feigned victimhood of those who considered basic COVID-19 restrictions to be some sort of great "persecution." And she speaks just as loudly (without words) to those whose intolerance of different perspectives has expanded into a narrative of how they have been spiritually abused by those who dared disagree with them. "Deconstruct this!" she shouts in my mind.

Sister Ann is at least a foot *shorter* than I am, and over a decade *younger*, but, before her, I feel small and immature. And rightly so, I think. It's not shame that I feel. Just the recognition of our relative spiritual stature and her invitation: *"Let's go out to him."*

BLANDINA OF LYON

Sister Ann's narrative reminds me that the Christian story runs both broader and deeper than the problems I may have with my own particular church assembly, denomination, or culture. She also opens the door to a long history of Christian faithfulness. We should certainly condemn corruption in the institution (the church as an "it"), but we ought not forget the devoted martyrs for love in our spiritual genealogy (the church as a "she").

Sister Ann's outstretched arms also recalled for me two other women—in these instances, they died for their faith in the cruciform posture. Their stories are moving, but I warn that they include some graphic descriptions of violence. So, again, for those who know they shouldn't be exposed to such triggers, I believe Sister Ann's example is sufficient reading for this chapter.

In his classic history of the early church, *Historia Ecclesiastica*, Eusebius recounts the gruesome and glorious martyrdom of an enslaved teenage girl, Blandina of Lyon. She is venerated as one of the band of martyrs tortured and killed by the Romans in AD 177 when Marcus Aurelius was emperor.

Eusebius preserves Blandina's memory by citing an epistle from "the Churches of Vienne and Lyons to their brethren in Asia and Phrygia."[330] In that letter, we have eyewitness accounts of a series of events, both tragic and triumphant.

Popular malice toward Christians had been stirred up in the city, where the strategy was to arrest and torture the slaves of Christians until they were willing to confess falsely that their households practiced incest and cannibalism. Christians—slaves and masters alike—were imprisoned and horribly tormented to try to make them recant their faith in Christ. The steadfast in faith were transported to the Amphitheater of the Three Gauls for their execution at the claws and jaws of wild beasts.

The Christians framed these trials as "combat"—they considered renunciation under duress a defeat, while Blandina's victory was described as "the courage and resolution to make a free and open confession of her faith," even unto death.

Fellow believers were concerned that Blandina would be too frail to endure the cruelty commanded by the Roman legate, but the letter reports how, despite every imaginable torment, her executioners exhausted both their methods and their energy, to no avail. She held firm to her confession: "I am a Christian; no wickedness is transacted among us." And so, she was sent off to the amphitheater for another round of tortures. What happened next marks the apex of our story:

> Blandina was suspended on a stake, and exposed to be devoured by
> the wild beasts who should attack her. And because she appeared as

if hanging on a cross, and because of her earnest prayers, she inspired the combatants with great zeal. For they looked on her in her conflict, and beheld with their outward eyes, in the form of their sister, him who was crucified for them, that he might persuade those who believe in him, that every one who suffers for the glory of Christ has fellowship always with the living God.[331]

After she had remained thus exposed for some time, and none of the beasts could be provoked to touch her, she was untied, carried back to prison, and *reserved for another combat; in which she was to gain a complete victory* over her malicious adversary the devil, (whom she had already foiled and discomfited on several occasions,) and to animate the brethren to the battle by her example. Accordingly, though she was a poor, weak, inconsiderable slave, yet, by putting on Christ, she became an overmatch for all the art and malice of her enemy, and, by a glorious conflict, attained to the crown of immortality.[332]

After days of suffering at the stake and being forced to witness others being tortured, she was dragged to her third round of "battle." Blandina was scourged, then grilled on a fiery grate, wrapped in a net, and tossed around on the horns of a wild steer. In the end, we read that her captors finished her with a dagger.[333]

Such a waste.

Was it?

I can feel in her faithful testimony a stinging rebuke to shallow Christianity and the feeble reasons I might give to compromise or abandon my faith. But again, as with Sister Ann, Blandina's outstretched hands evoke and invoke the vision of Christ crucified—her companions saw Christ in her and were renewed by his real presence before them. She, too, speaks to me, "*Let us go out to him.*"

HOLY MARTYR LYDIA

Lydia Grammakova[334] (1901–28) was the daughter of a Russian priest in Ufa, Russia. Widowed by civil war at nineteen, she found work in the offices of the Forestry Department. There she was known for taming the foul-mouthed and ill-tempered lumberjacks who came her way. Party chiefs took note and kept an eye on her, but the secret police (GPU) were unaware she attended (literal) underground meetings in the Catacomb Church. They were stymied in their plots and investigations against the growing faith movement.

Secretly, Lydia began typing and distributing brochures that included sermons, prayers, and stories about the saints. Unfortunately, her typewriter's letter *k* had a misshapen stem, and, eventually, authorities traced the leaflets back to Lydia and arrested her. The GPU knew that since she was the distributor, breaking her could potentially bring down the entire Catacomb network across the region. For ten days, they questioned her day and night without reprieve, but "like a sheep led to the slaughter, she did not utter a word."[335] At that point, she was shuffled downstairs into a cellar room for grilling by "special command." Lydia was so depleted by now that Private Cyril Atayev, a twenty-three-year-old Red Army guard, had to carry her to the interrogation chamber. Sensing a seed of compassion in his soul, she whispered to him, "May Christ save you"—words that pierced his heart as he listened to her screams through the next ninety minutes of ruthless torture. As with Blandina, this young saint exhausted her abusers as they took turns beating her. They asked, "Aren't you in pain? You are screaming and crying; that means it's awful, doesn't it?"

She whimpered, "Painful! Lord, how painful!"

"Then why won't you talk?" they demanded. "It will only be more painful."

"I can't…I can't," she groaned. "He won't allow…."

"Who won't allow?"

"God won't allow!"

In desperation and hatred, the interrogators decided to escalate their strategy to sexual assault. The four torturers called in Private Atayev to take part. There lay Lydia, splayed out in restraints—cross-like—prepared for the rape. When he realized what "special command" was about to do and that they expected him to participate, young Cyril's compassion for Lydia and his revulsion at their wickedness overcame him, and he snapped. He spontaneously drew his revolver and shot two of the soldiers. The third struck him from behind with the butt of his gun. Cyril turned to grab him by the throat, but the fourth fired a round that took him down.

Bleeding to death beside the young saint, Cyril Atayev's last words echoed the thief on the cross: "Saint, take me with you!"[336]

Lydia was able to smile, and her face shone like Saint Stephen's when he was stoned to death.[337] "I will take you," was her final utterance.

Author Vladimir Moss described the impact of this powerful encounter:

The sound and meaning of this conversation opened a door to the other world, and terror darkened the consciousness of the two GPU men who remained alive. With insane shouts, they began to shoot the helpless victims who threatened them, and they shot until both their revolvers had been emptied. Those who had come running at the shots led them away, shouting insanely, and themselves fled from the room, seized by an unknown terror.[338]

Those two GPU interrogators would ultimately die of the experience—one of insanity, the other of "nervous shock" (PTSD?). The latter shared his confession to a friend, Sergeant Alexis Ikonikov, through whom we came to know Lydia's story. The description of her faithful martyrdom-witness caused Ikonikov to turn to Christ, and his zeal in recounting it led to his own martyrdom.

I needn't analyze the morality of Cyril Atayev's act of violence on Lydia's behalf. I can say that I'm grateful she was spared the demonic gang rape. Nor need I explain why the GPU deaths were demonic, not divine. What matters, what moves me to tears, and the reason I have an icon of Lydia on my wall is that, in her death, she became Christ to Atayev and likewise ushered him into paradise.

When I think of the toxic images and examples of God that have pervaded Christianity and driven so many people to abandon Christ, something about Sister Ann, Blandina, and Lydia splashes my face with glacier-fresh, living water. Their cruciform witness cleanses the spiritual cataracts that cloud my vision with false christs. They purify my heart to see Christ in their pain-contorted, radiant faces.

I hear them saying, *"Let's go out to him, outside the camp, bearing his shame."*

WHY THE MARTYR STORIES?

Why am I sharing these stories? What value does hearing them add to faith in crisis? Are these gruesome testimonies merely gratuitous violence, or do they have real value for those who meditate on them? What is gained by recalling them? What is lost by forgetting them?

I'll begin with the historical fact that the various collections we know as "The Lives of the Saints" began as martyr stories. The early accounts weren't loaded with fanciful, magical tales to titillate the imagination—that came later. Rather, early hagiography offers us thousands of examples of courageous faith passing through the fire of unimaginable duress. The "mother church" tradition (Roman Catholics, Orthodox, and High Anglican believers) honors these saints with songs, poetry, and prayers every day of the year. Later, the Anabaptists, Quakers, Ukrainians, Russians, and others would add their voices to these anthologies. In these ways, the historic church has kept their lost loved ones in their minds and hearts and regards them as having entered the "great cloud of witnesses,"[339] believes they are alive with the Lord, and invokes their help and ongoing intercession.

Second, rather than scattering under persecution, the church has historically experienced phenomenally rapid growth—in breadth of converts and depth of faith—as a direct result of these trials. In AD 197, Tertullian, a Catholic theologian based in Carthage, North Africa, wrote, "The blood of the martyrs is the seed of the church."[340] Killing Christians was as effective at stamping out Christianity as trying to eradicate dandelions by blowing their seeds to the wind. How could this be?

Unlike other pogroms that successfully broke the back of insurgencies such as the slave revolts and Jewish revolts, Christianity exuded unshakeable faith in the resurrection and experienced this supernatural inner conviction when faced with death. It was not a psychological state they could work up, but rather a real and existential grace given in the fires (sometimes actual) of persecution.

When witnesses beheld *the way in which these martyrs died*, they recognized something so profoundly absent in their own lives that, instead of being intimidated, masses of them converted. On a tragic side note, all too often, over the centuries, the persecutors of such martyrs claimed to be Christians themselves. Nonetheless, those who suffered were transfigured into the image of Christ in plain view.

If we take these three cruciform sisters as examples, the combination of their suffering, their faithfulness, and even their outstretched limbs fashioned them into living icons who made Christ present bodily to those who looked on. Zechariah's words, fulfilled in Christ, were fulfilled again in Sister Ann, Blandina, and Lydia:

> I will pour out a spirit of grace and compassion upon the household of David and the inhabitants of Jerusalem,
>
> And they will gaze on me, the one they have pierced,
>
> And seeing my death, they will beat their breasts as a spouse grieves the death of their beloved, and they will grieve with the grief of a parent who has lost their firstborn [or "the firstborn," hinting a messianic fulfillment].
>
> (Zech 12:10, my translation)

The "order of operations" in this passage is important. First, this encounter with Christ in martyrdom is an act of God's outrageous grace and compassion toward the martyrs, the witnesses, and even the perpetrators, if they can receive it. Further, the martyrs are not merely being persecuted, tortured, or killed. They are being set free and glorified!

> Precious in the sight of the LORD
>   is *the death of his saints.*
> O LORD, I am your servant;
>   I am your servant, the son of your maidservant.
> You have loosed my bonds.
>
> (Ps 116:15–16 ESV)

They experienced the light *from within*. God came to them, in Christ, in their suffering.

In the martyr's passage through death to eternal life, God's grace also extends to those who gaze on these events with wide-eyed wonder. They want to tear themselves away from the ugliness but are compelled by the beauty.

> Did e'er such love and sorrow meet,
>
> Or thorns compose so rich a crown?[341]

So, in gazing on the martyrs, those with eyes to see behold Christ. They begin to recognize their complicity in his death. They begin to mourn for him as if he were their own spouse or child. They begin to identify him as theirs and themselves as his. And he becomes their Christ. I don't know why or how some would continue to mock and hate and flail while others are healed and saved as Christ gazes back at them. It's inexplicable. So, I'll leave it there.

OUT OF THE EMBERS: INSPIRATION

I've pondered how the stories and songs of the martyrs can capture our hearts, even by third-party testimony. How do they inspire us? What values do they create in us? How might they form our ethics? Do they shift our perspective?

I sent the three stories to a friend who experienced long-term suffering, violence, and trauma. I asked, "How does hearing these stories speak to you? Are they just triggers? Or do they help in some strange way?" She responded:

> I think for me personally, they relate, although I would never put myself on this level. But especially Lydia: during her massive torture...she stayed close to Jesus! During ALL of it, she never wavered. And then in the worst, she showed the grace of Jesus. The courage to never stray from his love and to continue loving others is pure love and courage and trust in Christ. She became like Christ.[342]

Yes! And in some mystical way, *she became Christ.*

There's more. My youngest son, Dominic, pointed out how these accounts root our faith in real-life stories—in the history that is the soil where our faith grew and how we became "the Way." Christian faith is not a nebula of abstract ideas and doctrines. Such stories have practical value because they contextualize what we believe about Christ into how these women coped with real struggles.

The stories ask us hard questions and provide perspective. Were these martyrs idealists who died needlessly? Should they have compromised? Or lied? Why not pretend to renounce Christ as a pretense? Or is denying Christ to save your life an actual betrayal? What compromises has Christianity made to political, economic, or social trends that already constitute apostasy? And why would I balk at dying for Christ while others die for much more dubious causes?

The martyrs also guide us in terms of our values, ethics, and alliances. With a steady dose of their medicine, we are reminded of what should be obvious commitments that have become slippery in Christian culture. Here are a few:

+ *Don't torture and kill people. Reject violence as a means to govern.*

+ *Don't become insurgents. Reject violence against those who govern.*

+ *Don't abandon the afflicted ones. Stand, kneel, sit, and be with the oppressed.*

+ *Don't lash out in retaliation. Reject violence as a means to advocacy and allyship.*

+ *Be faithful to the Jesus Way.*

Finally, let's not mistake the meekness in these women who faced death peaceably and courageously as acquiescence to moral darkness or social injustices. They weren't arrested, beaten, or killed for quietly going about their business. Nor were Jesus, James, Stephen, Peter, or Paul. Something about their way of overcoming evil with good deeply disturbed the ruling powers, both those who practiced evil *and* those who thought violence was the way to overcome it. Before the cruciform throne of Christ the King, and before his victorious saints—these women—their opponents' way to peace-on-earth utopia is exposed as weak, naïve, and terribly small. As for the martyrs' faith, yes, it is inexplicable. But in the end, such faith has overcome the schemes of even Pharaoh and Caesar. And now we call our children Lydia and our dogs Nero. Whose way will we follow? Whose mark will we bear?

"Let us go out to him, outside the camp."

23

JESUS AND THE DISINHERITED: GOD'S BLACK VOICES

To say that The Great Deconstruction has decimated confidence and attendance in the Western church is a gross understatement, if "decimated" literally means culling just ten percent. The fallout has been much more severe than that. And the hemorrhaging is, by most accounts, primarily self-inflicted. It's not Roman centurions or Islamic radicals or atheist scoffers who are emptying the pews. If we listen to the "be-leavers" I referred to earlier, judgment begins with the household of God.[343] I needn't repeat the factors of our demise. My question is, does that mean that most of the church in America (for example) is an ash heap in denial, an empty lampstand, left without a witness?

As I scan the ruins, I hear the martyrs again beckoning, *"Let's go out to him, outside the camp"* (Heb 13:13). I interpret their call as an invitation to sit at the feet of those beyond the margins who've "borne his shame" as the disenfranchised. What if the outsiders have *not* lost the plot? What if those who've suffered "outside the camp" somehow preserve the gospel intact by their proximity to the cross? What if our *reconstruction* begins with a new pattern of intent listening to their stories?

Whose stories? Pick a marginalized group—those with a history of oppression as outsiders to privilege and power. It could be women, refugees, racial or sexual minorities, people with disabilities, victims of occupation or genocide—you name it. If they've experienced their disadvantage or subjugation as a point of communion with Christ, their gospel is a truth I need to hear. I've sought and found that gospel "voice from elsewhere" since the early 1990s. Maybe that's why I'm not cynical about Jesus or his Way—and why my crash wasn't the end of faith for me. You just need to know where to look. The gospel voices aren't really so hard to find. *Maybe we are.* Hard to find, I mean. For many of us, hunkering down for safety in our suburban ghettos can insulate us "inside the camp" until we imagine the only deconstruction available is apostasy. It's not.

More recently, I've chosen to tune my heart to the Black voices whose gospel experience and message align with Christian martyrs, from Blandina to Lydia. As a white male of considerable privilege, I will stack up caveats up front: (1) I won't presume to speak for or to the Black community. I'll only share what I hear them teach me about Jesus. (2) What I share won't represent the breadth of Black perspectives—Black activists, theologians, and preachers don't speak in unison. They don't all agree, for example, on Martin Luther King Jr.'s commitment to nonviolent resistance. My central focus will be what I've digested from books and lectures by James H. Cone and Howard Thurman (the spiritual mentor to MLK). (3) I don't presume to interpret them alone. My listening has leaned heavily on the wisdom and nuance of my friend Felicia Murrell,[344] whom I especially trust as Thurman's faithful interpreter.

As we hear God's Black voices through Cone and Thurman's analyses of culture, Christianity, and the gospel, we enter the treasury—and trauma—of the Black experience in America that unveils Jesus's life and death more clearly than what I inherited as a white Evangelical. The fundamental connection for me is the intersection of two images—the cross and the lynching tree.

THE CROSS AND THE LYNCHING TREE: HEARING JAMES CONE

I once imagined *lynching* as nighttime murders by anonymous Klansmen hunting down and hanging Black men in the secrecy of darkness. I was oblivious to the scope, popularity, and publicity of these crimes against humanity. One reason for many people's lack of awareness of this atrocity is that white Christians (the main perpetrators) would rather move on without being reminded about their history. If we can't even stomach seeing a Black athlete wearing an "End Racism" sticker on the back of their jersey, then facing the sordid facts about lynching will probably feel like a bout of shingles. Further, according to James Cone in *The Cross and the Lynching Tree*, Black people find "visions of black bodies dangling from southern trees, surrounded by jeering white mobs almost too excruciating to recall."[345]

The topic requires a careful reading, highlighting, and dog-earing of Cone's entire book—I must leave you to it. But summarizing the history of "lynching fever" in sickening detail, we discover that approximately five thousand Black people were lynched in America, most of whose names have been identified. And these were not merely covert nighttime hangings.

> Burning the black victim slowly for hours was the chief method of torture. Lynching became a white media spectacle, in which prominent newspapers, like the *Atlanta Constitution*, announced to the public the place, date, and time of the expected hanging and burning of black victims. Often as many as ten to twenty thousand men, women, and children attended the event. It was a family affair, a ritual celebration of white supremacy, where women and children were often given the first opportunity to torture black victims— burning black flesh and cutting off genitals, fingers, toes, and ears as souvenirs. Postcards were made from the photographs taken of black victims with white lynchers and onlookers smiling as they struck a pose for the camera.[346]

Unreal. Thus, lynchings were a spectacle event enacted in plain sight with the tacit approval of local and state authorities. Far from illegal, lynching was an extralegal extension of white supremacy, meant to keep a racist boot on the throats of those who imagined emancipation had freed them. As with Roman crucifixions, the purpose—other than being a euphoric catharsis of cruelty— was to intimidate. The idea was, "You could be next," even for *perceived* disrespect of white neighbors. Forgetting "your place" or casting a glance in the wrong direction might be all it took for a young Black man to be barbecued.

Horrid. How easily we can say, "Okay, I've heard enough," and plug our ears. Don't. Reckon, instead, the emotional cost to generations of Black communities who could never just avert their gaze. The chronic stress hypervigilance imposed over a lifetime is unimaginable.

But Cone's legacy runs far deeper than demanding we remember a national atrocity. He draws explicit parallels between the cross and the lynching tree in order to locate the heart of living faith in America. Both the cross and the lynching tree became symbols of torture and terror involving public humiliation—a degradation of dignity. Cone reminds us that Jesus, too, was "paraded, mocked and whipped, pierced, derided and spat upon, tortured for hours in the presence of jeering crowds for popular entertainment."[347]

The correspondence between crucifixion and lynching was not lost on Black people of faith—they quite literally knew what it was to be crucified. When their hymns say, "I was there when they nailed him to the tree,"[348] the cross and the lynching tree are one indivisible experience of Christ's co-suffering union with God's Black children.

Where is Christ? *There he is, hanging (as ever) from a tree.*

"Let's go out to him, outside the camp, bearing his shame" (Heb 13:13).

But also, *claiming his victory.*

This is and always has been the paradox of the cross and the martyrs—that the Lamb so brutally slain is the gospel's critique of worldly power and the revelation of true authority: divine love, liberation, and hope. As we seize the power of the cross, the lynching tree loses its power because it is not the final word. Defeat and death are inverted—no longer ultimate. "The final word about black life is not death on a lynching tree but redemption in the cross—a miraculously transformed life found in the God of the gallows.... The cross places God in the midst of crucified people, in the midst of people who are hung, shot, burned, and tortured."[349] A faith formed in that forge is not easily erased—not by murderous racists and, I would think, not by the cultured despisers of faith who pose as deconstructionists.

Rather than rejecting the gospel message because of the satanic hypocrisy of white Christians, the Black community saw the cross as a source of spiritual strength in their resistance to violence and hatred, including the temptation to mirror it. They didn't abandon the message of Christ crucified because of the failure of his church to live and carry his message—they *are* his church, *they* carry his message, because, like Simon of Cyrene[350] of Africa, they have carried his cross and, in fact, thousands have also hung on it. What no lynching tree could strip from them was their faith in the crucified One. Instead, the lynching tree became a reference point to their identity in Christ.

Further, the Black community saw in their struggle the story of Jacob the wrestler, who refused to let go of the Angel of the Lord without receiving the promised blessing of a new identity.[351]

O wrestlin' Jacob, Jacob, days a-breakin';
   I will not let thee go!
O wrestlin' Jacob, Jacob, days a-breakin';
   He will not let me go!...

O, Jacob do hang from a tremblin' limb,
   He would not let him go!
O, Jacob do hang from a tremblin' limb;
   De Lord will bless my soul.[352]

The resilient vision continues to flourish in the robust and active(ist) faith of Black America today. So, despite gleeful autopsy reports of the end of Christianity, I'm inclined to check for a pulse among those outside the camp, in closest proximity to the cruciform experience. I no longer see that investigation as optional. Cone pointedly asks,

> If the American empire has any similarities with that of Rome, can one really understand the theological meaning of Jesus on a Roman cross without seeing him first through the image of blacks on the lynching tree? Can American Christians see the reality of Jesus' cross without seeing it as the lynching tree?[353]

I once thought I could. But now? *God's Black voices have my attention.*

LOVE OR PERISH: HEARING HOWARD THURMAN

Among the greatest of God's Black voices in the twentieth century, Howard Thurman (1899–1981) stands tall as an activist, preacher, and scholar of just peacemaking. Thurman, along with Mahatma Gandhi, took up Leo Tolstoy's "religion of Jesus" (Sermon on the Mount living) and became a spiritual father and mentor to Martin Luther King Jr. and other civil rights leaders. Thurman was the grandson of a former slave named Nancy Ambrose, who rooted her commitment to a kingdom of justice and love in Christ's solidarity with the disinherited. Jesus's firsthand experience of Roman oppression struck a familiar chord to her and her family. Christ's life and message spoke directly into their daily reality.

Thurman was convinced that Jesus was neither deluded nor naïve in his goal (realizing the dream of a banquet where everyone belongs and no one need fear the Other) or his means (unconditional love, radical empathy, and scandalous forgiveness).

But what happens when the agents of domination are not a Roman legion but members in good standing of status quo Christianity—Christ's sterile counterfeit or principal persecutor?[354] For Thurman, there is no confusing his *religion of Jesus* with the church of white supremacy. And although he forged his vision in the realpolitik of racial discrimination and violence, he could not be compromised by the "three hounds of hell"—*fear, deception, and hatred.*

Thurman saw that the Jesus Way of loving one's enemies was the only practical path to liberation—personal and social, internal and external. Following Jesus's manifesto *"the kingdom of God is within you"* means that, ultimately, what reigns over you is *not* out there. That battle is won or lost in one's own heart. Thus, resistance begins by internalizing the victory of Christ over those damnable hounds, which Thurman deconstructs with strategic genius in his masterwork *Jesus and the Disinherited.*

THE THREE HOUNDS OF HELL

1. FEAR

The first hound, *fear,* forever tracks the poor and the dispossessed, growling at them in their isolation and helplessness, snapping at them with the perpetual threat of violence. Jesus knew that once that bone-shivering fear is internalized, we're no longer free.[355] The fear that once served as a safety alarm, "a kind of protective mechanism for the weak, finally becomes death for the self. The power that saves turns executioner."[356] Fear kills hope and ambition, and it corrodes the very self, stripping it of meaning and identity.

Is there any help for this condition? YES. The disease of fear is overcome when we know who we are. Thurman recalls his grandma citing a slave minister who held secret meetings: "How everything in me quivered with the pulsing tremor of raw energy when, in her recital, she would come to the triumphant climax: *'You—you are not niggers. You—you are not slaves. You are God's children.'"*[357]

Jesus's revelation that God is our Father and that each one of us is God's child can have a profound impact on us both personally and socially. Knowing that *I am God's beloved child* and that I (me specifically, individually) am held in *Love's care* drives out fear, stabilizes the ego, and empowers courage in the face of overwhelming odds—even the threat of death. Knowing who I am— *forever God's beloved son or daughter*—establishes inner security "in which fear cannot possibly survive."[358]

Yes, he says, *life is hard—hard as a crucible steel.* But Thurman recalls his mother's promise: "God will take care of us." And if we know *God cares about us,* we become "unconquerable from within or without," regardless of external pressures. Faith in God's care overcomes fear and transforms it into "the power to strive, to achieve, and not to yield." [359]

2. DECEPTION

Thurman's second hound—*deception*—surprised me. Those in power often use patterns of deception to deprive people of their basic human rights and to justify why such systems can't change. That message is surely relevant, but it wasn't Thurman's most urgent focus. He was concerned about bringing healing to the powerless who themselves practice deception to gain a foothold in their hostile world.

He empathizes with those who use deceit as a strategy for survival, but he rejects its use because he sees how deadly losing one's moral compass is to the soul: "The penalty of deception is to *become* a deception, with all sense of moral discrimination vitiated. A man who lies habitually becomes a lie, and it is increasingly impossible for him to know when he is lying and when he is not." [360]

Instead of deception for survival, Thurman opts for Jesus's mandate to *"let your yes mean yes, and your no mean no"* (Matt 5:37 CEB) be a liberating command to be "simply, directly truthful, whatever may be the cost in life, limb, or security." [361] Truth-telling may seem not to *work* in the moment—it might even be deadly. But he sees how truth is a long game with a proven track record and a threefold thrust:

+ For ourselves: sincere truth-telling means the individual stands innocent under divine scrutiny—blameless in the presence of God.

+ For our world: complete sincerity multiplies into movements that grow until the truth is vindicated and irrepressible.

+ For our enemy: the power of truth may even extend to deliver the oppressor—it transposed the martyrdom of Stephen into the conversion of Saul of Tarsus. [362]

3. HATE

By now we recognize how closely Thurman follows Christ's Sermon on the Mount. By seeing the parallels between Christ's context and his own, he understood Jesus's strategy for taking the axe to the root of the tree [363]—to the fear, the deception, and now also the hate that underlies and feeds injustice.

Thurman laments the ways our nations masquerade racial hatred as patriotism during times of war, draping it in a flag to make it respectable and even sacred. Further, he shakes his head at Christianity's ineffectual efforts to get rid of hatred "by preachments, by moralizing, by platitudinous judgments" [364] instead of evaluating its causes in the lives of the people possessed by it.

Thurman felt that hatred could not be defined—only described, as follows:

1. Hatred begins in situations where we have *contact without fellowship*.

2. Contact without fellowship is *"strikingly unsympathetic"*—incapable of empathy for the Other—and governs relations between the powerful and the weak.

3. This unsympathetic understanding expresses itself as *ill will* in action.

4. The ill will, "when dramatized in a human being, becomes *hatred walking on the earth*."[365]

So far, Thurman's outline is clear and simple, but he presses further to understand how hatred functions and why it is so alluring to the powerless. The perceived payoffs cause us to cling to our hatred once we're in its iron grip—every vice becomes a vise. What does hatred seem to offer the disinherited whom Thurman hopes to free from its chains? He theorizes five ways that hatred ensnares his people.

+ Hatred, born out of bottled-up resentment, is distilled into a vitality that provides *a basis for self-realization*. Hatred promises to rebuild a sense of individual significance in those who were so despised that they had despised themselves.

+ Hatred thus becomes a *source of validation*, significance, and defiance "hammered out of the raw materials of injustice."

+ Hatred as self-realization generates *surplus energy and endurance* at the disposal of the individual's needs and ends.

+ Hatred as self-realization can then create an *illusion of righteousness*, spinning bitterness and resentment as righteous indignation.

+ Hatred serves as *protective armor*, seeming to defend us from moral disintegration. Our self-righteous hatred *immunizes* us from loss of self-respect as we do unto others what we would never dream of doing ordinarily.[366]

Well, I'm sold! But Thurman wasn't. He saw how deeply hatred sinks its hooks into the souls of the disinherited. As long as the weak are convinced that hatred serves a creative purpose, indispensable to surviving with dignity, it cannot be dislodged. But, he insists, Jesus understood this danger perfectly. He saw the gruesome truth, the terrible cost that hatred exacts on its victims:

> Hatred destroys finally the core of the life of the hater. While it lasts, burning in white heat, its effect seems positive and dynamic. But at last it turns to ash, for it guarantees a final isolation from one's fellows. It blinds the individual to all values of worth, even as they apply to himself and to his fellows. Hatred bears deadly and bitter fruit.... Hatred cannot be controlled once it is set in motion. The logic of the development of hatred is death to the spirit and disintegration of ethical and moral values.... The urgent needs of the personality for creative expression are starved to death.[367]

In that case, I'd like to refund my hatred, please. This is why Jesus completely rejected hate and its deceptive charms. He saw clearly *how hatred is death*, shriveling the mind and shrinking the heart, severing our communion with his Father, who is the lifeblood of our identity. Christ came to grant us life, while hatred is the thief that steals, kills, and destroys.[368]

Exorcising the disease of hatred—as well as the other two hounds of hell—requires an alternative response: a positive, thorough course of treatment and action. For Thurman, *love* alone is sufficiently potent. And the love he describes is not denial, repression, or sentimental niceness. So, what is it?

LOVE

Against fear, deception, and hatred, and in his realistic diagnosis of his dire social situation, Jesus's clear-minded prescription for liberation, inside and out, is love: love God with all that you have. Love your neighbors—potentially anyone.[369] Love the stranger—even the Samaritans. Love your enemies—even the Romans and their collaborators. Jesus "projected a dream, the logic of which would give to *all* the need for security. There would be room for *all*, and no man would be a threat to his brother."[370]

"His brother" (male and female)—there's the rub. That's where Thurman's Jesus is most challenging, offensive, even dangerous. How does one begin to see the perpetrator as a brother or sister, especially when rage has functioned as a shield for the dignity of one's personhood? It's one thing for the abolitionist to sing, "Chains shall He break for the slave is our brother."[371] Paul could say that to Philemon of his slave Onesimus. But who presumes to tell the slave? Who has the moral authority to tell an occupied Galilean that the Roman sentry is their brother? Who dares tell the Palestinian refugee or the Black child of enslaved people or civilian victims of a drone attack to imagine their oppressor could, or even should, be considered a fellow child of God?

Not me. But Jesus does. And Thurman does, without ever once losing sight of the cause of justice. In fact, *their commitment to universal brotherhood is the foundation of resistance.* Thurman once preached:

> Now this was the great creative and radical discovery of Jesus Christ.
>
> The term *"brother"* is a very exclusive term. It says that there are those who are *not* brothers. It says this by definition. The unique ethical contribution of the Master was to make the exclusive term *"brother"* become a universal term.
>
> And it cost him his life.... And if it costs you your life, then it costs you your life. The early church saw this—the later church has forgotten it. Why do you think the communion table looks like a coffin?[372]

To love and bless and pray for the enemy Other who mistreats us ought not—*must not*—silence the cry of lament or the persistent demand for justice. But, for Thurman, it *is* to spit out the poison of bitterness, to see our opponents as fellow children of God, to implore God to penetrate their recalcitrance and lay bare the heart that can yet be redeemed. We love even the "Roman"—redeeming them from blanket categories ("enemy") so that the "Roman" might emerge as a person.[373] Thus, Thurman directs his assault on the "enemy" status itself. In that same spirit, Valarie Kaur—a Sikh faith leader and civil rights activist, and the founder of *Revolutionary Love Project*—has proposed that a vital step toward reconciliation is replacing the word "enemy" (a fixed identity) with "opponent" (a fluid category).[374]

Thurman conspired with Jesus to overcome the evils of injustice by establishing beachheads of *fellowship* with the Other. They resisted segregation in their respective contexts by creating common space, such as table fellowship, where people of a different social status, political bias, or ethnic background, the powerful and the poor—the Pharisee, the collaborator, the zealot, the blue-collar worker, and the beggar—experienced their mutual worth together.[375] Jesus's kingdom banquet protocol of indiscriminate hospitality strategically erodes us-them barriers of exclusion *and also* the us-*over*-them foundations of injustice. Here we learn the art and obligation of reverencing personhood—opening our eyes to the Other in their truest self. Do this, Jesus says, and you will be like your Father in heaven in an inclusion so radical that even you are compelled to attend Love's feast!

Love as fellowship also involves love as forgiveness. The disinherited often hear "forgiveness" as the f-word—a profane demand for silence and order that bypasses truth and suppresses our hunger for justice. We see this aberration regularly and can be sure that Thurman experienced it directly. Nevertheless, forgiveness stands at the heart of Jesus's love ethic and rings out from the cross. Forgiveness is essential for personal and societal healing from the ravages of hatred, so Thurman makes a case for it. He mandates forgiveness on three bases:

1. God forgives us seventy times seven.[376] How can we withhold from others that which we seek for ourselves?

2. "No evil deed represents the full intent of the doer." The acts we see don't define the whole person. They are but snapshots of a complex story we have no access to.

3. "Vengeance is mine, I will repay," says the Lord. Not that God is literally vengeful, but, in Thurman's words, "Life is its own restraint. In the wide sweep of the ebb and flow of moral law, our deeds track us down, and doer and deed meet." If so, my unforgiveness is needless and useless in the cause of cosmic justice—and may even oppose it, if justice is about making things right.

Having deconstructed the three hounds of hell and applied cruciform love against their domination, Thurman reiterates his audacious dream of hope for the disinherited:

The disinherited will know for themselves that there is a Spirit at work in life and in the hearts of men which is committed to overcoming the world. It is universal, knowing no age, no race, no culture, and no condition of men. For the privileged and underprivileged alike, if the individual puts at the disposal of the Spirit the needful dedication and discipline, he can live effectively in the chaos of the present the high destiny of a son of God.[377]

I so appreciate Thurman's generosity and grace. When I read him, I can't escape my reality of power, privilege, or complicity in systems of injustice. Yet he never seeks to imprison me in perpetual shame or exclude me from the table. His agenda isn't to assert moral superiority over white people (which I'd gladly concede). Instead, he invites us to become "more free than we have ever been, free to engage our fullest powers in the transformative tasks that await us at the wall."[378] And by "we," that includes me—if I hope to be freed from my own racist blind spots and freed to know my belovedness in Jesus as he did.

I once thought I was already free. But now? *God's Black voices have my attention.*

RADICAL EMPATHY: HEARING FELICIA MURRELL

In Howard Thurman's message "Love or Perish," he offers a working definition of love specific to my understanding of empathy:

> Love is the experience of dealing with a man at a point in that man that is beyond all his faults and all his virtues. Love, then, is to deal totally with a man. And you can't do this without a disciplined and sensitized imagination—a sense of self-projection—to project yourself inside another human being and there take soundings and report those soundings back to your mind and spirit so as to inform the quality of your relationship to him.[379]

This capacity to project ourselves into the perspective and feelings of another person—especially the powerless whose experience we can only imagine—is Thurman's reiteration of Dostoevsky's *"co-suffering love."* Without empathy, people of privilege make poor allies, more in tune with how we feel about ourselves in our *"saviorism"* than actually mourning with those who mourn in genuine solidarity.

Again, the limitations of my empathy also regulate how much I presume to speak for minority communities beyond simply saying, "Here's what they are teaching me." I'm not an expert or a teacher on Black perspectives—I'm simply a grateful student who takes a lot of notes. It also means saying a belated, "Not my turn," which is why I surrender this space now to my friend Felicia Murrell, my mentor on issues of race and faith from a Black perspective. Specifically, she takes up Thurman's mantle in awakening love as empathy and compassion for the Other—she sees and says it so well.

Felicia, my sister—preach!

"Radical Empathy"

"...when they suffer, we suffer with them.
Whether we know it or not, we suffer with them."
—*The Dearly Beloved*, Cara Wall[380]

I don't know if this truth is THE key, but surely it's *a* key to awakening compassion and radical empathy. To understand that when "they," whoever "they" may be, suffer, I also suffer. That "they" are merely a part of me I do not yet know.[381]

"They" are an invitation to be acquainted with the afflictions of another. To perhaps model the way of the Samaritan (man judged him "good") who suffered in the suffering of a stranger, paid for his board and meal and medicine. Told the innkeeper he'd check back on his return trip to make sure the debt was completely paid. Surely this is the fellowship of suffering, or at least a part of it...

Any anti-racist work, any theology that does not allow for a person's full humanity—the whole of their lived experience from triumph to tragedy is only skimming the surface and will never go deep enough to yield transformation.

Circumstances all around present us with opportunities to *suffer with*. The pain and terror of the Palestinians and Israelis who fear for their lives. The trauma and terror of our transgender brothers, sisters, and non-binary siblings who fear for their safety and their right to exist in their bodies. The suffering of Black and Brown bodies who fear the police, who struggle to convince others that their experiences are real and not contrived, that they matter.

The list can go on and on here, for truly no one is exempt from suffering. There is no hierarchy in suffering, at least there ought not to be.

But there is an invitation to identify, to be with, to hold space for, to allow your heart to break open in the sorrow and pain of another.

Love weeps with those who mourn. Are you awake to hear?

May our ears become attuned to the cries of the suffering without the burden of false responsibility that demands we solve all of the world's problems. May our solidarity not turn into *saviourism*. May we be free from guilt and shame that detracts us from empathy and derails our participation in unconditional acceptance.[382]

Amen, Felicia. I hope to be better and to do better. You—one of God's Black voices—have my full attention.

POSTSCRIPT TO MY WHITE FRIENDS ON MLK DAY

I refuse to accept the view that mankind is so tragically bound to the starless midnight of racism and war that the bright daybreak of peace and brotherhood can never become a reality.... I believe that *unarmed truth* and *unconditional love* will have the final word."[383]

— Martin Luther King Jr.

"Be love."[384]   — Bernice King

Reading or listening to Martin Luther King Jr. and his daughter Bernice (who writes and speaks in the same spirit), I recognize that the relentless struggle for the love they preach never passively accepts injustice to maintain pseudo-peace with people who look and live like me. Rather, they teach me to identify love with actively overcoming evil through nonviolent resistance to (1) external oppression, inequity, and exclusion, and (2) internal enslavement to fear, deception, and hatred (Thurman). Their interpretation of Jesus is best verified by their proximity to the cross and its recapitulation of the Passover Exodus in Black history (Cone).

To my white brothers and sisters, whatever we say on Martin Luther King Jr. Day to honor King's memory, we will no doubt appear performative— "virtue-signaling" as if *ally* were an identity badge we could ever claim for ourselves. I feel the acid in my throat over it. I accept that dilemma. And we did it to ourselves. But let us at least avoid turning our engagement with civil rights into blatant hypocrisy. Let's not co-opt the man's own words to oppose his call to the work of justice—which included public opposition to *all* death-dealing via racism, war, and executions. Better to remain silent in the guilt of our complicity. But far better still to hear and heed God's voice through his Black prophets—and not merely one token day per year.

As we brag or complain about our deconstruction, we must consider *their* gospel, forged in the furnaces of Egypt, Babylon, Rome, and America over millennia. While the cultured despisers of faith cheer the end of Christian faith in the West, I would ask, since when did Black faith not count? And why would we hope for and serve in its erasure? How "progressive" is that? Rather, Rev. Thurman and Rev. Martin Luther King Jr.'s "religion of Jesus"— the gospel of nonviolent justice and anti-othering love—feels to me like a final beacon of the Jesus Way amid the church's broader meltdown.

But beyond the church, I am witnessing a sharp increase in boldness among secularists to shame BIPOC[385] people for their faith. I've been seeing public rebukes online and in social media scolding Black and Indigenous people of faith with slogans like "Learn your history," accusing them of betraying their own race and heritage by naïvely adopting the faith of European slavers, settlers, and residential school abusers. The dripping scorn involves overt patronizing, condescension, and sheer contempt as they talk down to BIPOC, presuming to correct them for being so ignorant, so unenlightened, so poorly informed of their own history that they've somehow stumbled into the colonized religion of their oppressors. As if the magnificent heritage of vivacious black preaching, spirituality, gospel music, and worship were merely derivative of white slavers—something to be derided and expunged. As if the greatest of the Latin and Greek patristic theologians weren't Africans!

Such arrogance imagines it will cleanse them of religious brainwashing by, what? *Colonizing* them! And *to* what? White European rationalist materialism? Remember from our discussion of Voltaire that the *progressive* bourgeois elite actually *expanded* the slave trade across three continents while condemning all spiritual tradition (Christian, Muslim, Jewish, Black, and Indigenous alike) as a "primitive" blight to be erased.

Yes, someone *does* need to learn their history. And it's not Cone, Thurman, King, or Murrell.

SMH (Shake my head).

Here's another narrative, truer to history and more respectful of our neighbors. Despite the corrupt pseudo-faith of European Christendom, BIPOC people resonated deeply with a more ancient tradition: the story of Hebrew slaves who overcame their oppression and made their exodus out of Egypt, Judean refugees who returned home after a long exile in Babylon, and the faith of the Teacher in Rome-occupied Galilee—the One who endured state-sanctioned execution and rose on the third day to embody liberation for all, even from death. The Christianity of Black and First Nations people *bypasses* European hegemony to directly identify with the Brown Jewish Jesus of occupied Palestine. His message rang true to the disenfranchised minorities who suffered under a tyranny similar to the tyranny Jesus suffered, and he announced a Way—a strategy of liberation—that freed them from the inside out. Certainly, for the Black church, the Lamb crucified and risen formed their Blues-Gospel-liberation culture, not some colonizer ruling over his plantation.

To now say, "Let that go! Be like us enlightened white modernist skeptics," and not see that as further violence to the BIPOC soul is a tragic kind of hubris. For the spiritually illiterate, perhaps a reminder of our foundational sacred texts serves as a great caution (or holy duct tape) to Christian and anti-Christian colonialists alike.

Psalm 102
A Prayer of the afflicted, when he is overwhelmed and pours out his complaint before the LORD.

¹ Hear my prayer, O LORD,
And let my cry come to You....
¹⁷ [The LORD] shall regard the prayer of the destitute,
And shall not despise their prayer.
¹⁸ This will be written for the generation to come,
That a people yet to be created may praise the LORD.
¹⁹ For He looked down from the height of His sanctuary;
From heaven the LORD viewed the earth,
²⁰ To hear the groaning of the prisoner,
To release those appointed to death,
²¹ To declare the name of the LORD in Zion,
And His praise in Jerusalem,
²² When the peoples are gathered together,
And the kingdoms, to serve the LORD.

(Ps 102:1, 17–22 NKJV)

God has heard their groans and come down. God is at work releasing people once enslaved. They have heard God's voice and have a message for us. Let us give them our full attention.

24

A WORLD UNRAVELING, A KINGDOM UNFURLING

A REMNANT PEOPLE

"If the LORD of hosts had not left us a few survivors, we would have been like Sodom, and become like Gomorrah."
—Isaiah 1:9 (NRSV)

Hearing accounts of God's faithful martyr-witnesses and attending to God's Black voices, who serve as envoys for marginalized people everywhere, brings to mind the biblical language of *remnant*. The Hebrew word for *remnant* comes from words such as *yether* (what's left over), *she'ar* (the rest), and *she'-erith* (residue)—what's "yet left" or has survived.[386]

The ancient myth of a survivor remnant began in ages past with stories of a single family averting human extinction through a global flood—for example, the biblical Noah narrative and, prior to that, the *Epic of Gilgamesh*. These stories became archetypal patterns for people groups who faced eradication through prolonged siege, catastrophic conquest, and centuries of occupation, exile, or enslavement. But human hope is wonderfully hard to kill, so whether it's diaspora or dystopia, out of the embers of destruction come prophecies of messianic leaders and their remnant bands of faithful warriors—from Judas Maccabeus (Maccabean Revolt, 167–60 BC—Happy Hanukkah!) to Robin Hood and his merry men to Rick Grimes (of *The Walking Dead* zombie fame).

The earliest era of survivalism involved dodging menacing and malevolent gods bent on wiping the world clean of our parasitic presence. Later, the stakes were only a little lower: the enemy beasts were emperors and their war machines. Until the last century, at least, they couldn't kill *everyone*. Their sights were more focused: other tribes, other races, other social classes, other sexual identities, and so on. Pick your enemy Other—but it's hard to find a more persistent (and resilient) target than the Jews. Their oppressors span about three and a half millennia if you start with their Hebrew roots. The lineup of would-be eradicators is impressive: Egyptians, Canaanites, Assyrians, Babylonians, Persians, Greeks, Romans, *way* too many Christians (shamefully), Nazis, communists, and Islamist nations or terrorist groups. I've probably missed some. The beasts come and go—but Jews remain, a stubbornly resistant *remnant*. An estimated thirteen million remain today.

The Jews' penchant for endurance is anchored in their story, remembered in their sacred Scriptures. Behold, the prophets have spoken! It starts as long ago as Joseph bar Israel: "God sent me before you to preserve for you a *remnant* on earth, and to keep alive for you many survivors" (Gen 45:7 NRSV).

Centuries later, Isaiah spoke:

20 In that day *the remnant* of Israel,
  the survivors of Jacob,
will no longer rely on him
  who struck them down
but will truly rely on the LORD,
  the Holy One of Israel.
21 *A remnant will return*, a remnant of Jacob
  will return to the Mighty God.
22 Though your people be like the sand by the sea, Israel,
  only *a remnant will return*.
Destruction has been decreed,
  overwhelming and righteous.
23 The Lord, the LORD Almighty, will carry out
  the destruction decreed upon the whole land.

(Isa 10:20–23 NIV)

And Micah cried out:

18 Who is a God like you,
  who pardons sin and forgives the transgression

of *the remnant* of his inheritance?
You do not stay angry forever
    but delight to show mercy.
[19] You will again have compassion on us;
    you will tread our sins underfoot
    and hurl all our iniquities into the depths of the sea.
[20] You will be faithful to Jacob,
    and show love to Abraham,
as you *pledged on oath* to our ancestors
    in days long ago.

(Mic 7:18–20 NIV)

Joel makes it a prophetic triad:

And everyone who calls
    on the name of the LORD will be saved;
for on Mount Zion and in Jerusalem
    there will be deliverance,
    as the LORD has said,
even among *the survivors*
    whom the LORD calls.

(Joel 2:32 NIV)

And the priest Ezra had this word for the Jews returning from the exile:

But now for a brief moment favor has been shown by the LORD our God, to *leave us a remnant* and to give us a secure hold within his holy place, that our God may brighten our eyes and grant us a little *reviving in our slavery.*　　(Ezra 9:8 ESV)

You get it. Anti-Semitic cruelty is *always ugly*, but it also *always fails*. Historically speaking, I can't think of a more self-defeating political agenda. It's the very definition of folly.

Now, I'm not a Jew, but if "all the promises of God are yes and amen in Jesus,"[387] and if, by faith in Christ, I've been "grafted in" (Rom 11:17, 19, 21, 24) to their new covenant…then don't I also benefit from those promises? Doesn't that make me part of the *remnant*? After all, the apostle says I'm in by faith, and I have loads of faith, so….

AN APOCALYPTIC THREAT

That said, where evil designs against one nation cannot succeed, today, obliterating *all* people seems more realistic. With the nuclear arms race and escalations of the Cold War, the gods of war became sufficiently powerful to leave the earth barren of life. And militarism is not the only path to extinction. Movies like *Don't Look Up*[388] remind us that a well-placed asteroid could send us back into the dust of our beginnings—whether in crowded bunkers or in tar pits with the dinosaurs is yet to be determined. And don't forget disease, right? Most zombie movies start with some rogue virus, a global pandemic that gets ahead of our wisdom and our healthcare systems. Like that could ever happen.

But even without cosmic fallout or microscopic antigens, humankind is quite capable of doing itself in, thank you very much. At least insofar as we contribute to the environmental catastrophes—the energy we draw from the earth and the chemicals we pour back into our land, waters, and atmosphere have given us a whole new vocabulary: greenhouse gasses, global warming, climate change, heat domes, particulate pollution, fire and smoke indices.... I can't keep up with debates between wunderkind Greta Thunberg and the "climate deniers." I just know that three hundred forest fires simultaneously burn in my province of British Columbia, Canada, most summers, so air purifiers and emergency smoke warnings are a normal part of my life.

It's sure sounds like all four horsemen of the apocalypse from Revelation 6 are out of the barn and galloping hard. Not that John the Revelator was actually referring to end-times global disaster scenarios, but the imagery makes for a great B-movie:

> [12] When he opened the sixth seal, I looked, and there came a great earthquake; the sun became black as sackcloth, the full moon became like blood, [13] and the stars of the sky fell to the earth as the fig tree drops its winter fruit when shaken by a gale. [14] The sky vanished like a scroll rolling itself up, and every mountain and island was removed from its place. [15] Then the kings of the earth and the magnates and the generals and the rich and the powerful, and everyone, slave and free, hid in the caves and among the rocks of the mountains, [16] calling to the mountains and rocks, "Fall on us and hide us from the face of the one seated on the throne and from the wrath of the Lamb; [17] for

the great day of their wrath has come, and who is able to stand?"

(Rev 6:12–17 NRSV)

Yikes! That passage would be so terrifying if we took it literally or seriously or whatever. Sure, the disasters sound familiar. I witnessed similar ones nightly until I cancelled cable news. No matter. You can pile these threats high and deep, but guess what? They don't scare me—because God will *always* preserve a remnant. Right? And since I'm one of God's "elect," I know I'm one of the chosen. Right? (/s) Even if our worldly death machines reduce us to a tiny company of the faithful who escape this self-inflicted global holocaust in a single ark-like rocket (as in Walter Miller's literary classic *A Canticle for Leibowitz*), God will ensure that life continues somewhere, yes? Priestly missionaries to the galaxy, right? Surely, our new messiahs—Elon or Jeff or Sir Richard—will take me and my family to the stars. God's promise! (/s)

Sarcasm doesn't always translate well into print, so, even though I included those special notations, I better make myself clear on two points: First, what I've just described is NOT where I anchor my hope. Second, while I'm not naïve, I'm also not cynical or hopeless. I believe Jesus is the Lord of history and will not fail in his promise to "make all things new."[389]

But before we get there, I think we need to pass through the Valley of the Shadow—not the shadow of half-dead or mostly dead—but through death to resurrection. The first death I'd propose is that of remnant survival fantasies, not least of which is nineteenth-century "rapture" theology. I'll begin with a science-fiction thought experiment. A fantasy. It's not the truth. It's not my eschatology. But I hope it sends us scurrying *to* the truth.

SCI-FI THOUGHT EXPERIMENT

The beautiful plot of so much literary fiction is the "hero's journey," where unlikely characters—Frodo and Sam, Luke and Leia, Neo and Trinity, Harry Potter with Hermione and Ron—face a series of trials in which they must overcome some dark force—Sauron, Vader, the Matrix, Voldemort—that threatens universal existence. If they fail, it's all over. But before they succeed, they will be confronted by their own shadow side—that part of them mirrored by their nemesis. Along the way, the heroes' vices will show, and their virtues will grow as they face life-and-death choices and prove willing to make the ultimate sacrifice.

I'm not the first to say that these stories are great because they echo the greatest story ever told—they are reflections of the gospel cross and the ultimate Savior. Every messiah before or since points back and up to Jesus Christ.

Now, imagine me trying my hand at such a happily predictable tale. I could just follow a manual on how to construct the hero's journey, pick a world-threatening crisis, gather my remnant of characters, develop a *très chic* villain, and then create a cunning plan to avert certain destruction. Plug and play, right?

Yawn.

Maybe I'd surprise you. I like twists. Maybe I'd break the rules and write my story in the following way (and sell dozens of copies). Here lies my thought experiment:

What if I told you up front that the New Testament has already showed us the end—the living *telos* or *end* or *fulfillment* or *outcome*? Easy enough: Christ IS our *telos*, so we read from the end, distilled in chapter one of my tale: *Jesus Christ restores all things and resurrects everyone, and we all fall down in joyful worship.* Amen. If by *telos* or *ultimate*, we mean the VERY end, that's what Scripture reveals.

Where the story gets interesting and risky and less predictable *in real life* is what happens before that. That's because *how* we get to the end is contingent. While God promises a good end, the journey depends on real people making authentic choices—with *help* from God, but without *interference from him*. For real. King Jesus *only* reigns by the wise persuasion of the cross—by *love*—never at any point by force or coercion. Those are the actual rules of play. No magic.

The "wrath of the Lamb" (citing Revelation 6) is that Christ invites our participation but consents to our rebellion, and there are rivers of blood flowing as deep as the horses' bridles. And it's the blood of his faithful martyrs, *not* his vanquished enemies.

In my imaginary novel, the hero is my actual grandson Felix's fictional great-grandchild (either Felix IV or Felicia)—about my age now but in the year 2172. Having trampled the earth for another one hundred and fifty years, the four horsemen of the Apocalypse bring world history to its devastating conclusion. How suddenly the last cataclysm comes is not as relevant as the fact that the world unravels through an obvious law of sowing and reaping, through human action and/or inaction. That's where the realism kicks in—the only plausible climax in the next century will be the unintended consequences of some triumph of progress (as usual). Advances in mRNA technology will have eradicated every virus and cured all cancer. Breakthroughs in energy will have replaced fossil fuels with cold fusion. And artificial intelligence (AI) will...well, no idea.

What never seems to leave on its own is our greedy consumerism, incurable xenophobia, and lust for power. As for the maladies of the soul, such as alienation, despondency, malice, and distraction—there's just no app for that. But, in my story, a few good women and men have not forgotten what's required for human flourishing: practicing presence, communion with God and one another, and renewal of heart, mind, spirit, and earth. Felix/Felicia remembers. And prays. And believes. And finds others who gather around these simple practices. This *remnant* isn't a company of John Connor militiamen battling terminators. Maybe their greatest achievement is growing plump bell peppers or Russian garlic. Or learning to knit and building bird feeders. And maybe that's what *heroic* looks like after the cell towers have fried our brains. Maybe just being kind is their grand discovery, and if they practice it, others may catch on, and they may yet save the world.

Now here's the twist. They don't. Save the world, I mean. They can't. They won't.

I mean, why would we even think so? What possesses us to imagine any scenario in which we *aren't* extinct in less than two hundred years? (Remember, this is a thought experiment, not my eschatology...we've a way to go yet).

Really think about that. The feeble voices gaining miniscule traction toward equity, generosity, or peace are countered by authoritarian heads of state, multitrillion-dollar military budgets, globalist corporations, and the environmental impact of bitcoin mining. Can you think of a single reason Felix IV *won't* be the last generation? Do we have any hope that *doesn't* involve superstitious faith in a magical outcome with no substantial course change by humanity? Why would we expect however many billion people to bottom out on the idolatry of "I" and "mine" and "us versus them"? Do we see any signs that we'll turn from hatred or wake up to kindness on a scale that reverses our trajectory and arrests the inevitable?

And so, in my story, maybe the shadow that Felix IV must face is the naivety of his own remnant mentality. "God will just rescue us from our own choices without our making different choices!" Will God do that? Has God ever done that? We'll come back to that.

In the story, our little remnant discovers why forty-two of the one hundred and fifty psalms are psalms of lament. Or why ten of Shakespeare's plays are tragedies. Or why Tolkien's "eucatastrophes"[390] are in the fantasy section of bookstores. Or why good literature avoids *deus ex machina* like the plague (or ten plagues). And maybe Jeremiah's Lamentations is what they're reading when the curtain drops. Maybe Felix IV is citing the words from chapter 3:

> ²² Because of the LORD's great love we are not consumed,
>   for his compassions never fail.
> ²³ They are new every morning;
>   great is your faithfulness.   (Lam 3:22–23 NIV)

The end.

If the last act featured a fire that incinerated the remnant right then, that would be quite the amazing irony. And didn't Peter say the following, at least rhetorically?

> But the Lord's day will come like a thief. On that day the heavens will pass away with a great rushing sound, the elements will be *dissolved in fire*, and the earth and all the works on it will be disclosed.
>   (2 Pet 3:10)

Except that's not *the END*. Remember, we already read about *the telos* back in chapter 1. In the faithfulness of God, there *is* a new dawn in which Christ restores all things and resurrects all people. But we don't get there by surviving. We get there by dying. And it's not only a remnant that's rescued— it's everyone. Didn't Paul say: "For God has bound *everyone* over to disobedience so that he may have mercy on them *all*" (Rom 11:32 NIV)?

As I said, this thought experiment does not represent my convictions. But it was a necessary step in order to shake me free of the fairy-tale ending that has Jesus swooping in over a rainbow on his unicorn to rescue us. Or pretending that humanity will somehow finally pass into the Age of Aquarius where John Lennon's "Imagine" mystically puts our heads back on straight.

I'll say what neither theologians nor humanists seem able to admit: *it doesn't work that way*. At this rate, we're done. Soon. But we had a pretty ~~good~~ (scratch that) interesting run. Kind of an anticlimax in the end, especially in light of the beautiful intrusion of the incarnation. But I don't count my sad story as any worse than Dispensationalism's tribulation/Antichrist/Armageddon nightmare.

FROM UNRAVELING TO UNFURLING

What if, instead of writing my doomsday novel, I return to the New Testament in search of the good news of the Lord of history—not the collapse of history but its redemption? Paraphrasing Jesus's message of the kingdom, *"God's reign is here, among you now! Reorient your lives to this great news! Invite it here into this world as it is in eternity."* Jesus didn't come to rescue a remnant out of a collapsing universe—he came to mobilize partners in his "Behold, I'm making all things new" movement.

One companion in Jesus's restoration project is my friend Richard Murray, an attorney and a theologian who is radiant with hope. His hope is not wishful thinking.[391] He shares story after story of transformation and redemption occurring where you'd least expect it: in the courtrooms of America. His experience has not left him pessimistic or cynical. He believes that our *telos* (completed end) has already appeared in Jesus Christ and that the kingdom of God is *not* something we await *after* human history or even *after* death! Christ has already established his kingdom and continues to *unfurl* it before our eyes. The kingdom of God is at hand, in our midst, and within us—if we have eyes to see it and hearts willing to participate.

But the reign of the Prince of Peace faces tremendous resistance. After John the Baptist's arrest, Jesus said, "And from the days of John the Baptist until now the kingdom of heaven has been treated violently, and violent men take it by force" (Matt 11:12 NASB). That is, first, wherever the kingdom city shines bright, opponents come and lay siege to it, spilling rivers of martyrs' blood. And, second, many people think the way to advance God's kingdom is by coercion, including violence in God's name! Indeed, both dynamics were in play in the crucifixion of Jesus and the stoning of Stephen.

Yet isn't it ironic and profound that God subverts these same acts—via forgiveness—and co-opts them for our salvation? So, for my friend Richard, the kingdom of heaven isn't an escape pod into a future we await, but a *rollout* that's already begun—it's an ascent further up and further in (C. S. Lewis) into divine love, our perpetual development in this life and the next, in this age and the next, in this world and the next (whenever, however that transition happens). The continuity features the "glory to glory" metamorphosis that Paul describes in 2 Corinthians 3:18. We are being fashioned into the very image of Christ—a spiritual evolution of growth and discovery. This is what Gregory of Nyssa called *epektasis*[392] (perpetual progress)—our unceasing evolution into eternal joy. In other words, we too continue to unfurl!

The Russian theologian Sergii Bulgakov uses *unfurling* in conjunction with the biblical phrase "ages of ages"—used, in some form, twelve times in the book of Revelation. Bulgakov writes in his commentary *The Apocalypse of John* that the "ages of ages" throughout Scripture refers to "a concrete, qualified eternity." It's not so much about eternity in the way God is eternal (divine, unchangeable fullness). Rather, "ages of ages" refers to

> ...eternity still becoming itself, *unfurling itself,* fulfilling its eternal content from age to age and in the ages of ages.... This is a matter not only of life in eternity but also of the salvation that is to be accomplished in it. This image of the all-conquering and all-filling divine omnipresence is applicable to *apokatastasis* [the restoration of all things],...synonymous with the "ages of ages" as an incremental and gradual revelation of eternity in time. And so *Revelation* ends with a promise of Christ's enthronement and the kingdom of God to the ages of ages and that without any limitation. For "There shall be no more curse" and "the servants of God will serve him (the Lamb)" (20:3).[393]

Imagine! What if we are destined for infinite love and our capacities for that are ever-expanding? For example, what if I could remember names and faces better—no, what if I never forgot a name or face? What if I were more understanding of others' struggles—what if I was perfectly empathetic, without any apathy or codependency? What if I saw *everyone* the way Jesus does—and could embody his self-giving, radically forgiving, co-suffering love? What if I were to access his *infinite relationality* and offer it across time and space to whoever needed it? What if this is what the image of Jesus looks like in us as we mature through "ages of ages" into the next life? Then maybe the historic dogma of the "communion of the saints" would deconstruct every limitation by which we currently box ourselves in!

What if that kind of presence in communion is the fullness of the kingdom that's not somewhere else or *somewhen* else but already a mustard seed that is growing in you today? Would you want in?

SUMMING UP: PARTICIPANTS NEEDED

If we grant an ultimate redemption in the *telos* beyond the veil (I do) but negate a magical utopian solution without changing our course (I do), then we're down to two Christian options, both of which are real possibilities, for the end of human history: (1) the rather glum hope of complete human extinction followed by universal restoration or (2) Richard's unfurling kingdom of perpetual (if halting) spiritual evolution and ascent. Which path will humanity pursue? "Choose you this day"[394] means that God treats our agency with utmost dignity. That is Love's nature.

Can we then hold the following truths in tension?

+ The road to human extinction is a genuine possibility, but it is *not inevitable*.

+ The ladder of ascent is an authentic invitation, but our involvement is *not* guaranteed or coerced.

+ The promises of God—what God will do, no matter what—are *unconditional*.

+ The promises of God are also *contingent*—our choices affect our experience of God's promises.

To summarize, chapter 8 of Paul's letter to the Romans is our clearest description of the dance between God's promises and our participation in experiencing them. In four movements:

1. I believe God has revealed the ultimate end (*telos*) in Scripture. Authors in both Testaments and Christ himself forecast the resurrection of all people and the restoration of all things. At the "Final Deconstruction," we will, at last, be cleansed of our lies, bathed of our shame, healed of our wounds, freed from our addictions, and released from our egoism—even our self-righteousness will be humbled. Malachi compares this purifying judgment to launderer's soap or a refiner's fire (Mal 3:1–4) such that we'll enter the kingdom of heaven free of every last construct. This is good news for everyone.

As Saint Isaac of Syria said many centuries ago:

> In love did God bring the world into existence; in love is God going to bring it to that wondrous transformed state, and in love will the world be swallowed up in the great mystery of the One who has performed all these things; in love will the whole course of the governance of creation be finally comprised. Among all His actions there is none which is not entirely a matter of mercy, love, and compassion; this constitutes the beginning and the end of his dealings with us.[395]

2. The path toward that end is a work in progress (or regress). At every given moment, God's kingdom both suffers violence and invites participation.

The apostle Paul uses even stronger terms. He says that *all of creation is wait-ing eagerly*—is *groaning*, just as we are, in the hope of redemption—which requires us to show up!

> ¹⁹ Yes: creation itself is on tiptoe with expectation, eagerly awaiting the moment when *God's children will be revealed....*
>
> ²² Let me explain. We know that *the entire creation is groaning together, and going through labor pains together, up until the present time.* ²³ Not only so: we too, we who have the first fruits of the spirit's life within us, are *groaning within ourselves, as we eagerly await our adoption, the redemption of our body....* (Rom 8:19, 22–23)

3. Moreover, *the Spirit groans with us* and *from within us*, interceding for our redemption, and pleading for us to participate:

> ²⁶ In the same way, too, the spirit comes alongside and helps us in our weakness. We don't know what to pray for as we ought to; but that same spirit pleads on our behalf, with groanings too deep for words. ²⁷ And the Searcher of Hearts knows what the spirit is thinking, because the spirit pleads for God's people according to God's will.... (Rom 8:26–27)

4. Finally, verse 28: "We know that all things work together for good for those who love God, who are called according to his purpose" (NRSV). This is *not* a whistling-in-the dark platitude that "everything always works out." Not in *this* life, anyway. It *doesn't* mean that. And it *doesn't* happen that way in real life much of the time. But what it does mean is this: those who love God and hear him calling us to his purposes—redemption and renewal—find our-selves *working together* in collaboration with ALL creation *and* with the Spirit as they groan toward the restoration of all things here in this world. This cooperative participation is the contingency that unfurls God's reign in our world and reconstructs the cosmos rather than settling for the hard reboot.

I know that "kingdom now" theologies can easily become botched by glassy-eyed Christian triumphalism—still merely magical and, in a sense, stuck at Jesus's triumphal entry in Jerusalem because they aren't prepared to pass through the cross to resurrection life. I'd rather not stumble into that familiar pothole. But I'll need help. Time to dial up my godfather, David Goa.

25

FRIDAYS WITH GODFATHER: PRESENCE IN COMMUNION

"O heavenly King, Comforter, the Spirit of truth,
Who art everywhere present and fillest all things,
Treasury of good things and Giver of life:
Come, and abide in us,
Cleanse us from every stain and save our souls, O Good One."
—From the Trisagion Prayer

TWO-STOREY[396] UNIVERSE

Often, *necessary* deconstruction can become a knee-jerk overreaction to past wounds, toxic teaching, and fraught church experiences. As I've shown, the temptation to despair and depart can retraumatize sincere *be-leavers* with the second death of alienation. The equally unhelpful overreaction to that heartbreak is for church leaders, deconstruction influencers, and ideologues to rush about, trying to herd strays into their respective corrals. It's the old tale of two ditches—we don't want to fall into either extreme. Hopefully, our seven sleepers have shown us how to reframe deconstruction such that we experience it as an opportunity for liberation, transformation, and communion.

On a similar note, many of us grew up hearing about some Christian version of an otherworldly paradise, where "heaven" was somewhere else ("up there") and *somewhen* else (at our death or at the "second coming"). We eventually woke up to see this perspective as a huge problem. We realized to what degree our heaven-out-there theologies diminished and degraded the value of life in the "here below" and deferred the kingdom of God until later, in some other realm. That approach can be dehumanizing to our daily existence and devastating to a planet we use up and jettison all too quickly.

Fr. Stephen Freeman identifies the underlying fallacy here as a "two-storey universe,"[397] where heaven and earth are separate "places." In a two-storey universe, we live on earth, and we hope there's a God up in heaven. We believe he "came down" in the incarnation, "went up" in his ascension, and will "come back down" at his "second coming." We hope that when we die, we too will go "up there" to live forever, or, even better, get raptured away to avoid death altogether. Our biggest fears, according to Freeman, are (1) that God is not actually up there at all, (2) that maybe there is no "up there" after all, and (3) if there is an "up there," what if I get left behind or take the down elevator when I die? And, of course, we're convinced that no one ever escapes that furnace room in the basement!

If we assume such a two-storey universe, it becomes easy to secularize our lives, acting as functional atheists who go about our days with little real sense of our connection to a living God except as an idea—and no mere idea can (or should) survive earnest deconstruction. We call the rare exceptions to this divided structure "miracles" or "revival," where morsels of manna descend on the dumbwaiter from on high.[398]

In my early Baptist years, the safeguard against this distance between the spiritual and the earthly was the continual assurance that the God who lives in heaven also lives in me. "You ask me how I know he lives?" we would sing, "He lives within my heart."[399] This old hymn also taught me that Christ is not just sequestered *in* my heart, but that *he walks with me and talks with me*. If I paid attention, I could *see his hand of mercy* everywhere and know that the risen One *lives* (present tense) and *is always near*. I can't overstate how those words saved me—how their truth sank into my elementary faith as an experiential reality: I knew eternal life as *divine presence*.

Otherwise? If we're unconscious of God's immanent, personal, loving care, we will seek and find for ourselves first-storey substitutes for the presence of

God, identifying them with faith, hoping they will rescue us from this world and transport us to the second floor. Our substitutes of choice may include doctrinal adherence, religious observance, behavioral conformity, personal piety, social activism, and more. Faith practices of this sort aren't intrinsically bad, despite what "faith alone" grace teachers or irreligious ex-vangelicals might tell you. Indeed, these spiritual disciplines often orient and prepare us for authentic grace encounters with both God and other people. The problem is how they can also slip in as surrogates for the divine presence. We see this occur wherever people following a form of Christianity live and worship as if Jesus were not, or no longer is, or is not yet *Emmanuel—God with us*.

Part of my water-to-wine experience was a renewed conviction that God's kingdom is not just "later on" or "up there" but is "within me"[400] and "at hand"[401] in the immediate experience of my life with God. The kingdom of God is the "presence in communion" that every human longs for and needs. Freeman insists that historic Christianity offers exactly this instead of the two-storey gap:

> When we gather for worship, there are not two-storeys…Heaven and Earth are together…[and] we actually eat of the marriage feast—indeed its food is nothing other than the Body and Blood of God. To the question: "Do you believe in God?" we may answer: "Believe in Him? We eat His Body and drink His blood!"
>
> …We pray in the beginning of almost all our prayers, "O Heavenly King, the Comforter, the Spirit of Truth, *who art everywhere present and fillest all things…*" [We learn] to pray in such a manner and to gradually come out of the darkness of the lie and into the brightness of the truth…leaving the two-storey universe and coming to live where there is but one storey.[402]

THE OTHER DITCH(ES)

All of this resonates with me. I'll now respond with my "Yes, AND…" caveats on two fronts—instances of overreaction to the two-storey problem (of which Fr. Stephen is *not* guilty).

1. *One storey, but still no God.* First, I've observed a mirror error to two-storeyism among those who deconstruct their second-storey paradise yet fail to see or believe that God inhabits and interacts with the first storey. The

ancient truth Freeman expresses is that God is *everywhere present, filling all things*, alive and involved in every room of our one-storey "ranch." But church and ex-church people alike may continue to practice their theology, ideology, religiosity, spirituality, or activism *sans God*. Two-floors become one, good. But without experiencing God *with us* in real life (mundane or dramatic), our one remaining floor becomes an exhausting flurry of spiritual activities where God, miraculously, is everywhere *absent!* Religious or spiritual practices easily become *idols* that displace God's living presence rather than *icons* that unveil God as being as near to us as our next breath. In that case, demolishing the "pie in the sky" otherworld didn't help at all.

How different from the God "who is '*not far*' from any one of us, *in whom* 'we live and move and exist.'"[403] In Christ, the living God is united with us in mutual, indwelling communion—Christ is in us, and we are in him, just as Christ is in God, and God is in Christ.[404] Or maybe the experience of *communion* is contingent—God awaits our attendance and willing participation. It's unfair to claim God is absent when we're the no-show to the banquet. I'm so glad God patiently forbears my tardy RSVPs.

2. *One storey, and this is it.* Sergius Bulgakov acknowledged the kingdom of God here and now, *everywhere present and filling all things*. But he pushed back against the idea that "*this is it*," as in, "*God has arrived, so we have arrived.*" You hear this idea in those who tout the "finished work of Christ" as if *we* are a finished work. I know I'm not! Freeman never makes this error, but some of us do. Bulgakov, forced into exile during the Russian Revolution, issues a stern warning: yes, welcome God into every aspect of your life in the here and now. But don't settle for *this-is-it* complacency about yourself or your world.

He reminds us that when we pray, "*Let your kingdom come on earth*" (do we, still?), we should see the kingdom of heaven on earth as both a reality and an aspiration. Yes, God is with us, *and* the world is burning. We know the kingdom *has come*, and we continue to pray, "*Come reign*"—first of all in me.

He reminds us that when we pray, "*Lord Jesus Christ, have mercy on me*" (you do, right?), we're not just asking him to go easy on us as we carry on unchanged. We're practicing *metanoia* (turning the *nous* to the light), actively inviting the fire of transformation.

He reminds us that the book of Revelation ends with a promise we continue to seek. Jesus says, "*Look, I am coming soon! My reward is with me, and I will give to each person according to what they have done*" (Rev 22:12 NIV).

Then, "The Spirit and the bride say, '*Come!*'" (v. 17 NIV).

First to Jesus, "*Yes, come!*"

Then to the world, "*Come!* 'Let the one who is thirsty *come*; and let the one who wishes take the free gift of the water of life'" (v. 17 NIV).

And then, "He who testifies to these things says, '*Yes, I am coming soon*'" (v. 20 NIV).

And we reply, "*Amen. Come, Lord Jesus*" (v. 20 NIV).

These promises and prayers do not at all deny the truth of a one-storey scenario where God is with us at all times and in all circumstances. What they reflect is the importance of actively, urgently surrendering our world and our lives to the reign of the ever-present Lamb of God who is (now) making (process) all things new. And we make ourselves present to the Lamb through this invitation. "Come, Lord Jesus" describes the posture of those who welcome Emmanuel to unfurl the kingdom and bring the unfolding, saving work to its *telos*. So says Bulgakov:

> "Even so come." This must not be only words, but a living, ardent prayer, which imparts a living feeling of certainty, of knowledge of the One Who comes…. When we pray to the Holy Spirit: "come and dwell in us," this is enough for us, because we have reasoned to ourselves beforehand that his presence is *partial*, like some kind of gracious help in our weakness, which nevertheless leaves us in our own place. But in the prayer to Jesus, "Even so, come," there cannot be anything partial, leaving our whole life in the place where it was and completely unchanged….
>
> But now the time is coming, when these words will burst into a new flame within us, will light up with a new inspiration and demand from us a living *amen*. And once that call has been heard, we cannot shield ourselves from it, nor do we want to.[405]

I'm sure Fr. Stephen would not only agree, but he'd also reference these two counterpoints in his own work. His teaching, especially in *Everywhere Present*, helps us enormously by deconstructing the imaginary second floor of our universe. We can grow toward a perpetual awareness of Love's "withness" to us, in this very second, as I knew it in childhood. I can hardly imagine a spiritual home renovation more significant!

FRIDAYS WITH GODFATHER

Freeman's one-storey hypothesis leads me to a parallel conversation I've enjoyed with David Goa. In 2012, David became my adopted godfather when I was chrismated[406] into the Orthodox church. After Bishop Varlaam (of blessed memory) entered the great cloud of witnesses in 2020,[407] David took up his role as my confessor, primarily through phone conversations most Friday mornings. Our talks are an invaluable source of spiritual and emotional stability for me, highly therapeutic and just as educational. The remainder of this chapter represents his input over the last two years.[408]

I'll begin with some key themes relevant to deconstruction and connect them to my favorite David Goa phrase: *The kingdom of God is presence in communion.*

SPIRITUAL EXHAUSTION AND ESTRANGEMENT

The phone rings. Call display says it's David Goa.

"Oh good, it's you!" I say immediately.

"Good morning, Irénée," he says, using my Orthodox name.

"Greetings, Godfather!"

I put on my earbuds and head outside for a walk. It's a blue-canopy day, and I'm ready to bare my soul and open my mind. On this day, I want to talk to David about those dear souls whose deconstruction has left them disillusioned and dry. I want to know how that happens and whether I can help. Some don't need my help, and they say so. Others are desperate enough to ask. But I want David's diagnosis.

He begins talking about the ways we approach God: through prayer, worship, holiness, ritual, the *via activa*, etc. Ways we open ourselves to the Divine. Ways, as I've said, that can be icons or idols.

David affirms these approaches, but notes, "They can also lead to spiritual exhaustion, especially when devoid of *presence*." When the weariness sets in, we need a break. And it's a real need.

As David continued, he suggested that deconstruction, in such instances, may mean taking a break from our pattern of communion with God and our faith community. Maybe even setting faith itself aside for a time. Understandably, distancing in this way can slide into a painful sense of what he called *estrangement*. We may conclude that it's time to take up faith again. We hunger for the felt presence of communion with God. But we may be surprised to find that it's...gone. And now *"I want it back. And I can't find it! Can't find God!"*

I feel a niggling hesitation when I hear this description. As if God is saying to me, "Their stone tablets are broken. Don't you dare offer a golden calf in exchange."

I say this to David. I don't want to play Aaron. Then how might I best facilitate? What do I say?

As usual, David pauses for a long time. Probably tamping his pipe, contemplating.

"Remind them," he says, *"that God is everywhere present and fills all things."*

He then explains that, in these crises of lost faith, two other factors are at work—a lie and a fact—both part of the garden of Eden story.

1. *Lie: "You don't have a living connection with God."*

The truth is that they already have a living connection with the God who is everywhere present and fills all things. The problem is that they don't recognize it. Remember, the serpent convinced Adam and Eve that they needed to become like God when they already were made in his image. They believed the lie. For many people in deconstruction, bad theology has reinforced the lie they have already accepted.

Most often, estrangement begins by believing (or being taught) they need to *get* something they have already been given. They assume there must be *some way to get* what's already theirs. They've done all the right things and still imagine they are without it. This is the story of the fall.

Remind them that every time they are in the presence of mercy or compassion, that which is beautiful and shimmers, every inkling of attention or joy, that is prayer. That is what life is. We don't earn it or make it. But we can ignore, deny, or turn away from it—or we can turn toward it. When we turn toward it, this is God's *"presence in communion."* And it's always modest.

2. *Fact: You cannot "have" communion. It is given.* Our stance must be attention and openness to what is given, rather than grasping or groping for it.

David explains how we might communicate this reality:

How we respond depends on who we're addressing. Some people dwell in estrangement from Reality. They have lost their feel for the world, for themselves, for others, and for God. But that's relatively rare.

In order to find what satan told them they needed to be fulfilled, they engage in this self-estrangement and reject the normal communions given to them.

How can I get this? Behind the question is that terrible sense that it was some *thing* they were taught, some *thing* they eventually rejected, and now they still want some *thing*. Living communion is not a *thing* you can *have* or *take* or *manufacture*. Spiritual disciplines are not techniques of *getting* some *thing*.

The stance we need is one of openness to the *Who* we have been given, *who is in all places and fills all things*, rather than trying to grasp and possess some elusive *it*.

I infer from David's commentary that every worthwhile spiritual discipline—from praying the Psalms to serving the poor to gazing at a sunset—is not *it*. They are wonderful aides that open us to the *Who* with whom we commune, rather than co-opting communion as ends in themselves. They help us to see, attend, wait, and be present, even in the darkness.

It's ironic that so many Evangelicals grow up hearing how spiritual disciplines are "works-righteousness," despite also being encouraged to have an active commitment to "daily devotions." We preached anti-works and grace alone, yet we frequently became worse than the medieval Catholics in our efforts to *achieve* relationship with God. I've seen the spiritual exhaustion generated in Evangelical revivalism and the charismatic renewal where "religion" was decried, even while the revivalists were driving the herd into a frenzy of "pressing in" to convince God to "show up" (measured by the altar call). The prophets of Baal would have been impressed. Too harsh? No. I led those meetings, urged by host pastors to *"make God come."*

Jesus said, "The kingdom of God is not elsewhere. It is at hand. It is within you," but the premise of revival meetings seemed to be, "God is *not* here, and we need to get him here. We need to do something to entice him." I knew how to do this. In our preaching, we re-erected a veil of estrangement and then made an industry of rending the veil that Christ has already removed once and for all. It's painful to remember. What can I say? It was the 1970s. And then the 1990s.

If people feel estranged from God, one major factor is that they faithfully believed the lie we taught them. It's not just a charismatic or revivalist lie. It's the same lie that's gripped every Christian movement founded on a belief in our separation from God and what we need to do about it. That's not the gospel. The Jesus story is about God's union with us and how Christ has achieved it.

The fruit of the lie of separation is estrangement. Deconstructing that lie is absolutely necessary to spiritual wholeness—even if it gets labeled *backsliding*.

I'm encouraged to see an increasing company of deconstructionists pass through disillusionment and estrangement into a new phase of opening their hands again. We can't just dupe them with another construct. I hope they're too smart for that. For my part, if there really is a *There* there, I will watch and wait. I will not grasp or grope. I will not press in for a breakthrough. I will attend. Attend to what? To the revelation that God is love, unveiled in the cross of Christ.

Thus ended our call that day.

COMMUNION VERSUS ALIENATION

Another Friday morning. The phone rings.

"Oh good, it's you!"

"Good morning, Irénée."

"Greetings, Godfather!"

After checking in with me about my family, my work, and my heart, David asks me what I'm reading and writing—what's on my mind. I'm thinking aloud:

"Whenever I speak with our friends in the Evangelical faith or from that background, there seems to be a *much* stronger (even compulsive) emphasis on afterlife affairs—heaven, hell, and who goes there—than is emphasized in the biblical and apostolic tradition." I recall that not one evangelistic message in the book of Acts ever uses the threat of hell as a motivator. Yet, inevitably, the question of knowing now who is "in" and who is "out" (and how), and where they're going, holds great prominence in their minds. I understand that—these are my people. And it makes all the more sense to me when I consider those concerns as their framework for interpreting Scripture. But it is most definitely a framework and not the only (or best) biblical/gospel-driven perspective.

In my discussions with David and other priests and scholars in my current faith community, I can say with confidence that their framework is assuredly biblical, theological, and most definitely gospel-centered. And yet their orientation to these questions is very different.

For instance, David reads Scripture as focused primarily on God's ways in *this* life and *this* world, very much in the tradition of John's Gospel and epistles, where words such as *perishing* and *eternal life* speak to the here and now. Similarly, the *kingdom of heaven* and the *kingdom of darkness*, death, and hell are present-tense (first-storey) concerns in the Synoptic Gospels and in the Pauline corpus.

In twenty-first century context, rather than literalizing heaven and hell as "up there" or "down there" places in the afterworld, Goa sees them as realities of the human condition, again, preferring the terms *communion* and *alienation*. And under these terms, the ethical backbone of the Law, the prophets, and the gospel come into much clearer focus for me. Loving (communion with) God and neighbor is not merely an addendum to grace or the currency for my postmortem destiny. Rather, the language of *communion* relates directly to the way I navigate life and especially how I experience human relationships and fulfill the command to love.

David distills his perspective:

Wherever there is *communion*, there is the kingdom or commonwealth of God, in this life. We know this. *Alienation*, abandonment, the curse…is wherever we see destruction in relationships in this life. This much we also know.

This perspective makes complete sense of the discussion between Jesus and Nicodemus in John 3:16–21, where Jesus says that he hasn't come to threaten the world with condemnation but to address humanity's current dilemma—that we're already *perishing*. He's come to walk us out of perishing and into eternal life, which he defines later *not* as being in heaven when you die but *knowing God now* (John 17:3). The question is not so much about life after death as it is, "Is there life *before* death?"

Goa transposes that conversation into the contemporary world where people understand the gaping difference between deathly *alienation* (a "living hell") and life-giving *communion* (especially a sense of belonging). What is disconcerting about this way of reading the New Testament is that if the heaven/hell problem is principally *lived realities* each day, then the in/out question is both more complex *and* much simpler than affirming correct doctrine to secure one's entry ticket through the pearly gates.

The complexity appears in those texts where Jesus deconstructs our presumptions about the end. Some people will be surprised to hear, "Depart from me," despite their assertion, "Did we not _____ in your name?" Others will be surprised to hear, "Well done, good and faithful servant," despite their mystified inquiry, "When did we feed/clothe/visit you?"[409]

The *simplicity* appears in the presence of unselfish love (mercy, compassion), even across faiths and on the wrong side of the tracks. It makes sense of John's insistence that *"everyone who loves is born of God and knows God"* (1 John 4:7 NKJV, NRSV). Wait. Even if they don't identify with Jesus? His next sentence is *not*, "But you need to become a Christian." Rather, it is, "Whoever does *not* love does *not* know God" (v. 8 NRSV). Even if I *do* identify with Jesus? Goa replies,

> The kingdom of God was written on the hearts of human beings before the foundation of the world. We, as human beings, *all* experience this—every one of us has known at least a bit of communion, just as we all have some experience of alienation.

That is, Christ IS known, even incognito, even by the "holy pagan," through participation in love, grace, and communion, because *all* of us were created in the image of Love (Christ crucified and risen). Conversely, Christ is *not* known when we participate in alienation—whenever we turn *from* love or *from* serving Christ in the Other.[410] These outcomes may be perplexing for two reasons:

First, what am I to make of loving pagans and unloving Christians? At one time, I would have said, "We are saved [for heaven], not by works, but by faith in Jesus." But the Lord Jesus, his brother James, and John the Beloved all push back. *What is faith in Jesus?* Is it signing a doctrinal statement and sealing it with baptism and the words "Lord, Lord?" No. *Living faith* is authenticated by love.[411] *Love IS our confession of faith in Jesus Christ*, even for those who don't yet know that they know him.

Second, this framework of the kingdom of God as communion throws into question my own previous means of assuring my own salvation. I can no longer say, "I am IN for all time because I prayed the right prayer on a particular date." Doubtless, that was an important waypoint for me. I reject the mocking tone of those who treat "inviting Jesus into their hearts" as if it was a meaningless mistake. It wasn't for me. I no longer believe Christ wasn't in me then; he was. But it was absolutely a life-changing instance of communion and transformation.

However, the stubborn fact is that my turning to and turning from divine Love seems to fluctuate with the tides. I'm frequently in and out of active communion (even though God is not). Then *how can I be sure I'm okay?* The problem rests in that mistaken question. The better question is, *"Will I live in the grace of today?"*[412] Or, *"Will I surrender myself to the care of God for this day?"*[413] Or, *"Will I stay under the waterfall of mercy today?"* I'm speaking here of my existential path, the way of my being, my actual life with God.

In that light, statements such as "Choose you *this day* whom you will serve"[414] and "*Now* is that accepted time, *now* is the day of salvation"[415] are no longer one-off altar call ultimatums but the invitation to a daily practice of trust in the mercy of God. The standing invitation greets me every morning when I wake up. This day and tomorrow and the next day. And, knowing me, it's a good thing there's fresh mercy with every sunrise.[416]

So, "believers" and "non-believers" (I don't equate that lingo with religious affiliation) alike share genuine experiences of communion. But as David points out, "We Christians are delighted with *our* theology, *our* secondary reflection—that is, *our* revelation about our experience of the Divine." And I truly am. In my real experience, I see a direct correlation between communion with Jesus Christ, the eternal life of knowing God, and opening my heart to love. As an evangelist to the alienated (Christian or not), I encourage and facilitate such encounters of communion whenever I'm able. I call this *gospeling*—sharing the Good News. My godfather's gospel sounds as deliciously generous as John's: "The gospel is that God is love. Where there is that communion of love, you are in the kingdom." That was Jesus's message. That's good news. And it makes a beautiful invitation—to me as much as to anyone. I suppose repenting (*metanoia*) in that gospel means turning from alienation to join Love's banquet, every day, repeatedly.

COMMONWEALTH

Friday. Phone rings. David again.

After niceties, I jump right in. "You used 'commonwealth' as a synonym for the 'kingdom of God' last week. Tell me about that."

I was drawn to his choice of words because, first, as a Canadian, I recognize the term *commonwealth*. We use it to describe a post-colonial community of nations with roots in the former British Empire.[417] Those nations that didn't secede from Her Majesty's empire via revolution discovered a path to autonomy within a network of political relations with "the Crown." But the U.K. could no longer relate to those nations as colonies under its hegemony (defined by the accumulation of capital to centers of power), demanding taxes or stripping the colonies of their resources.

While the old empire and its devastating colonial history deserve their full measure of condemnation, I suspected that David's use of *commonwealth* as a synonym for *kingdom* (also problematic) might be helpful. I asked why he chose that term. He replied,

Because it emphasizes two aspects of the kingdom of Christ:

1. That the *commonwealth of God* is something given; it is gratuitous, and not something we created

2. That the term *commonwealth* speaks literally of our "shared riches"

David developed that thought further, explaining that, in both cases, the term *commonwealth* clarifies that the kingdom of God is *not* like a worldly empire or hegemony. Sadly, whenever the church has fancied itself as God's kingdom here on earth, it has regularly mirrored capitalistic greed (figuratively and literally) rather than *kenotic* (self-giving) love. Indeed, when we apply the Jesus Way of *being, giving,* and *serving* to public faith, those who are still committed to economic exploitation may mislabel our values with ideological pejoratives ("leftist," "socialist," "Marxist"), rather than recognizing that generosity, justice, and equity are firmly rooted within the Jewish/ Christian prophetic tradition.

For those less familiar with the term *commonwealth*, I'd like to further define it according to Jesus's agenda for the kingdom of God in this world. Jesus signified life in communion with family, neighbors, and strangers as the banqueting table of God.

Commonwealth refers to the health, peace, and safety of an entire community or nation. That Christians in political power (in any party) or serving as lobbyists (for any interest) would actually oppose such a goal, especially where it would lift up the least, the lost, and the last of the oppressed and afflicted on the margins, is evidence of how far the religion called Christianity has failed to *conserve* the Christ of Isaiah 58, Micah 6, and especially Matthew 25. These texts measure Christianity as a movement on the scales of mercy *AND* justice, communion *OR* alienation, heaven *OR* hell, so that we must honestly ask ourselves:

+ What good news might we both bring and be?
+ How might we preach the *commonwealth of heaven* as Jesus did?
+ How IS *now* the accepted time? How IS *now* the day of salvation?

IMPOTENCE AND BANDWAGON MARTYRS

Friday. Phone rings. "David here."

I keep thinking about Nietzsche's warning that those who experience loss of meaning, estrangement, and alienation can't remain nihilists. They will *always* resume their quest for heaven—acceptance, belonging, and meaning—and so become vulnerable candidates for extremism. Granted, my readers will differ on what constitutes extremism. How does the adage go? "It's not paranoia if they really are out to get you." No matter. *Any* deconstruction that departs from Love's commonwealth into swamps of alienation and then lands in an ideology of hatred bears closer examination. But it's a million times more disconcerting to me when that hateful ideology retains the "Christian" brand. I bless deconstruction, but when it leads to *any* form of *cultism*, I'd like to know why.

What would David say about this? I ask, and he ponders aloud. As I listen, I also transcribe as fast as I can, hoping I will be able to catch every word:

How is it that particular issues become placeholders, baskets into which we put everything else? It reminds me of when the Lutheran church faced the specific question of being LGBQT+ welcoming. I watched how that issue became a placeholder for a score of other issues—divorce and remarriage, the status of divorced clergy, and on to the question of biblical inerrancy. More recently, one's opinions about vaccinations became a new placeholder. For some, "the jab" is inextricably linked to one's political loyalties, ideological stances, perspectives on healthcare, race, immigration, religious freedom, and even eschatology. Why is that?

Could it be that the scale of our institutions, society, globalization, and news coverage, and the combination of ecological and economic challenges (with no simple answers), has left an awful lot of people feeling unbelievably *impotent*? They're overwhelmed by these crises and have no simple way of responding. It's all too complicated. We're having to hold too much together and need to make snap judgments about that which we are unsure. This sense of impotence in the face of general social complexity conspires to lead people to jump on any bandwagon that makes *just one thing simpler.* We can feel righteous and right if we take a firm stand for or against even one thing.

My old friend of blessed memory, Heiko Schlieper, the marvelous historian and iconographer, loved to repeat Lord Acton's little formulation, but with a difference:

Power corrupts and impotence corrupts absolutely.

We've encountered young people who are so bright and capable— they have worked out a thorough critique of what's going on in society, politics, and institutions. The very thoroughness of their critique makes them feel like outsiders, to the point where they are not sure there's a place for them in society. How odd, then, that they hop aboard ideological bandwagons like the alt-right!

Or is it? They feel *impotent*—outside the pale. If they can't find something deeply meaningful to identify with or at least live in the hope that their understanding will deepen, they would rather choose something *negative* than something *without meaning*. Is there a felt need for some martyrdom they need to pay for the stupidities of science and politics?

"God, I have nothing to live for. Just give me a hill to die on."

In the second century, a council of bishops was called to address this very question in a different context. "Why are young people longing to be fed to the lions?" They *wanted* to be martyrs. They wanted some way to give their *life* to Jesus but thought the way was "death by cop." So, they would go to the magistrate presiding over those burn-ing incense to the emperor and essentially give him the finger. "We're not doing that! The emperor is a jackass!" It was like strapping on a suicide vest as a shortcut to heaven.

The bishops conferred and concluded, "This isn't martyrdom. This is spiritual selfishness. This is an illusion of the *presence* and *fullness* of the kingdom."

Thinking about cult leaders, it's amazing that when they attract followers, they can lead people over any precipice, and they will follow. What is the key ingredient? The leader convinces them to see the world in a profoundly negative way, shows them there is no space for them in that world, and then sells them a sense of belonging through a new identity that is of global significance and is wrapped in apocalypticism.

They can even die a meaningful death apart from the opportu-nity to live a meaningful life. Dying becomes the only way they can find meaning for their lives—they can be martyrs in a larger nar-rative. Their impotence is spiritualized into martyrdom, their mark of faithfulness, but on the negative side. If the impotent can't find a life-giving center to be faithful to, they take hold of its shadow image. Faithfulness is reduced to *not* doing, *not* participating, *not* having. Thus, those who embrace the negative side must demonize the doing, the participating, the having.

In a big society, where possibilities for young people (especially young men) are shrinking, disillusionment and impotence are inev-itable. If there's nothing to live for, you can die for anything called "righteous" that will get you into paradise.

Those early Christian youth who wanted to be martyred had the same impetus and psychological profile as the 9-11 bombers. The men who flew into the two towers in New York were not faithful Muslims. They included decadent young men who were into kinky stuff and needed a cathartic act that would cleanse and save their souls: a righ-teous stand against the decadent Beast. Osama bin Laden offered that.

A terrible, negative spiritual appetite overcomes those who wander into the valley of *anomie* (meaninglessness). Is this what we're looking at among young Evangelicals? The culture wars have sucked the life out of them and offered them misplaced concreteness and negative meaning. They were vulnerable, and now they're trapped.

In our frustration with them, we tend to forget that they are theological, spiritual, and moral anorexics. They are bred to chase after every new political-religious-moral fashion, hoping that this time is IT. *"At last! Triumph for the impotent."*

In the latest round, the gods of impotence and alienation still demand a beast to slay and martyrs to volunteer. Which candidates present themselves? Even a life-saving vaccine can be called "the mark of the Beast"—its users "sheeple," participants in fascism, oppressors of the martyrs.

What's going on? *It's all about meaning.*

IT'S ALL ABOUT MEANING

"What meaning?" I ask. *"What is the 'meaning world' pulling these bandwagons?"*

Lengthy pause. More pipe-tamping, methinks.

I'm a little impatient. "Still there? Please go on."

Their *meaning world* is a system comprised of dark forces, and they are those faithful chosen out of that world, called to resist and overcome it, even to the death. And to be fair, there's something very close to the Gospels and John's first epistle about that:

> [15] Do not love the world, or the things that are in the world.
> If anyone loves the world, the father's love is not in them. [16]
> Everything in the world, you see—the greedy desire of the
> flesh, the greedy desire of the eyes, the pride of life—none
> of this is from the father. It is from the world. [17] The world
> is passing away, with all its greedy desires. But anyone who
> does God's will abides forever.   (1 John 2:15–17)

The difference is their negative attachment to the world, where they find their identity in tearing it down or dying on its crosses—but without the light, life, and love that you see in the Jesus Way.

I interrupt. "That begs the question, what is the *meaning world* that *we* are tied into?"

David replies,

Isn't it just what we've been saying? That God is everywhere present? That the commonwealth of God is *presence in communion*? In our faith tradition, we affirm:

+ That our meaning world is *not closed*—we are not finished; we are not "some *thing*"

+ That, at the center of our faith, we recognize how easy it is to be deceived by our own suffering, our passions—personal and collective

+ That rather than turning our face to the wall or charging at windmills, we are to respond to God's constant invitation to *deeper* communion with *everything* and *everyone* we encounter.

+ That the gift of that tradition is *not* to set our world of meaning in *us-them* opposition that alienates others. To do so would be to convince ourselves that our meaning world is some *thing*. It's not. It is *presence in communion* (i.e., the kingdom of God).

TENDING WOUNDS, DEEPENING FRIENDSHIP

So far, this chapter has recounted Fr. Stephen Freeman's and David Goa's mature deconstruction of obstacles to our communion with ever-present Love that involve alienation. It's ultimately about our emergence from the ashes of our broken experiences with faith and culture. We've covered miles of territory. The next episode of my conversation with David was another phone meeting, one where I called in with no agenda but simply to hear his heart. Please excuse the snippet format—these are highlights from a long chat. And where his poetic language may seem obscure, I've opted not to try to explain it. Let it be poetic. Let it remain mystery. Trust that it's medicine. Don't figure it out; just listen.

For example, David reflected on The Great Deconstruction with these words:

We need to tend to our wounds,
but we cannot build a life on our scabs.
There are no veins in them.

In our disillusionment, the last thing the world and the church need is for us to age into bitterness. It is hard to swallow bitter medicine. For all its stupidity, hypocrisy, and inept leadership, the tradition [historic Christianity] is unbelievably sweet.

Our role is to spend quiet, easy time with anyone and to open up the gifts of our tradition so they can learn what it says to us and how we should live in this world.

* * * * *

Our problem is we may know about the existential experience of being in communion, but we become uncomfortable with it, partly because it decenters us. We're uncomfortable when it's not about *I* but truly becomes about *us* or *thou*.

We're uncomfortable encountering the fragility of that which is eternal. The experience of the eternal is so fragile, speaking directly about limitation, about mortality. The eternal can't speak to us except in that kind of language.

Theologies that project onto the future, or into heaven or hell, are also looking for some way of protecting themselves from the being of communion, because it's too real and thus seen as fragile and can so easily slip away. A big spiritual issue here—the tragedy of those theologies is less what they are saying as it is what they are doing. They become a condom protecting you from the raw experience of communion, with its joy and wonder, from the fact that you can't hang on to it or possess it, and that it's gratuitous.

Though centered on the idea of grace, they may construct theological cathedrals that protect people from the fire of grace. Happily, they are unsuccessful because the fire of grace is greater. What a difference it would make if they were given a language large enough that they could rest in the grace that is given, instead of running from it or putting it in a box.

When we speak of those who've "departed," we add to their name "memory eternal." What are we saying? We're not talking about heaven. We're saying, may the memory of this person flower in life-giving ways in our life. May it be part of that which is eternal, which is God's love, which is all we know of the eternal...and it's here, and it's now. It's a world without end, whether or not we see it.

* * * * *

Presence in communion is about spiritual friendship.

Aelred of Rievaulx (1110–67) was a Scottish Cistercian monk who lived in the first generation under Bernard of Clairveaux. Aelred had six hundred monks in his community, and he wrote the medieval classics *Mirror of Charity* and *Spiritual Friendship.*

He wrote beautifully about the significance of Jesus's humanity in its fullness. That Jesus is:

1. A father who educates

2. A mother who consoles and nourishes with the milk of sweetness

3. A friend who gives his life, shedding his blood for us

4. A brother, flesh of our flesh, who shared in the frailty and dignity of the human condition

This then becomes the foundation of our pastoral vocation and the work we do. We're to follow Jesus in the ministry of spiritual friendship—the goal of which is to make possible the restoration of the universe on the basis of a friend who becomes universal once more. Aelred exhorts us to mix the milk of compassion with the honey of holiness as a vocation that guides those who embrace it.

GOD WITH WOUNDS

As I listened to the empathy in David's voice for those whose deconstruction had reduced their faith to ashes and anger, I came to the following tentative conclusions:

1. *Wait for me.* First, reorientation is not simply about anxiously urging people to "go back" to who and where they were before their deconstruction. Nor is it about rushing them into the next construct, program, and community. What if "Be still, and know that I am God" (Psalm 46:10 various translations) means we can *wait* and let the Good Shepherd do the seeking and saving? Can we trust that he's capable enough to do this, so that we stop our hand-wringing and let go of our desperate clinging?

2. *Come to me.* Next, it is about embodying the welcome and belonging that Christ offers the weary and burdened. I don't mean signing them up to attend our next gig. But we can communicate Christ's invitation: "Come to my Father's house for rest and recovery."

3. *Follow me.* In due time, Christ's "come to me" will become "follow me." It takes time for us to rebuild our trust in him when his name has been misused to abuse. Eventually, though, Christ will ask us to follow him on the Way of the Cross. We can reassure each other that the path up to Golgotha is *not* the annihilation of the self. Christ is *never* the death of your personhood. It's about dying to what is not real—what is not love.

4. *Love with me.* The Way of the Cross also empowers others-centered love. Our role is not to convince or rescue or chastise others out of their deconstruction. We're to offer the spiritual friendship of empathy—companioning with those whom God sends us, even in their pain, and so discovering the God who bears our wounds.

5. *Work with me.* As deconstruction runs its course, living in the Father's house and following Christ's Way of the Cross brings us to two questions that will help us counter meaninglessness and alienation.[418]

    ✦ How will I order my life? This speaks to purpose or identity.

    ✦ What will I gather around? This speaks to community and belonging.

These questions don't address the quality of our purpose or community, but they implicitly nudge us out of spirals of stuckness. Considering these questions is a great step toward mental health. My sense is that Christ would love to help each of us find our unique answers to them.

26

THE DOORWAY:
LOVING LIMINAL SPACE

At its best, deconstruction serves our personal transformation "from glory to glory into the image of Jesus Christ" (*theosis*) and leads to "the restoration of all things" (*apokatastasis*), prophetically symbolized by Jesus's water-to-wine miracle at Cana. At its worst, deconstruction reenacts Adam's departure from the Tree of Life; it is like emptying our jugs of water onto the sand.[419] Actually, that's not what is worst. Even worse than that is people making an industry of knocking over other people's jugs of water and leaving them empty. Or presuming to refill them with their brand of snake oil as a prescription for restoring what has been lost.

But, in the best case, which I experience and witness every day, The Great Deconstruction is a marvelous example of "liminal space" we can learn to befriend. Although I had heard the term *liminal space* many times previously, the expression didn't register in my heart until I ran across the clear and positive descriptions of it that Fr. Richard Rohr offers in his writing and teaching ministry. The word *liminal* may be new to you, but I am confident the experience of it is not. As Fr. Richard defines it, liminal space is:

> ...an inner state and sometimes an outer situation where we can begin to think and act in new ways. It is where we are betwixt and between, having left one room or stage of life but not yet entered the next...when our former way of being is challenged or changed....

...Liminal space is where we are most teachable, often because we are most humbled.[420]

When we understand the concept of liminal space, it helps to clarify for us the nature of what many people (ourselves included) experience as deconstruction. In this chapter, I will reflect on liminal space (1) as a way of speaking about transition times, (2) as a season of transition in our experience of God, and (3) as an aspect of our approach to God. In all cases, liminal space is an opportunity, as I described earlier, for God to *come down* and *come from within* us to bring needed restoration.

1. LIMINAL SPACE AS TRANSITION TIMES

By now, it may seem tiresome to use the COVID-19 pandemic as an illustration for anything, but it's something we all have personal experience of, and it's a stark example of liminal space, defined as a transition time in the extreme that impacts how we live. "The pandemic" is an umbrella term for all the ways in which that viral blizzard has affected our cultures, our communities, our economies, our churches, and our families. Together, we've lost our loved ones, jobs, connections, health, and even friendships with people who responded to it differently than we did. Liminal space includes the experience of grief and/or trauma over the severity or longevity of these losses. I don't doubt that therapists could already diagnose PCTD—*Post-COVID Trauma Disorder*—especially considering the stress of holding our collective breath, wondering when or how it will end. Some people will see parallels between the liminal space of the pandemic and the onset or acceleration of their deconstruction.

Being in a place of liminal space invites and requires us to make adjustments—new ways of being we have to adopt and old ways of being we need to release. Once I recognized that the pandemic functioned as liminal space, I began asking myself and others the following five questions with empathy and attention, beginning with these two:

1. *How has the pandemic changed your life?* What rhythms of life or regular practices were interrupted by infections, lockdowns, and mandates? What do you miss the most? What do you look forward to resuming?

2. Conversely, *what new practices did you have to adopt* that have become regular (but not necessarily normal) routines?

After two years of COVID, I missed hugging. I'm a hugger. Or I used to be. I hope that comes back. I hope it doesn't feel too awkward. I also miss seeing my far-away-friends face-to-face. I have adapted to and appreciated video conferencing—it's how I continued teaching and how Christmas with our children (from Toronto to Korea) became possible. But it isn't the same as sharing the physical space of a living room. For Eden, the biggest difference was the damper it put on hosting dinners. She felt the infringement on her hospitality deeply. I hope you're able to consider these questions in the past tense: What did you miss the most? What brought you the greatest joy once it was restored?

I also wonder what aspects of life you might have dreaded resuming. Millions of employees became accustomed to working from home (in pyjamas) and dreaded commuting back to their cubicles. In fact, a significant percentage of the workforce would apparently rather resign! The introverts among us became so accustomed to their solitude or staying within their inner circle that resuming life outside their "bubble" became intimidating. In my case, what I dreaded most was getting drawn back into an aggressive travel schedule, which brings me to my next question:

1. *What old ways will you leave behind permanently?*

One redemptive gift of liminal space (including the pandemic) is that you taste of a life other than what you knew and lived before. And when the changes are involuntary, they may also feel guilt-free. After a while, one wonders, why was I living that way? Did I have to? How healthy was that lifestyle? What was driving me? What if I were to leave those practices behind permanently?

In the period from March 2020 until the end of that year, I had to cancel over thirty flights. The immediate downside was missing friends, missing conferences, and missing a large percentage of my income from speaking engagements. As my itinerant schedule dissolved, I wondered how soon our savings would dwindle. We tightened our belts (but only a bit) and trusted ourselves to God's care…because we had to. Six months in, we realized that our new budget was workable. More than that, I surfaced from a swamp of chronic jetlag. I knew my travel schedule had been unhealthy, but, at the time, I couldn't seem to make the needed changes voluntarily. Now that I was grounded—literally and figuratively—Eden and I resolved that I would *not* resume the old pace, even after we were cleared for liftoff.

How about you? Have you distanced yourself from any old patterns and practices that are best left behind? What has stopped that needs to stay parked forever? Perhaps you've even developed a healthy distance from relationships with individuals or circles (even churches) for which this liminal space created a much-needed boundary. What if the liminal space gave you the extra nudge you needed to *not* go back?

2. Conversely, what new practices did you adopt that you will continue permanently?

Before the pandemic, I was troubled by how many people who were deconstructing also drifted into *alienation* and then isolation, with no resistance. Some complained, others shrugged. Alienation was a side effect people seemed willing to accept as they exited their faith communities. Alienation is especially disconcerting if you associate it with Jesus's language of "perishing" or "outer darkness." Yet, in The Great Deconstruction, it was becoming the new normal—and, indeed, the primary response was to justify it. Alienation was the accepted cost tied to deconstruction.

Then something wonderful happened. The forced isolation of the pandemic stirred in us an active resistance to alienation that we had lacked before. What we found acceptable or necessary in our deconstruction was no longer something we were willing to live with under virus mandates. Quite suddenly, we woke up to the sickness inherent in *distance*.

Let's ignore the artificial persecution complex of many Christians over health regulations pertaining to the pandemic. Instead, let's bring it closer to home. Perhaps you've had experiences similar to mine. Eden and I had lived next door to Darryl and Christine for fifteen years. We had not once shared a meal with this couple or conversed with them for longer than thirty seconds in all that time. We found this acceptable. We live in a cul-de-sac of less than a dozen homes, but I couldn't have named even half the people who live within a stone's throw of our house. We had no hostility toward them, but we lived in the alienation of apathy toward our neighbors.

Then the pandemic hit. Amazing! Resistance to alienation began to stir in our neighborhood. With the help of another neighbor, Eden and I created a map of our street with everyone's name on it so we could stand outside, greet them by name, and enter into conversations with them; soon enough, we added outdoor deck "happy-hour" neighborhood get-togethers. Eden and our next-door neighbor Darryl even conspired to use the smoker for our first dinner together. We co-installed a shared fence and dismantled the relational fence that had divided us. I hope these new practices become permanent. The gift of liminal space inside the curse of a pandemic awakened and emboldened us to battle the long-form disease of alienation.

3. Seeing what liminal space is and how it works (for or against us), we can now explore the question *What other liminal times have you experienced?*

Think of changing residence—sorting, packing, junking, moving. Or vocational change—resigning or being laid off, being unemployed, applying for a new job, training to work in a new field. Other major transitions include hitting puberty, leaving home to live on one's own, getting married, having children, realizing you may never get married or have children, becoming an empty nester, experiencing divorce, going through a midlife crisis, undergoing menopause, retiring, caring for elderly parents, aging, facing mortality, and becoming a widow or widower. These are all major liminal spaces, in-between times that are necessary, perilous, and pregnant with possibility. A time to reflect, to adapt, to let go, and to pick up.

For me, leaving behind pastoral ministry after twenty years was a liminal space for the ages—a bit of an identity crisis, really. It took time for me to realize I couldn't and wouldn't and shouldn't return to the ministry. Four years lapsed between my resignation and my establishing a career in academia. That liminal space provided time for me to reorient my life and begin a healing journey; it was an opportunity to rethink my foundational beliefs and a season to rework my relationship with God and my family. In retrospect, I now see that time as a gift. Today, I sense intimations that this current reset due to the pandemic holds similar promise.

2. LIMINAL SPACE IN OUR EXPERIENCE OF GOD

Let's turn next to how The Great Deconstruction has impacted our relationships with God. I'm not talking about doctrinal shifts. I'm referring to significant transitions in our experience (or non-experience) of God. Specifically, we have seasons when our hearts feel either *filled with* or *emptied of* God's "felt presence"—times when God is more noticeably everywhere *present* or apparently grievously *absent*. What changes? God? Us? Circumstances?

In such cases, how did an obvious heightening of awareness of the divine presence reorient you to God, to yourself, to others, to the world? How have experiences of divine absence impacted you? Were you troubled? As we've previously discussed, we might initially assume that the former (presence) is "good" and the latter (absence) is "bad." But are they? Who or what are we judging by that assumption? How fair is it to assign a specific meaning to the ebb and flow of our spiritual sensitivity? Is how much or how little we *feel* God's presence something we control?

I think back to a dark time when our dear friends Dwight and Lorie lost a child, Adriana. In the earliest days of that awful situation, Lorie seemed to experience the death of their daughter as "presence" while Dwight experienced it as intense "absence." At first, Lorie witnessed a strong sense of the presence of both God and Adri—she could feel their nearness, sensed that Adri was okay, and spoke about receiving divine comfort. Meanwhile, Dwight described an anguished absence of both his daughter and his God. No nearness, no comfort, just unrelenting grief.

Presence good, absence bad, right? I wasn't so sure. I wondered if Lorie needed to dissociate just in order to function—that worried me a bit, but it was not something for me to "manage." She needed to go through the grief process in her own way and timing. Dwight was just the opposite: keenly in touch with his grief, with himself. It felt like the pain was doing the work. Denial bad, grief good, right? No, that's still a judgment. Each of our friends walked their own experience, and it wasn't as if they chose it. It just was. I'm so grateful that they learned to walk together despite their very different experiences. Lorie didn't goad false comfort in Dwight, and he didn't despise her mystical moments of presence.

Eventually, they both met in what she calls "the great sadness," a reference to Paul Young's book *The Shack*. And through a convergence of surprising connections, Dwight and Lorie found themselves in Paul's (and "Papa" God's) embrace on the set of *The Shack* movie. That story is theirs to tell, and you can read about it online or in the appendix to the 2016 edition of *The Shack*.[421] Briefly, Lorie tells us that, over time, divine love transformed her "great sadness" into a "grand embrace." We have also watched with gratitude as Dwight found his warm smile again and recovered his creativity, without ever practicing forgetfulness. Their faith experiences were certainly dismantled and then recreated—not into what they were before but into something different, something deeper.

In considering their experiences, images of trees come to mind. I see willows that bend but don't break. I see oaks that stand strong and sturdy through the storm. I watch the leaves of their old notions of God blown away, and a springtime of new spiritual growth emerge.

I see in my precious friends how life-changing events challenge and alter our connection with God—permanently, for better or worse. How we respond matters, for sure, but even our deepest trials can be the occasion for a sacred experience, whether felt as presence or absence.

And in your case?

+ Can you recall an experience of God's felt presence?
+ Have you experienced God's felt absence?
+ Has a life trial ever driven you away from God?
+ Has a life trial ever drawn you even closer to God?

When "sh*t gets real," we see that deconstruction is not just a mental game we play with doctrinal constructs. Our experience of life, especially through the disorientation of liminal space, can open up or shut down the ways in which we experience God, even without our making conscious choices about what we believe. Any given triumph in life can make us mindful or forgetful of God—and any given trial can send us scurrying toward or away from God. These dynamics are amplified by the vulnerability of our hearts during liminal time.

3. LIMINAL SPACE AND OUR APPROACH TO GOD

The etymology of *liminal* is "doorway" or "threshold." Liminal space is about the *space between*—between inside and outside, entry and exit, before and after. Liminal space is an opportunity to leave what was behind and enter into what is to come. It's about crossing the threshold, passing through the doorway, and walking into a new place—in our world, in our story, in ourselves, in God. While our *experience* of God (as presence or absence) during liminal seasons is largely involuntary, our *orientation* and *approach* to God is not. We can enter the door, exit the door, stand at the door. We do have some agency.

Obviously, if I choose to clench my fists, shut my eyes, and turn away from Love, I will have a different experience than if I turn toward Love with my hands and heart wide open. Running from God or running to God doesn't change God's heart toward us. It may not determine whether God feels present or absent to us. But our response is sure to impact our lives. If, throughout a trial, I bury my head in the sand, the outcome will be different than it would have been if I had buried my head in the divine bosom. More subtly, liminal space may call us to give ourselves to earnest asking, seeking, and knocking at the door,[422] while, at other times, the Spirit may say to us, "Just hush. Cease striving. Be still and wait patiently for the Good Shepherd." These images suggest that our approach to God may have an influence on our experience of God.

I raise this point because a common experience in deconstruction is a feeling of spiritual brain freeze—a kind of paralysis like, "I'm stuck. I don't know what to do. I don't know what to feel or think. I don't know how to pray or if I even should pray. I don't know where or what God is. Help!" If you're not feeling something similar, don't worry. I'm writing this for those who are.

Aside from the obvious—turn *toward* God, not *away from* God—our approaches to God are less about doing it right or wrong than they are about our unique spirituality and what we find most helpful or fruitful for enjoying a connection with the divine. The varied temperaments and experiences of individuals and even movements may favor a particular *via* (way) that best accommodates their spiritual needs. What stimulates communion with God for one heart may be alienating to another, more acutely so during times of liminal transition.

Let's review a few of the major approaches to God and what gift each way might have for you, even in deconstruction, regardless of your temperament.

Via Negativa. In an earlier chapter, I described the *via negativa*—the negative way—as drawing closer to God by *negating* what God is *not* and by removing obstacles in our minds and lives that impede our pathway. Maybe you need to hear that Nietzsche was wrong: God is *not* dead. I hope you're also discovering that God is *not dread*.

The *via negativa* was an approach to God that worked for ascetics—those minimalists whose experience of God was best served by decluttering their hearts, their minds, and their lives. Their simplicity reduced the noise that hindered a "clear signal" between God's heart and theirs. It's unlikely you're in the market for a hermitage right now, but I believe you can relate to metaphors such as removing clutter or letting go of baggage.

Here is one of the simplest conversations to have with Jesus: "Lord, would you show me something that is cluttering up my path to communion with you, with myself, with others?" If you're brave, you can ask him to show you external clutter (a habit, a possession, a commitment, etc.) that it's time to let go of. Or you can ask him to show you internal clutter (a resentment, a regret, a worry, etc.) that is an obstacle to deeper communion. You can consider letting it go or asking God to take it (but be prepared to participate). Or maybe the "positive way" is more your style.

Via Positiva. In this approach, we consider new tools that we could make use of to enhance our approach to God. I'm referring first to old standbys (Scripture reading, prayer, fellowship, teaching) that we may have ditched in our deconstruction. Maybe we felt they had become dry and stale—or maybe we had become dry and stale. Who knows, right? I just know that, for myself, I needed a break from the ways I used to read and pray and fellowship and worship and learn. Gradually, I'd become inoculated to their positive effects.

The problem is that we can only fast from Christian practice so long before we become spiritual anorexics who lose our taste for food and are malnourished or develop spiritual scurvy. But buckling down and "pressing in" to practice the disciplines is rarely a solution. I'm more inclined to experiment with ways of *refreshing* the disciplines so that they're more like delights. In my experience, I didn't change the ingredients so much as I rearranged the recipe. I sat under new teachers, focused on different texts, practiced new (and ancient) forms of prayer and worship, and started serving in small ways in a counter-cultural parish.

All of this has helped me—but that's just me. If you were to emulate my path, I doubt it would benefit you in the same way. What you can do is ask God, "Is there some element I'm missing that I'm now ready to pick up? What one additive would enrich our communion together?" What comes to mind? OR, could the first step be in our next category?

Via Activa. I see more enthusiasm these days for the *active way*—an approach to God that says, "I can't sit still through church services or prayer meetings, and I'm not much of a reader or a prayer. But give me a hammer, and I'll swing it; a loaf of bread to bake, and I'll share it; a mountain path, and I'll climb it."

I once heard Tony Campolo encourage service work as an active approach to God. He was promoting Habitat for Humanity, and he claimed, "You will sense the presence of God in what you're doing." Or, to paraphrase Bono, "Don't ask God to bless what you're doing. Find out what God is already blessing and go do it." I think of relief and development workers, human rights and peace activists, contemporary heroes like the late Bishop Tutu, or "Red Letter Christians" like Tony Campolo and Shane Claiborne.[423]

Even if the *via activa* is not your primary vocation, Eden and I can testify to the profound communion we experience during times of service work through people we meet in liminal space—in *their* transition times as much as ours. Something sacred occurs when we make ourselves present to vulnerable souls—we can't help but bump into Jesus there. According to Matthew 25, the disenfranchised are icons of his presence. To serve them is to welcome him. I wonder: is there an act of service, even a one-off, to which Jesus invites your participation today? Give it an ask. If you hear nothing at all, no worries. Contact me, and I'll give you a list.

Via Creativa. Let's wrap up these approaches with the "creative way." Not surprisingly, this approach often works for those known as "Creatives." The creatives I'm referring to are iconographers and mosaicists, painters and sculptors, musicians and composers, authors and poets, playwrights and actors, photographers and graphic designers, knitters and quilters, dancers and performers, and more! It's not that they'd rather dance or paint than pray or worship. Rather, their choreography and their brushstrokes *are* prayer and worship. Their creative edge is the threshold where heaven and earth meet— where Papa and the children play and sing and co-create!

You may be as inept an artist as I am, but I don't believe that anyone made in the Creator's image can be completely uncreative. Even for those of us who don't generate artistic content, at the very least, we can appreciate creativity in others who facilitate wonder and communion—their art leads us into "the presence." Do you have a creative gift to offer today? Who is it for? Could you receive one? Is your heart open to a song, a poem, a photograph, or a painting that's looking for a home? Could you imagine God waiting to meet you there?

Of these four approaches, which ones resonate with you *most?* Which come most naturally to you? When did you last meet God there? Would you be willing to book an appointment with God to revisit that place? If God said, "Yes, I'll be there Saturday morning anytime between seven and ten," would you show up?

Of these options, which are *least* familiar to you? Could one of them be a place to refresh your communion with God? Or has that approach just not worked for you? No worries—you aren't obligated to force the door open!

Your particular temperament does not make you less spiritual or God less accessible. But consider this possibility: during deconstruction, we may be more open to sampling new and unfamiliar doorways to encounter.

CHRIST THE DOOR

The primary point of this chapter has been to say that what we call deconstruction is a kind of transition, a liminal space, a doorway—an entrance as much as an exit. Consider now, also, this claim of Jesus Christ: "I AM the gate [or door]. If anyone comes in by me, they will be safe, and will go in and out and find pasture" (John 10:9, emphasis added). Thus, the *doorway* is not merely an entrance or exit on our journey to somewhere else. The door is Christ himself. Liminal space need not be reduced to the transition episodes of life I've described. Rather, or in addition, the entirety of our lives, from birth to death, is liminal (1) because we are forever "on the way," *and also* (2) because we are "*in Christ*," the blood-marked doorway, whose eternal life is ours now (believe it or not), even while we are in transit to the end of the ages. Metaphors such as *journey, way (via)*, and *path* remind us that we are sojourners in motion, in development, and so forth, while the image of a *gate* or *door* (or even *hallway*) indicates that our passage moves through stages, phases, or seasons. And here we see Christ "everywhen"-present... he IS the Way, he IS the Door, so our liminality, our deconstruction, even our dark nights are fully found within his loving care and are, in themselves, venues for communion with God. If so, deconstruction is not something we need to fear or flee—we might just watch for Jesus to emerge on the waves from within the storm, calling us to join him.

OUTRO:

LIVING COMMUNION NOW

HOW CAN WE HAVE THIS LIVING COMMUNION?

I was asked, *"How can I have this living communion with God...now?"*

It's troubling, isn't it, that we aren't even aware that we already have it?

How did the leaders and teachers of Christianity so fail its adherents in the promise of "personal relationship with God" and "eternal life" and leave so many without a witness of *how* we experience the kingdom of heaven here and now—the "presence in communion" that welcomes us out of alienation into the lived experience of grace?

And how is it that so many of today's proponents of The Great Deconstruction fail to deliver on that same promise rather than wholeheartedly seeking to serve it?

The answer in both cases may be that they can't offer what they don't actually believe in. Or maybe they do believe in it, but somehow they've narrowed their expectations around what it must look like.

How can we have this living communion?

Sometimes I find myself tongue-tied in responding to this question because it's become so much the air I breathe, even when—or especially when—I'm struggling badly. I struggle daily. I am struggling today, worrying about my grandson, who is in emergency room at this moment after vomiting blood [note: he's fine]. But my struggle is inside of that communion.

This is how I write. As life happens.

This is how I live. As God happens.

Resting or writhing, I'm in the arms of the One in whom I live and move and have my being. This is living communion.

So how can *you* have this? Maybe I just don't know how it happens. For me, I turn my head or heart or attention toward God, and the One who is with us and in us is there. There's a *There* there.

But that answer doesn't satisfy me, so why would it satisfy you?

I put the question to my dear friend Paul E. Ralph.[424]

How can I have this living communion...now?

Paul reflected on the nature of communion (versus alienation) and identified four common ways we talk about it:

+ Communion with self
+ Communion with others
+ Communion with creation
+ Communion with God

He surmised that Christianity's great misstep has been reversing this order, or truncating it, as we seek to bypass ourselves, others, and creation in our quest for God. Because we believe God is our ultimate reality and should be our first love, we've created this hierarchy that elevates God right out of our lives, our existence. We've so objectified God and made God so wholly/holy Other that God is now beyond, separate, distant, and silent in our experience of ourselves, others, and our world.

If I am alienated from or inattentive to myself, detached from others, or disconnected from God's good earth, how will I commune with God when that's precisely where God lives? The faith in which I was trained described the Christian life as three cars on a track: fact > faith > feeling, in that order. The eggheads among us (yours truly) exulted in our mastery of the objective truth of God's existence but subordinated, distrusted, and finally negated subjective experience as a way to know the Truth. God was "known" as a fact to be proven and assimilated rather than as a Person we encountered. My parents and grandparents knew better, but I was a giddy zealot of Christian rationalism.

Paul (Ralph, but the apostle, too) critiques that way of being as too prescriptive (metaphysical claims) instead of descriptive (our witness of living communion). If we neglect the latter, "belief" in the former is a brittle set of propositions that we have to prove to ourselves with sufficient ardor to find assurance or certitude about them.

He proposed that humans are unique, so each of us must discover which entry point is best for us. Some people will first find God in communion with themselves. Other people will first find God in communion with others. And still others will first find God in communion with creation. God indwells and expresses Godself in all three venues.

During our conversation about living communion, I told Paul that I could understand his point because of an experience Eden and I shared. Eden surprised and delighted me during the Advent season one year. Advent is that pre-Christmas time when we practice attentive waiting and prepare for the coming of Christ. Eden saw that our waiting is not simply preparation for the Nativity celebration of Christ's birth. Nor is "the coming" deferred to the end of history when Christ restores all things and all people. Rather, the coming we wait for is our attentive openness to the always-coming of God's presence in communion.

To my great joy, Eden said that she can no longer imagine a day going by when she *doesn't* experience the presence of Christ. Good news!

I asked her, using Paul's word *communion*, to *describe* what that's like for her. What surprised me was how every single example came via a human interaction, often incredibly mundane but always significant to her. The moment where a store clerk goes out of her way to find everything Eden needs (and God winks at her). The elderly Sikh man who makes eye contact and offers a radiant smile (and God winks at her). The responsive laughter of baby Felix when he recognizes her (and God winks at her). The boy who asks for our recyclables but then drops off chocolate and a card (and God winks at her). This is living communion with God and deep joy in the mundane, even on Mondays.

I understand her descriptions, especially given the visitations of Christ I experience through people who bear the burden of disabilities, addictions, poverty, or injustice. Christ-in-them or Christ-as-them moves me to tears when he can catch my attention.

But, for me, living communion often happens when I'm all alone and willing to overcome alienation from myself, when I fast (from self-loathing) and pray (without words).

I remember when my cousin Melanie, a charismatic Catholic, once said to me, "Brad, I've been praying for you, and I think Jesus has a message for you. I think he's saying, 'It's really important for you to *know* and *love* and *listen* to little Bradley—your inner child—because that's the part of you who sees and hears me most clearly.'"

When I shared this with Paul, he said, "*YES! This is what Mark Heard meant by the lyric 'He saw the world through unused eyes.*"[425] And maybe it is what Jesus meant when he said, 'Unless you come to me like little children, you won't enter [experience] the kingdom of heaven [presence in communion].'"[426]

Those are hints at entering into communion, but I returned to the initial question. "Paul, what would you say to that question, *How can I have this living communion with God...now?*"

He recalled an evening of conversation with the band Jars of Clay, in which someone asked, "How do you overcome writer's block?" One of the band members replied, in essence,

I don't believe in writer's block. Instead, I kneel down, pick up the broken shards of pottery that are strewn in the dirt around my own two feet, dust them off, and describe them to whoever will listen—myself included.

To me, this response integrated *so many* streams of thought and tied together our whole conversation. What the songwriter described is how we come into living communion with the divine presence of perfect Love.

YES, our communion with God is unapologetically subjective and existential...or please don't call it a "personal relationship." Because God IS personal, relational, and responsive.

And we encounter this God through *attention*. As I attend to the needs and wisdom of my inner child who speaks from God's lap. Or as Eden is attentive to how God expresses Godself through *everyone* she encounters. Or as our photographer friend Jean pays attention to the Belted Kingfishers feeding their young.

Do you want a divine encounter? Pay attention. Surely this is what Simone Weil meant by the aphorism *"Attention IS prayer."*[427] And as my recovery community would add, "With gratitude." Attention with gratitude to ourselves, to others, and to the world opens our hearts to God's presence in communion.

In those moments, ask yourself, "What is God saying?" This is what Eugene Peterson dubbed "alert listening."

FROM ATTENTION TO ACTION: "HOW WILL YOU SHOW UP?"

> Why do you call me, "Lord, Lord," and don't do what I say?
>
> (Luke 6:46).

It's disconcerting when our discovery of God's everywhere-present grace leads us to inaction in that grace, rather than motivating and mobilizing us to be instruments of grace in our world. Or when "spiritual people" become self-absorbed, so hypnotized by the mirror of self-reflection that their fingernails never get dirty with life. Weil would say that true attention *always* manifests in action. James would say, "But be doers of the word and not merely hearers who deceive themselves" (James 1:22 NRSV). The Sikh "Revolutionary Love" activist Valarie Kaur calls this "showing up."

> The only way we will survive as a people is if we show up.… I believe that you are the midwives in this time of great transition, tasked with birthing a new future for all of us.
>
> So I've come to ask you, how will you show up? How will you let bravery lead you? And how will you show up with love?… The greatest social reformers in history have built and sustained entire nonviolent movements to change the world that were rooted, that were grounded in love; love as a wellspring for courage, not love as a rush of feeling, but love as sweet labor, fierce and demanding and imperfect and life-giving, love as a choice that we make over and over again.
>
> Revolutionary love is the choice to enter into labor, for others, for our opponents, and for ourselves. The first practice: see no stranger. All the great wisdom traditions of the world carry a vision of oneness; the idea that we are interconnected and interdependent, that

we can look upon the face of anyone or anything and say as a spiritual declaration and a biological fact, "You are a part of me I do not yet know."[428]

Valarie champions the transforming power of love in the tradition of Jesus, Guru Nanak, Gandhi, and MLK. I share the bare bones of her vision here because, when it comes to reorientating our lives, our faith, and our practice toward the light of Love, her voice and her mission draw me deep into the heart of the Jesus Way. Christians and ex-Christians alike would do well to sit at her feet for a season. Kaur's learning hub[429] guides readers and educators into the practice of "revolutionary love." Here she describes a threefold strategy for "showing up" centered on the words (1) *wonder*, (2) *grieve*, and (3) *fight*.

> **To *wonder*** is to cultivate a sense of awe and openness to others' thoughts and experiences, their pain, their wants and needs. It is to look upon the face of anyone or anything and say: *You are a part of me I do not yet know.* Wonder is an orientation to humility: recognizing that others are as complex and infinite to themselves as we are to ourselves. Wondering about a person gives us information for how to love them. You can practice wonder for *all* others—animals, trees, living beings, and the earth. Wonder gives you information for how to care for them. Wonder is the wellspring of love.[430]

> **To *grieve*** with others is to share their pain, without trying to minimize or erase it. Grieving with others requires a willingness to be transformed by their experiences, especially those who have suffered trauma and violence. Grieving collectively and in community gives us the information to build solidarity, to fight for justice, and even to share in one another's joy.[431]

> **To *fight*** is to choose to protect those in harm's way. To fight with revolutionary love is to fight against injustice alongside those most impacted by harm, in a way that preserves our opponents' humanity as well as our own. When we fight for those outside our immediate circle, our love becomes revolutionary.[432]

If the fog of deconstruction has left you feeling lost and vulnerable, I commend Kaur's story, life, and training as a compass for the disoriented. As one of my colleagues said to me recently, "Valarie Kaur's Love Revolution is where I'd like Christianity to get someday."

WHY AM I HERE TODAY?

My conversation with Paul Ralph came to its apex as we discussed his personal mission statement. To me, it answers the question, *how can I have this living communion with God...now?*

> To notice and affirm the beauty of dignity and grace (the imago Dei) in the world around me. In the obvious and the unexpected, in the triumph and the tragedy, and in the delicious ambiguities of life. And, to invite others to consider the same.

If this orientation to life doesn't count, then surely nothing counts, because God is not elsewhere.

But if it does count, when we lean into it, we'll soon feel God's breath in our lungs and God's love in our hearts—in our attention and in every action devoted first to the intentions of God.

Paul then challenged me with this follow-up question: *How will I live today?* He offered the following blessing, which I share as my blessing to you:

> Gift it forward. Let Bradley—the little child in you who sees Jesus—wait for Jesus, be nourished by Jesus, and gift forward the mercy that's been lavished on him.

BENEDICTION

True faith is a constant dialogue with doubt, for God is incomparably greater than all our preconceptions about Him; our mental concepts are idols that need to be shattered. So as to be fully alive, our faith needs continually to die.[433]

—METROPOLITAN KALLISTOS WARE

We need not be anxious for anyone who's deconstructing. Jesus takes all human questions, doubts, deep hurts, and cross-examinations into himself as his own, takes them into his conversation with the Father. He is not ashamed to stand with us, one and all, and share our griefs and puzzlements.

As the human God in eternity he does not abandon us when we express disappointment, anger, frustration, or despair, does not ignore or sweep our injuries under the rug, but joins us in these wrestlings, and with patience he gives himself to all of our pains, sorrows, and losses.

We can trust ourselves and others with the human God. He is more beautiful and good than we have been told. He waits every morning and night of the world for our words and glances, sighs and groans. He rejects nothing we bring to him, even the hard and inexpressible things. His love handles it all.[434]   —FATHER KENNETH TANNER

Amen.

NOTES

Foreword by Brian Zahnd: "Something Is Happening Here"
1. Friedrich Nietzsche, *The Anti-Christ* (New York: SoHo Books, 2010), 30.
2. Martin Heidegger, "Nur noch ein Gott kann uns retten," Der Spiegel 30 (May 1976): 193–219. Trans. by W. Richardson as "Only a God Can Save Us," in *Heidegger: The Man and the Thinker* (1981), ed. T. Sheehan, 45–67, http://www.ditext.com/heidegger/interview.html.
3. See John 6:51–55.

Preface: The D-Word: Possibilities and Pedigree
4. *A Grief Observed* by CS Lewis © copyright 1961 CS Lewis Pte Ltd. Reprinted with permission.
5. See also Bradley Jersak, "Trending: #Deconstruction," in *A More Christlike Way: A More Beautiful Faith* (Pasadena, CA: CWR Press, 2019), 35–53."
6. "Nones" are those who have no religious affiliation or are not part of a specific denomination, and "dones" are those who declare they are finished with the church and religion, at least as they have experienced it to this point.
7. Derrida questions fundamental Western conceptual distinctions—the binary oppositions (presence/absence, speech/writing, etc.) that undergird our dominant ways of thinking. See Jack Reynolds, "Jacques Derrida (1930–2004)," *Internet Encyclopedia of Philosophy*, https://iep.utm.edu/derrida.
8. David Hayward started using the word deconstruction in 2006 to refer to the act of removing all that is superfluous in our spiritual lives. See David Hayward (@nakedpastor), Twitter, November 9, 2021, 8:00 a.m, https://twitter.com/nakedpastor/status/1458056842693816322.
9. See Richard Rohr, *The Wisdom Pattern: Order, Disorder, Reorder* (Cincinnati, OH: Franciscan Media, 2020).
10. See Brian McLaren, *Faith After Doubt: Why Your Beliefs Stopped Working and What to Do About It* (New York: St. Martins, 2021).
11. See Richard Kearney, *Anatheism: Returning to God After God* (New York: Columbia University Press, 2010).
12. See especially Brian Zahnd, *Water to Wine: Some of My Story* (self-pub., Spello Press, 2016) and *When Everything's On Fire: Faith Forged from the Ashes* (Downers Grove, IL: IVP Books, 2021).

PART I:
MEMOIRS: TRAUMA, PURGATION, AND LIBERATION

1. Freefall: My Messy Memoir
13. David Hayward, Facebook, June 29, 2021, https://www.facebook.com/nakedpastor/posts/4547368311959310.
14. See Mark 4:38.
15. Many of the stories I recount in this book happened on the day or week that I wrote them, and I'll say so, but understand that the writing process was protracted—over the course of late 2020 through spring 2022.
16. Pete Enns (@peteenns), "5 Truths About a Deconstructed Faith," Instagram, May 4, 2021, https://www.instagram.com/p/COeO1Bkhuw1.
17. Post-traumatic stress disorder. I suffered from a subset of this condition called *chronic* traumatic stress disorder, or CTSD.

18. See Mathew 12:20 NRSV, NIV.
19. Simone Weil (1909–43) was a French philosopher, political theorist, activist, and religious mystic.
20. See Romans 13:8.

2. Good, Bad, or Ugly: Sorrow and Joy Flow Mingled Down
21. See Bradley Jersak, *A More Christlike Way: A More Beautiful Faith* (Pasadena, CA: CWR Press, 2019), chapter 2.
22. See, for example, Revelation 21:5.

3. True Be-Leavers
23. See Simone Weil, *The Need for Roots: Prelude to a Declaration of Duties Towards Mankind* (New York: Routledge, 2001).
24. The "Other" refers to those we perceive as fundamentally different from ourselves—whom we hold in an us-them position of fear or hostility—and, therefore, whom we treat as if they don't belong. For a good overview of this concept, see "The Other," https://academic. brooklyn.cuny.edu/english/melani/cs6/other.html.
25. David Hayward (@nakedpastor), "Deconstruction," Facebook, July 16, 2021, https://www. facebook.com/nakedpastor/videos/941101323119428. Text and cartoon used by permission.
26. David Goa, conversation with author, February 25, 2021.
27. We see this theme, among many other places in Scripture, in Psalm 118:1–4, 29.
28. Paul also directed me to a series of podcasts by Aaron Holbrough entitled "beLEAVING the Faith, Part One," June 12, 2022, and "beLEAVING the Faith, Part Two," June 19, 2022, *The Parish*, podcast, https://parishpodcasts.podbean.com.
29. Paul E. Ralph, conversation with author, July 15, 2021.
30. The word *apheimi* has been translated as "abandoned," "allow," "divorce," "forgive," "leave," "let," "let alone," "let have," "neglect," "permit," "send away," "tolerate," "utter," and "yielded." *Aperchomai* has been rendered "came," "depart," "drew," "go," "go away," "go over," "go back," "gone," "gone away," "leave," "left," "passed away," "past," "spread," "went," "went their way," "went along," "went away," "went back," "went off," and "withdrew." That's just in the NASB!
31. Anonymous, email message to author, July 16, 2021.

4. Shake Off the Dust
32. An intimate friend of mine was invited to this private meeting. He recounted the conversation to me word for word. After hearing their agenda, my friend stood up and said, "This is bogus," and walked out.
33. See, for example, Daniel 9:5; Jeremiah 14:20.
34. See Mark 1:4; Luke 3:3; Acts 13:24; 19:4.
35 Felicia Murrell, "When the Sh*t Stink Lingers," *Clarion Journal for Religion Peace & Justice*, October 2, 2021, https://www.clarion-journal.com/clarion_journal_of_ spirit/2021/10/when-the-sht-stink-lingers-felicia-murrell.html. Bold and italics are in the original. Used by permission.

5. Exodus: Spiritual Liberation
36. See Matthew 2:11–14.
37. See Isaiah 41:14; 43:1, 14; 44:6, 24; 47:4; 48:17; 49:7, 26; 54:5, 8; 59:20; 60:16; 63:16.
38. Fyodor Dostoevsky, cited in Sergius Bulgakov, *The Sophiology of Death: Essays on Eschatology: Personal, Political, Universal*, ed. Roberto J. De La Noval (Eugene, OR: Cascade Books, 2021), 2n1.
39. Charles Wesley, "And Can It Be That I Should Gain," 1738, https://hymnary.org/text/ and_can_it_be_that_i_should_gain.
40. See John 3:1–20.

41. *The Wisdom of Trauma*, directed by Maurizio Benazzo and Zaya Benazzo, featuring Dr. Gabor Maté (Sebastopol, CA: Science and Nonduality, 2021), https://drgabormate.com/the-wisdom-of-trauma/.

6. Trauma: Spiritual Mastectomy
42. Paul Kingsnorth, *Beast* (Minneapolis, MN: Graywolf Press, 2017), 2, 115, 123–24.
43. A New Testament scholar-skeptic.
44. See Michael John Cusick, *Surfing for God* (Nashville, TN: Thomas Nelson, 2012).
45. Simone Weil, *Awaiting God: A New Translation of Attente de Dieu and Lettre à un Religieux*, trans. Bradley Jersak (Abbotsford, BC: Fresh Wind Press, 2012).
46. See Numbers 21:9; John 3:14–15.
47. See Matthew 6:5–6.
48. See Kenneth Tanner, "The Universe Doesn't Love You," *Clarion Journal*, April 8, 2020, https://www.clarion-journal.com/clarion_journal_of_spirit/2020/04/the-universe-doesnt-love-you-kenneth-tanner.html.

7. Threshold: Can't Leave, Can't Enter
49. Gleb Bryanski, "Russian Patriarch Calls Putin Era 'Miracle of God,'" Reuters, February 8, 2012, https://www.reuters.com/article/uk-russia-putin-religion-idUKTRE81722Y20120208.
50. Weil's understanding of the Council of Trent (1545–63).
51. See, for example, Hebrews 13:12. We will explore this topic further in chapter 22, "'Let Us Go Out to Him': Three Cruciform Sisters."
52. Weil, *Awaiting God*, 146.
53. Brad Jersak, "Preface to Her Letters: Weil on Catholicism and Judaism," in Simone Weil, *Awaiting God*, 117–18.
54. Weil, *Awaiting God*, 124–25, 155. Italics are in the original.
55. See Revelation 2:5.
56. Conrad Hackett and David McClendon, "Christians Remain World's Largest Religious Group, but They Are Declining in Europe," Pew Research Center, April 5, 2017, https://www.pewresearch.org/fact-tank/2017/04/05/christians-remain-worlds-largest-religious-group-but-they-are-declining-in-europe/.

PART II:
SEVEN SLEEPERS OF DECONSTRUCTION

9. Seven Sleepers
57. Gregory of Tours, "The Patient Impassioned Suffering of the Seven Sleepers of Ephesus," *Contemporary Philology*, April 10, 2011, https://philologicumaequaevum.wordpress.com/2011/04/10/sevensleepers.
58. Jacobus de Voragine, *The Golden Legend: Lives of the Saints*, trans. William Caxton, ed. George V. O'Neill (Cambridge, UK: Cambridge University Press, 1914), https://brittlebooks.library.illinois.edu/brittlebooks_open/Books2008-04/voraja0001golleg/voraja0001golleg.pdf; Pieter W. van der Horst, "Pious Long-Sleepers in Greek, Jewish, and Christian Antiquity," in *Tradition, Transmission, and Transformation from Second Temple Literature through Judaism and Christianity in Late Antiquity*, ed. Menahem Kister, Hillel Newman, Michael Segal, and Ruth Clements (Leiden: Brill, 2015), 93–111 (available online at http://orion.mscc.huji.ac.il/symposiums/13th/papers/Horst.pdf); Witold Witakowski, "Legend of the Sleepers of Ephesus," in Gorgias Encyclopedic Dictionary of the Syriac Heritage: Electronic Edition, https://gedsh.bethmardutho.org/Sleepers-of-Ephesus-Legend-of-the?fq=;fq-Browse:Browse;J.

59. Bartłomiej Grysa, "The Legend of the Seven Sleepers of Ephesus in Syriac and Arab Sources: A Comparative Study," *Orientalia Christiana Cracoviensia* 2 (2010), 52, http://czasopisma.upjp2.edu.pl/orientalia/article/download/1011/895.

60. Grysa, "The Legend of the Seven Sleepers," 49.

61. See Joshua 10:1–15; Numbers 22; Daniel 3.

10. Into the Darkness, into the Light: Agnostic Faith (from Moses to John of the Cross)

62. Conversation with author, November 16, 2021.

63. Athenagoras the Athenian, "A Plea for the Christians," in *Ante-Nicene Fathers*, vol. 2, ed. Alexander Roberts, James Donaldson, and A. Cleveland Coxe, trans. B. P. Pratten (Buffalo, NY: Christian Literature Publishing Co., 1885), revised and edited for New Advent by Kevin Knight, http://www.newadvent.org/fathers/0205.htm. Athenagoras wrote his *Plea* to "the emperors Marcus Aurelius Antoninus and Lucius Aurelius Commodus, conquerors of Armenia and Sarmatia, and more than all, philosophers."

64. *Merriam-Webster.com Dictionary*, s.v. "revelry," https://www.merriam-webster.com/dictionary/revelry.

65. See Nehemiah 9:18–19.

66. *Apophasis*, or "negative theology" or "via negativa," comes from the ancient Greek ἀπόφασις, via ἀπόφημι (*apophēmi*, "to deny"); Online Etymology Dictionary, s.v. "apophatic," https://www.etymonline.com/search?q=apophatic.

67. See especially Gregory of Nyssa, *Life of Moses*, and Dionysius, *Mystical Theology*. "Both seize on Exodus 20:21 as symbolizing the utter incomprehensibility of God. But they resolve the enigmas of Exodus 33–34 differently. Gregory uses Exodus 33:18–23 as a springboard to his articulation of a never-ending journey into the infinite divine, while Exodus 34:29–35 provides the biblical impetus behind Dionysius' concept of 'union.'" A. Conway-Jones, "Exegetical Puzzles and the Mystical Theologies of Gregory of Nyssa and Dionysius the Areopagite," *Vigiliae Christianae* 75, no. 1 (2020): 1–21.

68. For more on these two forms, see Jonah Winters, "Saying Nothing About No-Thing: Apophatic Theology in the Classical World," Bahá'i Library Online, 1994, https://bahai-library.com/winters_apophatic_theology.

69. Online Etymology Dictionary, s.v. "apophatic," https://www.etymonline.com/search?q=analysis.

70. David Cayley, *George Grant in Conversation* (Concord, ON: House of Anansi Press, 1995), 34.

71. Jaroslav Pelikan, *Christianity and Classical Culture* (New Haven, CT: Yale University Press, 1993), 205.

72. Gregory of Nyssa, *The Life of Saint Macrina*, trans. Kevin Corrigan (Eugene, OR: Wipf and Stock, 2005).

73. See Thomas Merton, *New Seeds of Contemplation* (New York: New Directions, 2007).

74. See Matthew 5:1–12, "The Beatitudes."

75. Vladimir Lossky, *Orthodox Theology: An Introduction* (New York: Crestwood, 1978), 32.

76. See Hebrews 11:6.

77. See Deuteronomy 6:4.

78. See Colossians 2:9.

79. Michael Egnor, "Egnor and Solms: What Does It Mean to Say God Is a Person?" Mind Matters News, December 5, 2021, https://mindmatters.ai/2021/12/egnor-and-solms-what-does-it-mean-to-say-god-is-a-person.

80. See Genesis 1:26–27.

81. From the Greek *energeia*, translated variously as "working," "operations," "effects," or "activities" (compare 1 Cor 12:6). For more detail, see Larry Perkins, "115. God at work– Paul's Concept of the Verb *energein* and Cognates (Philippians 2:12–13)," *Internet Moments with God's Word*, June 30, 2011, https://moments.nbseminary.com/archives/115-paul's-concept-of-the-verb-energein-and-cognates---god-at-work-philippians-212-13.

82. Pelikan, *Christianity and Classical Culture*, 55.

83. See 1 Corinthians 2:6–16.

84. Of God, God's Spirit, or God's Spirit in us. See Ephesians 1:19; 3:7; 4:16; Philippians 3:21; Colossians 1:29.

85. Archbishop of Thessalonica (1296–1359).

86. See John 14:9.

87. Jonathan Bieler, "Apophaticism and Kataphaticism in Maximus the Confessor's Thought" (paper presented at Platonism and Christian Thought in Late Antiquity— International Workshop in Oslo on the Philosophy of Late Antiquity, University of Oslo, Norway, December 1–3, 2016), https://www.zora.uzh.ch/id/eprint/133816/1/Apophaticism_and_Kataphaticsim_in_Maximus_Confessor.pdf.

88. Ivana Noble, "Apophatic Way in Gregory of Nyssa," in *Philosophical Hermeneutics and Biblical Exegesis*, ed. Petr Pokorny and Jan Roskovek (Tübingen: Mohr Siebeck, 2002), 335.

89. See 2 Corinthians 3:7–18.

90. Saint John of the Cross, *Dark Night of the Soul*, trans. Edgar Allison Peers (New York: Image Books, 2005), 2.

91. See Saint John of the Cross, "The Dark Night of the Soul," trans. A. Z. Foreman, Poems Found in Translation, http://poemsintranslation.blogspot.com/2009/09/saint-john-of-cross-dark-night-of-soul.html.

92. The language of purgative, illuminative, and unitive stages is common across centuries of mystical writings. The following article is a good example and specific to John of the Cross: Tom Mulcahy, "Oh Blessed Night of Pure Faith: A Bird's Eye View of the Spirituality of St. John of the Cross," Catholic Strength, February 16, 2017, https://catholicstrength.com/2017/02/16/oh-blessed-night-of-pure-faith-a-birds-eye-view-of-the-spirituality-of-st-john-of-the-cross/.

93. Personal communication with author, April 8, 2021.

94. Anonymous, *The Cloud of Unknowing* (New York: Paulist Press, 1981), 159, https://archive.org/details/cloudofunknowing00wals.

11. Out of the Shadows: Plato (from Socrates to Weil)

95. I believe few people read or even teach Plato well these days, in great part because (1) they mistake him for a gnostic dualist, which he is not, and (2) they are using translations heavily influenced by Cartesian rationalists (e.g., translating nous as "reason," missing his entire point that contemplative knowing transcends reason).

96. See Bradley Jersak, "Pushing Back: 'Greek Thinking' vs. 'Jewish Thinking' Is a Dualistic Error," in Ron Dart and Bradley Jersak, *The Gospel According to Hermes: Intimations of Christianity in Greek Myth, Poetry & Philosophy* (Abbotsford, BC: St. Macrina Press, 2021), https://www.clarion-journal.com/files/hermes-chapter-1.pdf. Nerds note: Aristotle testifies that Socrates did not treat universals/ideas/forms as separate from the particulars in this world. All that is exists by participation in what is universal. See Aristotle, *Metaphysics* 1.987b, http://www.perseus.tufts.edu/hopper/text?doc=Perseus%3Atext%3A1999.01.0052%3Abook%3D1%3Asection%3D987b.

97. Tertullian, "Prescription Against Heretics," trans. Peter Holmes, in *Ante-Nicene Fathers*, ed. Alexander Roberts and James Donaldson (Peabody, MA: Hendrickson, 1994), 3:249.

98. Plato, *The Republic*, Book 2, 361–2a. Glaucon says, "It becomes an easy matter, I fancy, to unfold the tale of the sort of life that awaits [the righteous man]. We must tell it, then; and even if my language is somewhat rude and brutal, you must not suppose, Socrates, that it is I who speak thus, but those who commend injustice above justice. What they will say is this: that such being his disposition the just [righteous] man will have to endure the lash, the rack, chains, the branding-iron in his eyes, and finally, after every extremity of suffering, *he will be crucified....*"

99. In fact, Christian apologist Justin Martyr (second century) claimed that Plato got his understanding of creation through Moses: "And that you may learn that it was from our teachers—we mean the account given through the prophets—that Plato borrowed his statement that God, having altered matter which was shapeless, made the world, hear the very words spoken through Moses, who, as above shown, was the first prophet, and of greater antiquity than the Greek writers" (*First Apology*, ch. 59). Available online through Christian Classics Ethereal Library at https://www.ccel.org/ccel/schaff/anf01.viii.ii.lix.html.

100. Plato, *Republic*, 6.484b.

101. Plato, *Republic*, 6.484a–b.

102. Read it here: https://www.indwes.edu/academics/jwhc/_files/plato_s%20allegory%20of%20the%20cave.pdf.

103. "The reality of the world is the result of our attachment. It is the reality of the self which we transfer into things. It has nothing to do with independent reality.... Attachment is a manufacturer of illusions and whoever wants reality ought to be detached.... Attachment is no more nor less than the insufficiency in our sense of reality." Simone Weil, *Gravity and Grace*, trans. Emma Crawford and Mario von der Ruhr (New York, London: Routledge Classics, 2004), 14. "To come out of the cave, to be detached, means to cease to make the future our objective" (Weil, *Gravity and Grace*, 40).

104. Weil distinguishes between the "social," which she associates with the cave, and the domain of the "prince of this world" (the "devil")—vis-à-vis the "city" (*polis*) that she regards as potentially holy. Simone Weil, *Notebooks*, trans. Arthur Wills (New York, London: Routledge, 2004), 1:286, 296.

105. Weil plays with this ambiguity between *necessity*—the good world God created and loves—versus *force*—the fallen world order of oppressive societies (Weil, *Notebooks* 1:148–50). This ambiguity is typical of the New Testament. Compare cosmos in John 3:16 with 1 John 2:15. At the personal level, the NT also uses the term "flesh" (*sarx*) for one's God-given humanity (esp. 1 John 4:2) OR one's self-serving, self-destructive ego (e.g., Rom 8:6).

106. See Adam Ellwanger, *Metanoia: Rhetoric, Authenticity, and the Transformation of the Self* (University Park, PA: Pennsylvania State University Press, 2020); Brett M. Bertucio, "*Paideia* as *Metanoia*: Transformative Insights from the Monastic Tradition," *Philosophy of Education* (2015), 510.

107. Plato, *The Republic*, Book 7, 515c, 521c. My translation of the Greek text from Plato, *Platonis Opera*, ed. John Burnet (Oxford, UK: Oxford University Press, 1903).

12. Voltaire's Enlightenment: Love Your Frenemies

108. Tom Holland, *Dominion: How the Christian Revolution Remade the World* (New York: Basic Books, 2019), 391.

109. Immanuel Kant, "What Is Enlightenment," trans. Mary C. Smith, http://www.columbia.edu/acis/ets/CCREAD/etscc/kant.html. Italics are in the original.

110. John Ralston Saul, *Voltaire's Bastards: The Dictatorship of Reason in the West* (New York: Simon & Schuster, 2013), 6.

111. Voltaire was imprisoned in the Bastille briefly over an argument with an aristocrat, then spent a few years in self-imposed exile in England, where he became friends with the English master of satire Jonathan Swift.

112. Tejvan Pettinger, *"Biography of Voltaire,"* Biography Online, updated February 7, 2018, https://www.biographyonline.net/writers/voltaire.html.

113. N. E. Cronk, *"About Voltaire,"* Voltaire Foundation for Enlightenment Studies, University of Oxford, https://www.voltaire.ox.ac.uk/about-voltaire.

114. Saul, *Bastards*, 7.

115. Cronk, "About Voltaire."

116. Kat Eschner, "Voltaire: Enlightenment Philosopher and Lottery Scammer," *Smithsonian Magazine*, November 21, 2017, https://www.smithsonianmag.com/smart-news/voltaire-enlightenment-philosopher-and-lottery-scammer-180967265.

117. See Voltaire, *Treatise on Tolerance* (1763), trans. and ed. by Jonathan Bennett (July 2018), 3, https://earlymoderntexts.com/assets/pdfs/voltaire1763.pdf.

118. Will Durant and Ariel Durant, *The Age of Voltaire: A History of Civilization in Western Europe from 1715 to 1756, with Special Emphasis on the Conflict Between Religion and Philosophy*, Story of Civilization 9 (Boonsboro, MD: Sequitur Books, 1997), 126; available online at https://erenow.net/modern/the-age-of-voltaire-a-history-of-civlization-in-western-europe-from-1715-to-1756/126.php.

119. Durant and Durant, *The Age of Voltaire*.

120. Robert E. Lucas Jr., "Robert E. Lucas Jr., Banquet Speech," The Nobel Prize, December 10, 1995, https://www.nobelprize.org/prizes/economic-sciences/1995/lucas/speech/.

121. Saul, *Bastards*, n.p.

122. Pettinger, *"Biography of Voltaire."*

123. *Deism* is an umbrella term for rational belief in a supreme being that gave rise to the cosmos but does not interact, interfere, or intervene in creation or with humanity.

124. Holland, *Dominion*, 391–92.

125. See Romans 8:28; 2 Corinthians 4:17.

126. Contrast this to Simone Weil's anti-theodicy in which there is an "infinite distance" and real contradiction between the necessary and the good, but these are spanned by and intersected at the cross.

127. Voltaire, *Philosophical Letters: Letters Concerning the English Nation* (Mineola, NY: Courier Dover, 2003), 147.

128. Titled *"Juzio da verdadeira causa do terremoto"* ("An Opinion on the True Cause of the Earthquake"). See https://www.literaturabrasileira.ufsc.br/documentos/?action=download&id=92344.

129. Kathy Warnes, "The 1755 Lisbon Earthquake: Marquis Pombal Uses Science to Rebuild," Stories in Science, https://storiesinscience.weebly.com/the-1755-lisbon-earthquake-marquis-pombal-uses-science-to-rebuild.html.

130. Voltaire, "Poem on the Lisbon Disaster, Or an Examination of the Axiom, 'All is Well,'" *Toleration and Other Essays*, trans. Joseph McCabe (New York, London: The Knickerbocker Press, 1912), 86, https://oll.libertyfund.org/title/mccabe-toleration-and-other-essays#lf0029_head_086.

131. Voltaire, *Candide* (Electronic Scholarly Publishing Project, 1998), 1, http://www.esp.org/books/voltaire/candide.pdf.

132. Voltaire, 1–2.

133. Voltaire, *Candide*, 11–13.

134. Voltaire, "Tout est bien / All is good," in Voltaire, *Philosophical Dictionary*, ed. and trans. by Theodore Besterman (London and New York: Penguin Books, 1972), 68–74, https://www.whitman.edu/VSA/Candide/tout.est.bien.html. Italics are in the original.

135. In my summary, my primary source for this section is Voltaire's *Treatise on Tolerance*, where he lays out his case in detail. See Voltaire, *Treatise on Tolerance* (1763), trans. and ed. by Jonathan Bennett (July 2018), https://earlymoderntexts.com/assets/pdfs/voltaire1763. pdf. I also lean on Tom Holland's *Dominion* (chapter 16, "Enlightenment 1762: Toulouse") and Ken Armstrong's "Broken on the Wheel," *The Paris Review*, March 13, 2015, https:// www.theparisreview.org/blog/2015/03/13/broken-on-the-wheel.

136. Frederic Herbert Maugham, *The Case of Jean Calas* (London: Heinemann, 1928), 18–19.

137 Voltaire, *Treatise on Tolerance*, 2.

138. Armstrong, "Broken on the Wheel."

139. Armstrong, "Broken on the Wheel."

140. Armstrong, "Broken on the Wheel."

141. "Jean Calas, The Martyr of Toulouse," *The Southern Presbyterian Review* 25, no. 3 (July, 1874): 420, https://static1.squarespace.com/ static/590be125ff7c502a07752a5b/t/5f283336062baa1f2b232352/1596470071313/ Howe%2C+George%2C+Jean+Calas%2C+the+Martyr+of+Toulouse.pdf.

142. Armstrong, "Broken on the Wheel."

143. Voltaire, "Treatise on Tolerance," 33.

144. Voltaire, "Treatise on Tolerance," 35.

145. Voltaire, "Treatise on Tolerance," 36.

146. Voltaire, "Atheist, Atheism," in *Philosophical Dictionary* (London: Wynne and Scholey; James Wallis, 1802), 25–26, https://ia800905.us.archive.org/25/items/ philosophicaldic00voltrich/philosophicaldic00voltrich_bw.pdf.

147. Voltaire, "Atheist, Atheism," 26.

148. Voltaire, "Atheist, Atheism," 27–28.

149. Voltaire, "Epistle to the Author of the Book *The Three Impostors*," in *Euvres complètes de Voltaire*, ed. Louis Moland, trans. Jack Iverson (Paris: Garnier, 1877–1885), 10:402–05, https://www.whitman.edu/VSA/trois.imposteurs.html.

150. See the introduction and text at https://infidels.org/library/historical/unknown/ three_impostors.html.

151. Voltaire, "Epistle to the Author of the Book *The Three Impostors*." Boldface type is in the original.

152. Voltaire, "Theism," in *The Philosophical Dictionary*, trans. H. I. Woolf (New York: Alfred A. Knopf, 1924), 301. See https://www.gutenberg.org/files/18569/18569-h/18569-h.htm.

153. Gertrude Himmelfarb, *The Roads to Modernity: The British, French, and American Enlightenments* (Random House, Inc., New York, 2004), 154.

154. Richard Aldington, ed., *Voltaire and Frederick the Great: Letters* (London: George Routledge & Sons, Ltd, 1927), 285, https://ia801803.us.archive.org/20/items/dli. ministry.03748/8962.E13263_Letters_Of_Voltaire_and_Frederick_The_Great_text.pdf.

13. Unveiling the Darkness as Darkness: Friedrich Nietzsche, Part 1

155. Friedrich Nietzsche, *Thus Spoke Zarathustra*, in *The Portable Nietzsche*, trans. Walter Kaufmann (New York: Viking, 1988), 432, https://antilogicalism.files.wordpress. com/2017/07/the-portable-nietzsche-walter-kaufmann.pdf.

156. Sarah Kofman, "And Yet It Quakes! (Nietzsche and Voltaire)," *Paragraph* 44, no. 1 (March 2021); 117–37, trans. by Jacob Bates-Firth and John McKeane, https://www. euppublishing.com/doi/full/10.3366/para.2021.0358.

157. Jeff Matthews, "Two NY Times Accounts of the Great Ischia Earthquake of 1883," Naples: Life, Death and Miracles, http://www.naplesldm.com/ischiaquake.php.

158. "We *ourselves*, we free spirits, are already a 'transvaluation of all values,' *a visualized declaration of war and victory against all the old concepts of 'true' and 'not true.'*... *The transvaluation of Christian values*,—an attempt with all available means, all instincts and all the resources of genius to bring about a triumph of the *opposite* values, the more *noble* values." Friedrich Nietzsche, *The Antichrist*, trans. H. L. Menkcen (New York: Alfred A. Knopf, 1918), §13, 61.

159. Kofman, "And Yet It Quakes!"

160. "The Rise of Religious 'Nones' Looks Similar in Data from Pew Research Center and the General Social Survey," Pew Research Center, September 8, 2022, https://www.pewresearch.org/religion/2022/09/13/modeling-the-future-of-religion-in-america/pf_2022-09-13_religious-projections_01-01/.

161. "In U.S., Decline of Christianity Continues at Rapid Pace," Pew Research Center, October 17, 2019, https://www.pewresearch.org/religion/2019/10/17/in-u-s-decline-of-christianity-continues-at-rapid-pace/.

162. Lazar Puhalo, "We ARE the Bowls of Wrath," *Clarion Journal for Religion, Peace & Justice*, July, 28, 2021, https://www.clarion-journal.com/clarion_journal_of_spirit/2021/07/we-are-the-bowls-of-wrath-lazar-puhalo-.html.

163. Friedrich Nietzsche, *The Will to Power: Attempt at a Revaluation of All Values*, "Nov. 1887–March 1888," note 2. First German translation 1901, English translation unknown. See http://nietzsche.holtof.com/Nietzsche_the_will_to_power/the_will_to_power_book_I.htm.

164. See the German hymn "Ein Trauriger Grabgesang" ("A Mournful Dirge") by Johann von Rist (1607–67).

165. Friedrich Nietzsche, *The Gay Science*, ed. Bernard Williams, trans. Josefine Nauckhoff (Cambridge, UK: Cambridge University Press, 2001), 120.

166. See Exodus 33:7–10.

167. Brian Zahnd, *When Everything's On Fire: Faith Forged from the Ashes* (Downers Grove, IL: IVP Books, 2021), 30.

168. Friedrich Nietzsche, *On the Genealogy of Morality*, ed. Keith Ansell-Pearson, trans. Carol Diethe (Cambridge: Cambridge University Press, 2006), 17–21, https://philosophy.ucsc.edu/news-events/colloquia-conferences/GeneologyofMorals.pdf. See also Todd Calder, "The Concept of Evil," in *Stanford Encyclopedia of Philosophy Archive (Summer 2020 Edition)*, ed. Edward N. Zalta (Stanford: Metaphysics Research Lab, 2022), https://plato.stanford.edu/archives/sum2020/entries/concept-evil/.

169. See Terry Eagleton, *Reason, Faith, and Revolution: Reflections on the God Debate* (New Haven, CT: Yale University Press, 2010). Eagleton confronts the "superstitious" view of God held by his atheist opponent (the hybrid caricature he calls Ditchkins) and retrieves a revolutionary reading of the Christian gospel. But like Kierkegaard or Tolstoy, he also assaults "institutional Christianity" in its betrayal of Jesus's radical vision.

170. In a coming chapter on Fyodor Dostoevsky, chapter 17, "Possessed," we'll see him parse this out further in his novel *The Possessed*, distinguishing between bourgeois liberalism and its radicalized progeny, revolutionary progressivism.

171. On the fact that "faith in progress" cannot generate meaning, see also Leo Tolstoy, Confession, trans. David Patterson (New York and London: W.W. Norton, 1983), http://www.arvindguptatoys.com/arvindgupta/confessions-tolstoy.pdf.

172. To see the acceleration of the slave trade during the Enlightenment era, see "Trans-Atlantic Slave Trade–Estimates," Slave Voyages, https://www.slavevoyages.org/assessment/estimates?selected_tab=timeline, and McLain Sidmore, "Slaves Embarked on Voyages by Nation During the Trans-Atlantic Slave Trade," *HIST 139 Early Modern Europe*, https://earlymoderneurope.hist.sites.carleton.edu/items/show/175.

173. Valerie Strauss and Daniel Southerl, "How Many Died? New Evidence Suggests Far Higher Numbers for the Victims of Mao Zedong's Era," *Washington Post*, July 17, 1994, https://www.washingtonpost.com/archive/politics/1994/07/17/how-many-died-new-evidence-suggests-far-higher-numbers-for-the-victims-of-mao-zedongs-era/01044df5-03dd-49f4-a453-a033c5287bce/.

174. "Cambodia," University of Minnesota Holocaust and Genocide Studies, https://cla.umn.edu/chgs/holocaust-genocide-education/resource-guides/cambodia.

175. See, for example, Ephesians 2:6; Colossians 3:3.

176. Nietzsche describes resentment or *ressentiment* at length in his book *A Genealogy of Morals*.

14. Try Your Faith: Existentialist Courage

177. George Grant, *Philosophy in the Mass Age* (Toronto ON: University of Toronto Press, 1998), 75.

178. Antonio Spardaro, SJ, "'Freedom Scares Us': Pope Francis' Conversation with Slovak Jesuits," *La Civiltà Cattolica*, October 20, 2021, https://www.laciviltacattolica.com/freedom-scares-us-pope-francis-conversation-with-slovak-jesuits/.

179. See, for example, Mark 5:1–20.

180. See Galatians 5:1.

15. Con-Testing Faith: Friedrich Nietzsche, Part 2

181. See Mark 9:49–50, various translations.

182. Excerpt from *An Introduction to Nietzsche* by Lucy Huskinson, copyright © 2009 Used by permission of Baker Academic, a division of Baker Publishing Group. Lucy Huskinson, *Introduction to Nietzsche* (London, UK: SPCK, 2009), 89.

183. Friedrich Nietzsche, *Daybreak: Thoughts on the Prejudices of Morality* (Cambridge, UK: Cambridge University Press, 1997), 62. Italics are in the original.

184. Nietzsche, *Daybreak*, 57, 86.

185. Huskinson, *Introduction to Nietzsche*, 81–82.

186. You're most welcome to join us. See ssu.ca/graduate for details on online or on-site graduate studies modules.

187. This is called *Rumspringa*—literally, "to run around." See, for example, Bruce Stambauch, "The Traditional Amish Youth Period of Rumspringa," *Ohio's Amish Country*, https://ohiosamishcountry.com/articles/the-traditional-amish-youth-period-of-rumspringa.

16. The Grand Provocateur: Søren Kierkegaard

188. Mason Mannenga (@masonmennenga), Twitter, November 10, 2021, 10:44 p.m. https://mobile.twitter.com/masonmennenga/status/1458626554678984709.

189. I especially recommend Stephen Backhouse's biography *Kierkegaard: A Single Life* (Grand Rapids, MI: Zondervan, 2016), which includes a fascinating narrative on Kierkegaard the controversial recluse, lover, author, and social critic, not to mention a chapter on those whom he directly influenced, including Kafka, Barth, Bonhoeffer, Camus, and Martin Luther King Jr.

190. Søren Kierkegaard, *Provocations: Spiritual Writings of Kierkegaard*, ed. Charles E. Moore (Walden, NY: Plough Publishing, 2002). Plough has graciously granted permission for extensive citations from their compendium.

191. Kierkegaard, *Provocations*, 30.

192. Kierkegaard, 65.

193. Kierkegaard, 156.

194. Fyodor Dostoevsky, *Crime and Punishment*, trans. Constance Garnett (Planet E-book), 37, https://www.planetebook.com/free-ebooks/crime-and-punishment.

195. Kierkegaard, *Provocations*, 239.

196. Kierkegaard, 244.

197. Kierkegaard, 315.

198. Stephen Backhouse, conversation with author, January 20, 2022.

199. See Colossians 1:27.

200. Kierkegaard, *Provocations*, 227.

201. Kierkegaard, 16. Stephen Backhouse says, "It is the orthopraxis of culture, common sense, and habit that SK is attacking as saccharine, not orthodoxy as such. The problem with Christendom is precisely that it has substituted orthodoxy with sentimental patriotism." Conversation with author, January 20, 2022.

202. Kierkegaard, 232.

203. Kierkegaard contrasted the "Church Militant" with the "Church Triumphant" throughout his book *Practice in Theology*. Theologians had referred to the former as living Christians and the latter as those who've entered the heavenly kingdom. "Kierkegaard complains that Christendom has turned the Church Militant into the Church Triumphant, and has commandeered the Eternal Heavenly state without it being realized." Wyatt Houtz, "Soren Kierkegaard's Practice in Theology," *PostBarthian*, May 18, 2012, https://postbarthian.com/2012/05/18/soren-kierkegaards-practice-in-theology.

204. Kierkegaard, 204.

205. Kierkegaard, 204.

206. Kierkegaard, quoted in Charles E. Moore, "Introduction," *Provocations*, xix. This quote and the quote cited in the next endnote are from a series of pamphlets Kierkegaard wrote entitled *The Instant*.

207. Kierkegaard, quoted in Charles E. Moore, "Introduction," *Provocations*, xix.

208. I deconstruct these four counterfeit ways in *A More Christlike Way: A More Beautiful Faith*.

209. Kierkegaard, *Provocations*, 214.

210. Kierkegaard, 85.

211. Kierkegaard, 277.

212. Kierkegaard, 279.

213. Kierkegaard, 281.

214. I would have regarded Abraham as Kierkegaard's hero of faith, based on his work *Fear and Trembling*, from which we get the phrase "leap of faith." Indeed, the first draft of this book included a paragraph to that effect. But again, Backhouse to the rescue: "SK only valorizes Abraham in one book (*Fear and Trembling*) written under a pseudonym ([Johannes] de Silentio) who explicitly tells us he is not a Christian. SK basically never mentions Abraham after this book, and he never talks about the so-called leap of faith again. In fact, SK's foundational hero of faith was Jesus himself, as detailed in *Practice in Christianity*, where Jesus becomes the sign of offense against the popular crowd. The presentation of SK as someone who sees Abraham's sacrifice as *the* quintessential moment of a 'leap of faith' is one which is wrong (in fact opposite to SK's whole Jesus-centered project), but sadly deeply rooted in the popular conception of SK." Conversation with author, January 20, 2022.

215. The NIV most closely matches Kierkegaard's sense. Other translations render the first phrase as "willing to" or "desires to," but, for Kierkegaard, it's a clear choice we make, not divorced from the act.

216. Kierkegaard, *Provocations*, 271.

217. Kierkegaard, 247.

218. Kierkegaard, 65.
219. Leo Tolstoy makes a powerful case along these same lines in *What I Believe:* "My Religion," The Free Age Press "Later Works of Tolstoy (1878—)," ed. V. Tcherthooff and A. C. Fifield (Christchurch, UK: The Free Age Press, 1902), https://archive.org/details/whatibelievemyr00tolsgoog/mode/2up. Tolstoy would come to have direct influence on Gandhi's commitment to the Jesus Way applied outside of Christianity.
220. Kierkegaard, *Provocations*, 103.
221. Kierkegaard, 98.
222. Kierkegaard, 98.
223. Kierkegaard, 100.
224. Kierkegaard, 106.
225. See also Dostoevsky's "The Grand Inquisitor," a short story within *The Brothers Karamazov*, in which a Spanish priest interrogates Jesus and rebukes him for resisting Satan's wilderness temptations and bringing about a freedom that humans cannot handle and don't actually want. The church, he says, has rectified that problem. More on this theme in chapter 18 of this book, "Affliction—Full Stop: Dostoevsky, Part 2."
226. Friedrich Nietzsche, *The Birth of Tragedy Out of the Spirit of Music*, trans. Ian Johnston (Nanaimo, BC, 2008), https://www.holybooks.com/wp-content/uploads/Nietzsche-The-Birth-of-Tragedy.pdf.
227. Kierkegaard, *Provocations*, 289.
228. See Luke 10:42.
229. Kierkegaard, *Provocations*, 289.
230. Kierkegaard, 165.
231. Kierkegaard, 307.
232. See Matthew 5:20.
233. Kierkegaard, *Provocations*, 306.
234. Kierkegaard, 306.
235. Kierkegaard, 223.
236. Kierkegaard, 223.
237. See Revelation 6:9–11.
238. Kierkegaard, 260.
239. Kierkegaard, 254–255.
240. Kierkegaard, 255.
241. Kierkegaard, 255.
242. Brian McLaren, *Faith After Doubt: Why Your Beliefs Stopped Working and What to Do About It* (New York: St. Martins, 2021), 212.
243. An insight and distinction I gained in conversations with David Goa.
244 See John 6:67.
245. Johannes de Silentio (alias Søren Kierkegaard), *Fear and Trembling*, trans. Walter Lowrie (1941), https://www.sorenkierkegaard.nl/artikelen/Engels/101.%20Fear%20and%20Trembling%20book%20Kierkegaard.pdf.

17. Possessed: Fyodor Dostoevsky, Part 1

246. Fyodor Dostoevsky, "The Grand Inquisitor," trans. H. P. Blavatsky. Available at Project Gutenberg at https://www.gutenberg.org/files/8578/8578-h/8578-h.htm.
247. Matthew 8:28–34 refers to two *Gadarene* demoniacs, while Mark 5:1–20 and Luke 8:26–39 refer to one Gerasene demoniac, possessed by an unclean spirit named "Legion" or "Regiment."
248. Cited in Fyodor Dostoevsky, *The Possessed, or the Devils*, trans. Constance Garnett (London: William Heinemann, 1916), v, https://www.gutenberg.org/files/8117/8117-h/8117-h.htm.

249. Cited in Dostoevsky, *Possessed*, v. The account from Luke 8 is Garnett's translation of this passage as it appears in the novel.

250. Malcolm Muggeridge, "Dostoevsky 1821–1888," *Biography* (1975), YouTube video, 55:35, November 7, 2017, https://www.youtube.com/watch?v=8hDo436bnfk&t=0s.

251. Stepan's speeches include a host of phrases in French. For brevity, I have included my English translation of those phrases in brackets.

252. Dostoevsky, *Possessed*, 615.

253. Dostoevsky, 615–16.

254. Dostoevsky, *Possessed*, 482.

255. Dostoevsky, 482–83.

256. See Gary Saul Morson, "Suicide of the Liberals," *First Things*, October 2020, https://www.firstthings.com/article/2020/10/suicide-of-the-liberals; Nikolai Bergiaev, *Vekhi Landmarks: A Collection of Articles About the Russian Intelligentsia* (Armonk, New York, London: M.E. Sharpe, 1994); Sam Joshua Reed, "Ideological Infection in Dostoevsky's 'Demons'" (2017), *Senior Projects Spring 2017*, 359, https://digitalcommons.bard.edu/senproj_s2017/359.

257. Sergey Nechayev, "The Revolutionary Catechism," https://www.marxists.org/subject/anarchism/nechayev/catechism.htm.

258. Fyodor Dostoevsky, "Pushkin Speech," *Diary of a Writer*, ed. Alan Kimball (1880), https://pages.uoregon.edu/kimball/DstF.Puw.lct.htm#KmbIntro. Italics are in the original.

259. See Ephesians 2:15.

260. See Mark 9:17–27.

18. Affliction—Full Stop: Fyodor Dostoevsky, Part 2

261. "15 Aphorisms of Stanislav Jerzy Lec, Which Should Never Be Forgotten," Время, November 14, 2021, https://vk.com/wall-113266028_11165?lang=en.

262. From Malachi 3:2–3 (NIV): "But who can endure the day of his coming? Who can stand when he appears? For he will be like a refiner's fire or a launderer's soap. He will sit as a refiner and purifier of silver; he will purify the Levites and refine them like gold and silver. Then the LORD will have men who will bring offerings in righteousness."

263. Murray Jones, "40% of All Civilian Casualties from Airstrikes in Afghanistan—Almost 1,600—in the Last Five Years Were Children," Relief Web, May 6, 2021, https://reliefweb.int/report/afghanistan/40-all-civilian-casualties-airstrikes-afghanistan-almost-1600-last-five-years.

264. Erik Møse, "Update by the Chair of the Independent International Commission of Inquiry on Ukraine, at the 51st Session of the Human Rights Council," United Nations Human Rights Office of the High Commissioner, September 23, 2022, https://www.ohchr.org/en/statements/2022/09/update-chair-independent-international-commission-inquiry-ukraine-51st-session.

265. Fyodor Dostoevsky, *The Brothers Karamazov*, trans. Richard Pevear and Larissa Volokhonsky (Christian Classics Ethereal Library, 2010), 206, https://www.ccel.org/ccel/d/dostoevsky/brothers/cache/brothers.pdf.

266. Dostoevsky, *The Brothers Karamazov*, 211–12. His monologue has been abridged for brevity.

267. Dostoevsky, 212.

268. Albert Camus, *The Plague*, trans. Laura Marris (New York: Alfred A. Knopf, 2021), 227–28.

269. Elie Wiesel, *Night*, trans. Marion Wiesel (New York: Hill and Wang, 2006), 32.

270. Wiesel, *Night*, 4.

271. Wiesel, *Night*, 62.

272. Jonathan Martin (@thetableokc), *Instagram*, December 19, 2021, https://www.instagram.com/p/CXrMFa8L5bR. Used by permission.

273. Sergius Bulgakov, *Unfading Light: Contemplations and Speculations*, trans. Thomas Allan Smith (Grand Rapids, MI: Eerdmans, 2011), 14–15. Italics are in the original.

19. Atheism, Decreation, and the Absence of God: Simone Weil

274. Simone Weil, *Gravity and Grace*, trans. Emma Crawford and Mario von der Ruhr (London, New York: Routledge Classics, 2002), 114.

275. Hans Urs von Balthasar, *The Grain of Wheat: Aphrorisms*, trans. Erasmo Leiva-Merikakas (San Francisco: Ignatius Press, 1995), 46.

276. Publisher's preface to Simone Weil, *The Notebooks of Simone Weil*, trans. Arthur Wills (Abingdon, UK/New York: Rutledge, 2004), n.p.

277. Simone Weil, *Gravity and Grace*, 114.

278. See Philippians 2:7.

279. See excerpts on decreation from *Gravity and Grace* at "Simone Weil—Decreation," Fleurmach, March 20, 2016, https://fleurmach.com/2016/03/20/simone-weil-decreation.

280. Susan Anima Taubes, "The Absent God," *The Journal of Religion* 35, no. 1 (1955): 6, http://www.jstor.org/stable/1201142. Italics are in the original.

281. Simone Weil, *Awaiting God*, 31.

282. Simone Weil, "Lettre à Maurice Schumann," in *Seventy Letters*, trans. Richard Rees (Oxford, UK: Oxford University Press, 1965), 178.

283. Weil, *Gravity and Grace*, 115.

284. Cayley, *George Grant in Conversation*, 128–29, 176–79.

285. Excerpts from Tadeusz Borowski, "Auschwitz Our Home (A Letter)," in *This Way for the Gas, Ladies and Gentlemen*, trans. Barbara Vetter (New York: Penguin Books, 1992), 98–142.

286. "Jesus Wept," track 2 on Demon Hunter, *Outlive*, Solid State Records, 2017.

287. See Luke 23:34.

288. See Mark 15:39.

289. Weil, *Awaiting God*, 157–58.

20. Fevers, Tears, and Co-Suffering Love: Dostoevsky, Part 3

290. See Hebrews 10:4.

291. See, for example, C. Baxter Kruger, *Patmos: Three Days, Two Men, One Extraordinary Conversation* (Brandon, MS: Perichoresis Press, 2016), 211. "The Lamb of God, slain by Adam's race, lives now inside our abyss of shame, and is not swallowed by it: the light shines in our darkness, and our darkness cannot overcome it. This is our hope."

292. *Notes from the Underground, The Idiot, The Possessed, Crime and Punishment*, and *The Brothers Karamazov* can all be accessed at www.gutenberg.org.

293. Fyodor Dostoevsky, *The Project Gutenberg eBook of Notes from the Underground*, trans. Constance Garnett, II.IV, n.p., https://www.gutenberg.org/files/600/600-h/600-h.htm. All subsequent quotations from *Notes from the Underground* in this chapter come from this edition of Dostoevsky's book.

294. Dostoevsky, *Notes from the Underground*, II.I.

295. Dostoevsky, II.III.

296. See Genesis 4:1–6.

297. Fyodor Dostoevsky, *The Project Gutenberg eBook of Crime and Punishment*, trans. Constance Garnett, chapter V, n.p., https://www.gutenberg.org/files/2554/2554-h/2554-h.htm. All subsequent quotations from *Crime and Punishment* in this chapter come from this edition of Dostoevsky's book.

298. Dostoevsky, *Crime and Punishment*, II.I.

299. Dostoevsky, II.I.

300. Dostoevsky, II.III.

301 "Abp. Lazar Puhalo w/ Ron Dart in Conversation—Theological, Pastoral, Prophetic & Political," *Clarion Journal for Religion, Peace & Justice*, May 15, 2018, YouTube video, 46:08 (at mark 7:45), https://www.clarion-journal.com/clarion_journal_of_spirit/2018/05/abp-lazar-puhalo-with-ron-dart-in-conversation-theological-pastoral-prophetic-political.html.

302. Dostoevsky, *Crime and Punishment*, V.IV.

303. Dostoevsky, V.IV.

304. Fyodor Dostoevsky, *The Project Gutenberg eBook of The Brothers Karamazov*, trans. Constance Garnett, III.VII.II, n.p., https://www.gutenberg.org/files/28054/28054-h/28054-h.htm. All subsequent quotations from *The Brothers Karamazov* in this chapter come from this edition of Dostoevsky's book.

305. Dostoevsky, *Brothers Karamazov*, III.VII.III.

306. Dostoevsky, III.VII.III.

307. Dostoevsky, III.VII.III.

308. Dostoevsky, III.VII.III.

309. Dostoevsky, III.VII.III.

310. Dostoevsky, III.VII.III.

311. Dostoevsky, III.VII.III.

PART III:
PROVOCATIONS: OUT OF THE EMBERS: FAITH AFTER FREEFALL

21. Revenants: Faith Resurrected

312. "Pope Francis' Homily at Epiphany Mass 2022," *Rome Reports*, January 6, 2022, https://www.romereports.com/en/2022/01/06/pope-francis-homily-at-epiphany-mass-2022.

313. See Russell Moore, "The Capitol Attack Signaled a Post-Christian Church, Not Merely a Post-Christian Culture," *Christianity Today*, January 5, 2022, https://www.christianitytoday.com/ct/2022/january-web-only/january-6-attack-russell-moore-post-christian-church.html.

314. See 1 Peter 4:17.

315. See Revelation 1:18.

316. G. K. Chesterton, *Orthodoxy* (New York/London: John Lane Company, 1908), 275–76.

317. See John 11:1-44; Acts 9:36-41.

318. "Woke": The language of "woke" was initially a positive sentiment more broadly used by younger segments of Black culture (Millennials, Gen Z) but was co-opted by progressive ideologues and then weaponized by their opponents. It is rarely used today except in tones of contempt. Recognizing this, this is the last you'll see me use this term.

319. G. K. Chesterton, *The Everlasting Man* (London: Hodder & Stoughton), 288, https://www.gutenberg.org/files/65688/65688-h/65688-h.htm.

320. Fyodor Dostoevsky, *The Idiot*, trans. Constance Garnett (New York: Bantam, 1981), 370.

321. Burnout proper is defined as a "prolonged response to chronic emotional and interpersonal stressors, defined by exhaustion, cynicism, and sense of inefficacy." Adapted from Christina Maslach, "Job Burnout: New Directions in Research and Intervention," *Current Directions in Psychological Science* 12, no. 5 (October 1, 2003): 189–92.

322. Lazar Puhalo, "The Paradise of the Heart," *Clarion Journal for Religion, Peace & Justice*, August 15, 2021, https://www.clarion-journal.com/clarion_journal_of_spirit/2021/08/the-paradise-of-the-heart-lazar-puhalo.html.

323. See 2 Corinthians 6:18; Revelation 1:8; 4:8; 11:17; 15:3; 16:7, 14; 19:6, 15; 21:22.

324. John Behr, Open Table Conference conversation (Sun River, OR, July 3, 2022).

325. See Matthew 5:13–15.

326. See Matthew 5:1–12.

22. "Let Us Go Out to Him": Three Cruciform Sisters

327. Re: capitalizing "Black" herein, see Kwame Anthony Appiah, "The Case for Capitalizing the B in Black," *The Atlantic*, June 18, 2020, https://www.theatlantic.com/ideas/archive/2020/06/time-to-capitalize-blackand-white/613159.

328. Siobhan Robbins, "Myanmar: Nun Tries to Protect Protesters as at Least Two Killed in City of Myitkyina," *Sky News*, March 8, 2021, https://news.sky.com/story/youll-have-to-come-through-me-nun-tries-to-protect-myanmar-protesters-as-two-killed-12239838.

329. "'Today Is the Say I Will Die'–Nun Who Opposed Myanmar Military Says She Begged Them for Mercy," *Sky News*, March 6, 2021, https://news.sky.com/story/today-is-the-day-i-will-die-nun-who-opposed-myanmar-military-says-she-begged-them-for-mercy-12236955.

330. Alban Butler, "June 2: St. Pothinus, Bishop, Sactus, Attalus, Blandina, Etc., Martyrs of Lyons," in *The Lives of the Saints* (New York: Bartleby.com, 2010), vol. VI, https://www.bartleby.com/210/6/021.html.

331. Eusebius,"Letter of the Churches of Vienne and Lyons to Asia and Phyrgia," in *Nicene and Post-Nicene Fathers, Second Series*, trans. Arthur Cushman McGiffert, ed. by Philip Schaff and Henry Wace (Buffalo, NY: Christian Literature Publishing Co., 1890), 1:5.1.41, http://www.newadvent.org/fathers/250105.htm.

332. Butler, "June 2.

333. Johann Peter Kirsch, "St. Blandina," in *The Catholic Encyclopedia*, vol. 2 (New York: Robert Appleton Company, 1907), http://www.newadvent.org/cathen/02594a.htm.

334. For this account, see Vladimir Moss, ed., "Holy Martyr Lydia of Ufa (+128): And Those With Her," in *A Century of Russian Martyrdom: A Selection of the Lives of the Holy New Martyrs and Confessors of Russia* (Vladimir Moss, 2021), 1:192–94, https://www.orthodoxchristianbooks.com/downloads/894_A_CENTURY_OF_RUSSIAN_MARTYRDOM_VOLUME_1.pdf.

335. See Isaiah 53:7.

336. See Luke 23:39–43.

337. See Acts 7:54–60.

338. Moss, "Holy Martyr Lydia of Ufa."

339. See Hebrews 11:1–12:1.

340. Tertullian, "Apologeticum (The Apology)," The Tertillian Project, http://www.tertullian.org/works/apologeticum.htm.

341. Isaac Watts, "When I Survey the Wondrous Cross," *Hymns and Spiritual Songs*,1707.

342. Anonymous, personal correspondence with author, April 7, 2021.

343. See 1 Peter 4:17.

344. Other Black voices that have guided and corrected me (not always in agreement with each other) are Martin Luther King Jr., Bernice King, Cornel West, Drew G. I. Hart, Austin Channing Brown, LaToshia Everson, Esau McCaulley, and my friend and colleague Rev. Dr. David N. Moore.

23. Jesus and the Disinherited: God's Black Voices

345. James H. Cone, *The Cross and the Lynching Tree* (Maryknoll, NY: Orbis Books, 2013), 3.

346. Cone, *Cross and Lynching Tree*, 9.

347. Cone, 31.

348. "Were You There When They Crucified My Lord?" (likely pre-American Civil War).

349. Cone, *Cross and Lynching Tree*, 23, 26.

350. See Luke 23:26.

351. See Genesis 32:22–32.

352. "Wrestling Jacob," published in Thomas Wentworth Higginson, *Army Life in a Black Regiment* (1869), cited in Cone, *The Cross and the Lynching Tree*, 24.

353. Cone, *Cross and Lynching Tree*, 63.

354. "To those who need profound succor and strength to enable them to live in the present with dignity and creativity, Christianity often has been sterile and of little avail. The conventional Christian word is muffled, confused, and vague. …a religion that was born of a people acquainted with persecution and suffering [had] become the cornerstone of a civilization and of nations whose very position in modern life has too often been secured by a ruthless use of power applied to weak and defenseless peoples." Howard Thurman, *Jesus and the Disinherited* (Boston: Beacon Press, 1976), 1–2.

355. Thurman, *Jesus and the Disinherited*, 26–27.

356. Thurman, 35.

357. Thurman, 39.

358. Thurman, 45.

359. Thurman, 46–47.

360. Thurman, 55.

361. Thurman, 60.

362. Thurman, 60–61.

363. See Matthew 3:10; Luke 3:9.

364. Thurman, *Jesus and the Disinherited*, 64.

365. Thurman, 65–68.

366. Thurman, 70–75.

367. Thurman, 76–77.

368. See John 10:10.

369. See, for example, Matthew 22:37–38; Luke 10:25–37.

370. Thurman, *Jesus and the Disinherited*, 24. Note that Thurman's disciples testify that his gendered language does not reflect sexism in Thurman but rather the standard vocabulary and wording of the English Bible translations of that era. He would no doubt have been among the first to use inclusive speech to fortify his inclusive message. I've chosen not to edit his actual words when citing him.

371. Placide Cappeau, "O Holy Night" (1847).

372. Howard Thurman, "Howard Thurman Lost Lectures—'Love or Perish,'" YouTube video, 44:19, June 7, 2019, https://youtu.be/3t2AtErMO4Q.

373. Thurman, *Jesus and the Disinherited*, 86–87.

374. See Valarie Kaur, "The Revolutionary Love Learning Hub," ValarieKaur.com, https://valariekaur.com/wp-content/uploads/2021/06/The-Revolutionary-Love-Learning-Hub-Audio-Transcript.pdf, and Valarie Kaur, *See No Stranger: A Memoir and Manifesto of Revolutionary Love* (New York: One World, 2020). Thanks to Felicia Murrell for directing me to Kaur's work.

375. Thurman, *Jesus and the Disinherited*, 88–90.

376. See Matthew 18:21–22.

377. Thurman, *Jesus and the Disinherited*, 98–99.

378. Vincent Harding, "Foreword," *Jesus and the Disinherited*, xvii.

379. Thurman, "Love or Perish."

380. See Cara Wall, *The Dearly Beloved* (New York: Simon & Schuster, 2019), 94.

381. This phrase is from Kaur, *See No Stranger*, 7, 11.

382. Felicia Murrell, "Radical Empathy," *Clarion Journal for Religion, Peace & Justice*, May 20, 2021, https://www.clarion-journal.com/clarion_journal_of_spirit/2021/05/index.html. Italics are in the original.

383. Jennifer Fandel, *Martin Luther King, Jr.* (Makato, MN: Creative Education, 2006), 41.

384. Ram Dass and Rameshwar Das, *Be Love Now: The Path of the Heart* (New York: HarperOne, 2010), 22.

385. BIPOC refers to Black, Indigenous, and people of color.

24. A World Unraveling, a Kingdom Unfurling

386. See W. L. Walker, "Remnant," *International Standard Bible Encyclopedia*, https://bibleapps.com/r/remnant.htm#isb.

387. See 2 Corinthians 1:20.

388. *Don't Look Up*, directed by Adam McKay (Netflix, 2021).

389. See Revelation 21:5.

390. J.R.R. Tolkien: "I coined the word 'eucatastrophe': the sudden happy turn in a story which pierces you with a joy that brings tears (which I argued it is the highest function of fairy-stories to produce). And I was there led to the view that it produces its peculiar effect because it is a sudden glimpse of Truth, your whole nature chained in material cause and effect, the chain of death, feels a sudden relief as if a major limb out of joint had suddenly snapped back. It perceives—if the story has literary 'truth' on the second plane....—that this is indeed how things really do work in the Great World for which our nature is made. And I concluded by saying that the Resurrection was the greatest 'eucatastrophe' possible in the greatest Fairy Story—and produces that essential emotion: Christian joy which produces tears because it is qualitatively so like sorrow, because it comes from those places where Joy and Sorrow are at one, reconciled, as selfishness and altruism are lost in Love." Tolkien, "Letter 89," in *The Letters of J.R.R. Tolkien*, eds. Christopher Tolkien and Humphrey Carpenter (Boston: Houghton Mifflin, 1981).

391. See Richard Murray's vision in a panel discussion with Sheri Pallis, Matthew Distefano, and me on the topic of the afterlife. "The Afterlife, or Lack Thereof?" Fireside Creators, YouTube video, 1:04:12, September14, 2021. https://www.youtube.com/watch?v=iZ3LHEVXIOM.

392. Gregory speaks about epektasis in his classic work *Life of Moses*. For a scholarly introduction to his thoughts on "perpetual progress," see K. Robb-Dover, "Gregory of Nyssa's 'Perpetual Progress,'" *Theology Today* 65, no. (2008), 213–25, https://doi.org/10.1177/004057360806500207.

393. Sergii Bulgakov, *The Apocalypse of John: An Essay in Dogmatic Interpretation* (Münster, Germany: Aschendorff Verlag, 2019), 238.

394. See Joshua 24:15.

395. Saint Isaac the Syrian, Homily II.38.2, cited in Fr. Aiden Kimel, "In Love Did He Bring the World into Existence," *Eclectic Orthodoxy*, March 24, 2013. Adapted from Hilarion Alfeyev, *The Spiritual World of Isaac the Syrian*, Cistercian Studies 175, (Kalamazoo: Cistercian Publications, 2000), https://afkimel.wordpress.com/2013/03/24/in-love-did-he-bring-the-world-into-existence/.

25. Fridays with Godfather: Presence in Communion

396. Because I cite Stephen Freeman in this chapter, I will follow his use of the spelling of "storey" (chiefly British) to describe "floors" of reality, but "story" to speak about narratives (e.g., the Eden story).

397. See Stephen Freeman, *Everywhere Present: Christianity in a One-Storey Universe* (Chesterton, IN: Ancient Faith Publishers, 2010).

398. A dumbwaiter is a small freight elevator designed to deliver food.

399. A. H. Ackley, "I Serve a Risen Savior," 1933.

400. See Luke 17:21, translated variously as "within you" (KJV, NKJV) or "in your midst" (NIV, NASB).

401. See Matthew 4:17 and Mark 1:15, translated as "at hand" (NKJV, NASB) or "near" (NIV).

402. Stephen Freeman, "Christianity in a One-Storey Universe," Glory to God for All Things, Ancient Faith Ministries, https://blogs.ancientfaith.com/glory2godforallthings/christianity-in-a-one-storey-universe/. Italics are in the original.

403. See Acts 17:27–28.

404. See John 17:21.

405. Sergii Bulgakov, *The Apocalypse of John*, 251.

406. Chrismation is the liturgical service in which I confessed my faith and was anointed with oil for entry into the Eastern Orthodox Church.

407. Note: in a one-storey universe, where is the "great cloud of witnesses" (Hebrews 12:1)? Not "up there" but *with us*. The historic church refers to their presence with us as "the communion of the saints."

408. Because there are few transcripts of these conversations, with David's permission, I will freely alternate between first-person quotations and third-person paraphrases.

409. See Matthew 7:21–23; See Matthew 25:31–46.

410. See Matthew 25:45.

411. See Galatians 5:6.

412. A phrase I learned from William Paul Young.

413. Adapted from step three of Twelve-step recovery.

414. See Joshua 24:14–15.

415. See, for example, 2 Corinthians 6:2.

416. See Lamentations 3:22–23.

417. The founding Commonwealth members were Australia, Canada, India, New Zealand, Pakistan, South Africa, Sri Lanka, and the United Kingdom. Today, there are fifteen realms: Antigua and Barbuda, Australia, The Bahamas, Belize, Canada, Grenada, Jamaica, New Zealand, Papua New Guinea, Saint Kitts and Nevis, Saint Lucia, Saint Vincent and the Grenadines, the Solomon Islands, Tuvalu, and the United Kingdom. But beyond the British Commonwealth, a Pan-Commonwealth association developed consisting of more than fifty nations. See https://thecommonwealth.org/about-us.

418. These questions came via Jon Steingard.

26. The Doorway: Loving Liminal Space

419. Peri Zahnd, conversation with author, January 13, 2022.

420. Richard Rohr, "Liminal Space: Between Two Worlds," Center for Action and Contemplation, April 26, 2020, https://cac.org/between-two-worlds-2020-04-26.

421. See Lorie Martin, *A Piece of Our Shack Story*, http://loriemartin.com/about-lorie/her-shack-story; Wm. Paul Young, *The Shack* (Windblown Media, 2016).

422. See Matthew 7:7–8.

423. See Red Letter Christians, https://www.redletterchristians.org/tony-shane.

Outro: Living Communion Now

424. The reflections from Paul E. Ralph in this chapter all came via personal conversations with author, December 7–11, 2021.

425. Mark Heard, "Heart on the Line," *Masaics* (Montrose, CA: Fingerprint Records, 1985).

426. See Matthew 18:3.

427. Weil, *Gravity and Grace*, 170.

428. Valarie Kaur, "Valarie Kaur: Breath! Push! The Labor of Revolutionary Love," Bioneers, YouTube video, 29:42, November 13, 2019, https://www.youtube.com/watch?v=lIrl_Ob0jvg.

429. Citations come from The Revolutionary Love Learning Hub, valariekaur.com/learninghub. All rights reserved.

430. Valarie Kaur, "Understanding Wonder," Learning Hub, https://valariekaur.com/2022/03/wonder-toolkit/.

431. Valarie Kaur, "Understanding Grieve," Learning Hub, https://valariekaur.com/learninghub/part-1-grieve/.

432. Valarie Kaur, "Understanding Fight," Learning Hub, https://valariekaur.com/learninghub/3-fight/.

Benediction

433. Kallistos Ware, *The Inner Kingdom: Volume 1 of the Collected Works* (Crestwood, NY: St. Vladimir's Press), 29.

434. Kenneth Tanner, Instagram post, February 2, 2022, https://www.instagram.com/p/CZf67-MOncD/.

ABOUT THE AUTHOR

Bradley Jersak is the Dean of Theology & Culture, a graduate studies program at St. Stephen's University in New Brunswick, Canada. He is also an editor for the Clarion-Journal.com and CWR Magazine (PTM.org). Bradley and his wife, Eden, have lived in the Abbotsford area of British Columbia since 1988, where they served as pastors and church planters for twenty years. Bradley is the author of a number of books, including *A More Christlike Word*, *A More Christlike God*, *A More Christlike Way*, *Her Gates Will Never Be Shut*, *Can You Hear Me?: Tuning in to the God Who Speaks*, and *Jesus Showed Us*. He has an MA in biblical studies from Briercrest Seminary, an MDiv from Trinity Western University/ACTS Seminary, and a PhD in theology from Bangor University, Wales. He was also a visiting scholar at the University of Nottingham, United Kingdom, for postdoctoral research in patristic Christology (under Dr. Conor Cunningham).

www.bradjersak.com